The Rise of the Castle

M. W. Thompson

The Rise of the Castle

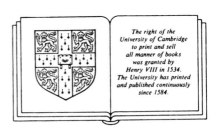

The right of the
University of Cambridge
to print and sell
all manner of books
was granted by
Henry VIII in 1534.
The University has printed
and published continuously
since 1584.

Cambridge University Press

Cambridge   New York   Port Chester   Melbourne   Sydney

CAMBRIDGE UNIVERSITY PRESS
Cambridge, New York, Melbourne, Madrid, Cape Town, Singapore, São Paulo, Delhi

Cambridge University Press
The Edinburgh Building, Cambridge CB2 8RU, UK

Published in the United States of America by Cambridge University Press, New York

www.cambridge.org
Information on this title: www.cambridge.org/9780521375443

© Cambridge University Press 1991

First published 1991
This digitally printed version 2008

A catalogue record for this publication is available from the British Library

Library of Congress Cataloguing in Publication data
Thompson, M. W. (Michael Welman)
The rise of the castle / M. W. Thompson.
         p.   cm.
Sequel: The decline of the castle.
Includes bibliographical references and index.
1. Castles – England – History.
2. Great Britain – History, Military – Medieval period, 1066–1485.
3. Great Britain – History, Military – Anglo-Saxon period, 449–1066.
4. Fortification – Great Britain – History.
5. Great Britain – Antiquities.   6. Castles – Wales – History.
I. Thompson, M. W. (Michael Welman).   Decline of the castle.   II. Title.
DA660.T464   1991
942 – dc20   90–36081   CIP

ISBN 978-0-521-37544-3 hardback
ISBN 978-0-521-08853-4 paperback

Frontispiece: the White Tower of the Tower of London from the north-west
(A.F. Kersting).

Contents

With some experience of medieval halls and mottes at Huttons Ambo (1953), Long Buckby (1955) and the Pickering castle guidebook (1957) my road to Damascus as far as castles are concerned was the uncovering of the vast masonry structure at Farnham castle, Surrey, in 1958, the highlight of thirty years in the service of the Inspectorate of Ancient Monuments. The correction of the dating of the construction of the great brick entry tower of this castle to 1470–5 from the Winchester Pipe Rolls concentrated my attention on the later history of castles, which ultimately led me to write *The Decline of the Castle* (1988). The earlier history of castles attracted then and since far more interest and far more controversy; the storms around the subject are as continual as those around Cape Horn. I was repelled by the debate, sometimes carried to unseemly lengths, between archaeologist and historian: to an outsider like a dispute between the deaf and the blind. One had misgivings about entering such a hubbub.

My first intention had been to write about the hall, the second anchor of English history, perhaps outranking the parish church itself in its antiquity. However, long association with castles in my work led to the thought that the hall could best be treated as part of the earlier history of the castle which may be viewed in some respects as an aberration of the hall culture; the *Decline* had been in a sense an account of the resurgence of the hall from its long confinement within castle walls. Furthermore, the residential element of the castle, less robustly built than the defences and less immediately evocative, has never received the attention it deserves.

In buying a house the method and date of construction cannot be ignored by a wise purchaser, although the name of the architect may well be a matter of indifference (the contractor's name could be more important), but it is primarily with the use of the rooms and their suitability for intended purposes that we are concerned. The survival from medieval times of prodigious quantities of documents dealing with the construction of buildings, especially accounts of expenditure, has led to a preoccupation with this aspect of them; the leading craftsmen have been elevated to the status of post-Renaissance architects. We speak of medieval buildings as if we were borough surveyors. The form of construction is fundamental to our understanding of any building, but its function and use throw a more powerful light on the people who occupied it. Planning and design in the middle ages were governed far more by tradition and habit than intended function, as is the case today, a point not sufficiently taken into account by would-be students of the domestic architecture of the period. This, together with the exiguous nature of the written sources, makes function very elusive; we happily apply the word 'hall' to two-storeyed and single-storeyed buildings, hoping that their functions were the same. Distinction between the two types of building is one of the central themes of this book.

After a short introductory chapter dealing with halls before the Norman Conquest, the second and third chapters turn to Germany and France. The castle was an alien introduction from abroad and cannot be understood without looking at its place of origin; comparison and contrast with the Continent in the eleventh and twelfth centuries are essential to an understanding of architecture in this country, as much in the ecclesiastical as in the secular spheres. The next four chapters cover well-trodden ground in England and Wales, although I hope with fresh insight and some new ideas. Chapters 8 and 9 are something of a fresh departure, since they are concerned with the new foundations spawned by castles, monasteries and towns, their most positive contribution to medieval civilisation, and in the case of towns sometimes a permanent legacy to the future. The last chapter describes the remarkable outburst of self-conscious castle construction in the fourteenth century, when appearance played a hardly less important role in the design than function. Thus this book concludes at about 1400 with the abrupt cessation of castle foundation described in *The Decline of the Castle*, now transformed into its sequel. It is evident from reviews of the latter that the reason for choosing this date for the division had escaped the reviewers.

The most photogenic aspect of a castle is its exterior, especially if enhanced by a dramatic feature like a mountain, cliff, a lake or river. This was the view seen by the traveller, the attacker in the event of siege, and today of course by the tourist; but the person living inside would have felt very enclosed, only glimpsing the fine views through arrow slits or from the battlements. The modern aerial view or colour photograph is designed to enhance the beauty of the monument (the modern photographer is no whit different from the eighteenth-century seeker after the picturesque) and is entirely misleading as to the claustrophobic sensations probably experienced by the people who lived in it. Obviously it would be absurd to exclude all aerial or external photographs, but I have tried to increase the proportion of internal views of cross-sections for, except in chapters 8 and 9, it is with the occupants what we are mainly concerned here.

The approach to the subject is archaeological, as it is the material remains that are the chief evidence and witness; the writer is neither a vernacular architect nor an art historian. By definition both of the last two fields of study are all but excluded from what can perhaps be called socio-architectural history. Written sources when relevant must have priority, but we certainly are not cabined and confined to 'medieval history' in the academic sense. The reader is at liberty to decide for himself what he would call this type of study.

My views on medieval halls owe not a little to discussion with the late Roy Gilyard-Beer, and on Norman keeps to the late Stuart Rigold, with both of whom I had the privilege of sharing offices in the old Ministry of Works. No one who has spent ten years in Wales, as the writer has, can fail to be beholden to Arnold Taylor for his lifetime's study of Welsh castles. Peter Curnow and I were partners at Richards Castle (1962–4), assisted by students of Allen Brown, so sadly recently taken from us, and not long since Peter and I inspected the Theodosian wall at Istanbul to compare with that of Caernarfon castle. I have had the pleasure of discussing medieval halls with John Blair of The Queen's College at Oxford, although we have not always seen quite eye to eye. No one in Wales can fail to be a wiser man after talking to Peter Smith of the Royal Commission at Aberystwyth.

The great volume of work on castles since the war has been catalogued by John Kenyon, amongst which the *King's Works* volumes, edited and in good measure written by Howard Colvin, must take precedence, while lists by Derek Renn (*Norman Castles*) and Cathcart King (*Castellarium Anglicanum*) and others have been of great help. The problem for the student is that the quantity of material is forbidding, almost overwhelming, and if he extends his field of study to the Continent he can only scrape the surface. The subject of this book is English and Welsh castles, only taking account of matters in France and Germany in so far as it is necessary to understand what is happening in Britain. All translations are my own unless otherwise stated.

Acknowledgements for the illustrations are made at the end of the book, but I must here thank my wife for taking a substantial number of the photographs.

M. W. Thompson

Chapter 1

Introduction

The eating habits among well-born Romans, a private activity among a few persons in the *triclinium*, each extended on a couch, had no special influence on the architecture. There could hardly be a greater contrast to the Germanic and Celtic peoples of the early middle ages. For them, feasting in hall was a public act, surrounded by protocol on seating, order of serving, and so on. It was the unifying factor that bound together the royal or chieftain's household and, from a sociologist's point of view, was probably the main common function of aristocratic secular society. Nor indeed was the importance of eating confined to secular society, as the scale and size of the refectory or frater in the monastic layout reminds us; the great Early English frater at Rievaulx Abbey almost rivals the church.

A Roman could draw a sharp distinction between his public and his private life: there were large and handsome buildings for the conduct of political, theatrical, legal, commercial and religious affairs. As municipal and state organisation disappeared with the collapse of the Empire, so many of these activities were drawn ineluctably into the only large building that could accommodate them and provide protection from the inclement weather of northern Europe, the hall.[1] It was the place where certain Germanic ceremonial functions were performed, like the giving of rings by the king.[2] It now had to serve as courtroom, theatre and, one of its most important functions, a bedroom at night. In medieval times, public and private life coincided to a degree which was as entirely alien to the Classical world as it is to us today.

Just to remind ourselves that an aisled hall, with a double row of columns supporting the roof, could be used for sleeping, figure 1 shows a splendid late twelfth-century example in the hospital hall at Angers in France, to which our own king Henry II may have contributed part of the cost.[3] Hospitals and monastic infirmaries were always aisled buildings, like a church, in the twelfth and thirteenth centuries. In this particular instance, the hospital still fulfilled its original function when this drawing was made in the nineteenth century.

1 Angers (Maine-et-Loire). A nineteenth-century view of the great hall, divided by double arcades of stone piers, of the hospital of St John, built in the late twelfth century. It was then still in use for patients

Returning to the varied function of the hall, there could be no more vivid illustration of it than the Welsh laws.[4] Although surviving in manuscripts from the late middle ages they go back in essentials presumably to the time of the great law-giver, Hywel the Good (mid–tenth century). In all three codes, the first of the three sections is devoted to the Court, listing the royal officers and where they sit in hall (*neuadd*), where they sleep, who sleeps in the hall, and so on. The protocol surrounding all activities in the hall and the overriding importance of the building in the life of the period could hardly be more powerfully demonstrated. Although the hall dominated the palace, there were other ancillary buildings around it, eight being named: chamber, kennel, barn, bakehouse, buttery, stable, latrine, dormitory.[5]

We may recall Snorri Sturluson's description of the palace built by King Olaf[6] written, it is true, 200 years after the event, but no doubt capturing the feeling of the royal house (*husa koningsgerat*). The principal structure was a great heated room (*mikil hirðstofa*) with doors at either end, in the middle of which sat the king with his chief officers sitting opposite and on either side of him, all drinking their ale by the flickering light of the open fire. As in the Welsh laws this room was not an isolated building, but one of a group that it dominated. It certainly differed in detail from the Welsh hall, the roof of which may have been supported by aisle posts, and the entries and seating arrangements were dissimilar, but the general resemblance between the two palaces is striking.

This then is the generalised picture of a palace or aristocratic seat that we should have in the back of our minds when considering the alterations necessary to turn it into a castle. The problems of how to treat the hall to some extent reflect the history of the castle itself. In England particularly, where the hall retained a much more archaic form than on the Continent, there may have been stronger sentiment, a stronger bond, between the users and the building itself. In this chapter something will be said about the hall as it is known to us from written sources on the one hand and the remarkable discoveries from excavation in the last few years on the other.

The starting-point for the discussion must be the great Old English epic, Beowulf, surviving in a single manuscript dated about 1,000 AD, although it is thought to have been composed between 650 and 700 AD.[7] Although entirely pagan in spirit and feeling there are hints of Christianity in it. The events described take place entirely in Scandinavia, with which there were close connections at that time as the treasures of Sutton Hoo have revealed, but it is thought that the Old English poet described the material world around him that he knew at first hand.

King Hrothgar in Denmark was unable to use his great hall, which had its own name Heorot, because every night a monster, Grendel, came and killed anyone in it. Life was able to go on because – an important point – there were other buildings in which Hrothgar and his kinsmen could sleep. The problem was the loss of face caused by the inability of the king to use his own hall for feasting. The hall itself, built of timber uprights tied by iron clamps, was a vast towering structure and was clearly an object of great prestige. Although referred to as the mead-hall, ale appears to have been the main beverage consumed in it. Hrothgar asked Beowulf, who came from Sweden, to help rid him of the monster, and when he and his men arrived they slept in the hall (lines 662–75, 1235), perhaps on a raised platform down either side. Something of the scale of the interior is revealed by the fact that eight horses with gold-plated cheek-pieces were brought inside (lines 1035–50).

The poem shows that the hall was no ordinary building, and from the Exeter Book we know that special skills were required in erecting its high timbers,[8] and that Christ himself is compared to the forces that held the great structure together.[9] In that fine Old English poem, *The*

Wanderer, we learn something of the poignant feeling of isolation and deprivation of the man who no longer has a place in the mead-hall, who no longer has a patron, the lord of the hall, the 'giver of treasure'.[10] It is the loneliness of the outcast.

Rather similar nostalgic, if a little less mercenary, sentiments were expressed in a ninth-century Welsh poem (*englyn*) of which a few lines in K. H. Jackson's translation may be quoted:[11]

> The hall of Cynddylan is dark tonight, without fire, without bed; I shall weep awhile, I shall be silent after.
> Hall of Cynddylan, you have become shapeless, your shield is in the grave; while he lived you were not mended with hurdles.
> The hall of Cynddylan is loveless tonight, after him who owned it; ah Death, why does it spare me?
> The hall of Cynddylan; it pierces me to see it without roof, without fire: my lord dead, myself alive.

The excavations at Mucking in Essex on the Thames estuary, carried out over many years, throw a fascinating light on the nature of the original settlement by the Saxons.[12] Occupation started at the southern end of site in the fifth century AD and gradually extended northwards up to the seventh century. The excavators who started work at the southern end did not at first recognise the post-holes of houses, and assumed that the people lived in the *Grübenhauser*, or small circular pits found in abundance on the site. It soon became clear that these were in the nature of workshops and that the inhabitants lived in rectangular, stave-built houses. There seems no clear evidence for aristocratic halls with their hierarchical implications, suggesting the settlers were not familiar with this kind of social division on their arrival, but rather that it was something that grew up afterwards. If so, this is a matter of great interest.

Although no actual buildings survive, excavations over the last thirty years have shed much light on the ground plans of royal palaces or buildings of high social status, covering more or less the whole period from the seventh to the eleventh centuries. They confirm in every way what we would expect: the dominating feature of these settlements was a large rectangular hall. The buildings were constructed of wood, and the interferences in the subsoil made to hold the uprights correspond to the outline of the ground plan. The relatively short survival time of wood thus thrust into the ground (like a wooden gatepost) meant frequent renewal was required, leaving a veritable palimpsest for the modern archaeologist to disentangle.

In many ways the most remarkable of these discoveries was the royal palace of the Northumbrian kings at Yeavering in Northumberland, identified with confidence as Bede's *Ad Gefrin*.[13] Discovered from the air, the marks on the aerial photograph were sufficiently clear to reveal almost the complete settlement on a low prominence about 70 m (230 ft) above sea-level (fig. 2). The marks showed a scatter of rectangular buildings, built originally of upright planks joined by tongue and groove, held at the base by horizontal planks set in a trench, and shored at the base by short diagonals to resist the roof thrust. The contrast with the round-hut bases in the nearby Iron Age hill-fort of Yeavering Bell was impressive. Apart from the curious theatre, a kind of Romano-British survival, the group of repeatedly reconstructed halls on the south at once catches the eye. The distance from the ancillary buildings reminds one of Hrothgar's hall in Beowulf. Seven or eight halls were identified, with two on occasion having been in use at the same time. Two features of these halls deserve a little more attention.

The buildings had opposed entries in the middle of the long sides facing the central hearth, vividly recalling Bede's memorable passage

2 Yeavering, Northumberland. Excavated traces of the wooden halls and ancillary buildings of the royal Northumbrian palace of the seventh to the ninth centuries AD. Note the repeated reconstruction of the halls. Scale *c.* 1:2,700

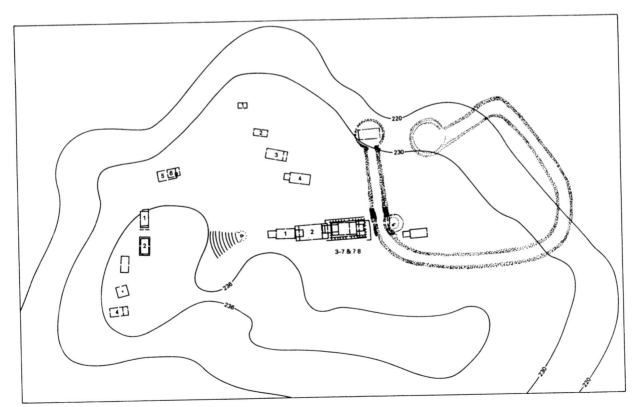

where the life of man was compared with the time taken by a swallow to fly through the hall.[14] The excavator's reconstruction shows the smoke rising to the roof but the draught created by the opposed openings in the doorways was probably specifically intended to draw out the smoke, and to assist in kindling, rather as the draught in the opposed doors of a barn was used in winnowing to separate out the chaff. Central doorways were a feature of early Germanic halls, and probably influenced the design even after they had been superseded (p. 17). In England the doors were moved to one end to create the time-honoured screens passage, no doubt to allow fuller use of the body of the building, and for ceremonies and processions, as with the opposed western doors of a church.

The second feature deserving comment is the wooden posts standing in the hall and rising up to support the roof. These posts are set in pairs dividing the building into 'aisles', two narrow ones down either side and a broader one down the middle, just as in a church. The longitudinal divisions are called aisles and the transverse ones bays; they will be referred to frequently in the following chapters. On the Continent, excavation has shown that all along the coastal areas of the North Sea, in Holland and Lower Germany huge rectangular houses, providing shelter for men and animals, with wooden aisle posts forming stalls in the bays, existed from the Bronze Age and continued in use to the present day.[15] Although confusingly called a *Hallenhaus* in German, such a structure was a peasant family house for man and beast; there were no royal or aristocratic connotations such as in our Yeavering palace. The inference must be that many, perhaps most, of the Germanic immigrants of the fifth and sixth centuries who had their place of origin precisely in those areas were familiar with this type of roof support formed by parallel rows of posts. However, far grander basilican buildings had been in use in Roman Britain, aisled but with stone columns, or in agricultural buildings no doubt with wooden posts. Every Roman town had its basilican hall in the forum, and many aisled barns have come to light in Roman Britain. It seems likely that the royal occupants of the palace at Yeavering were influenced by these, rather than by native practices.[16] The excavator was so impressed, indeed, by what he thought were Romano-British cultural elements at Yeavering that he referred to it as 'An Anglo-British Centre of Early Northumbria'.

As the reader may find the idea of wooden posts supporting a roof unfamiliar, figure 3 shows a section of a thirteenth-century barn at Ely constructed with wooden posts. These posts did not have their bases let into the ground and were protected by a roof from the weather, so they

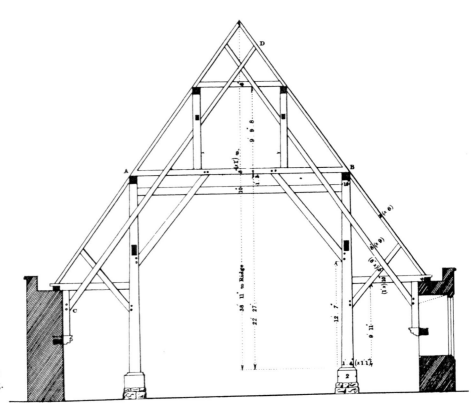

3 Sextry Barn, Ely, Cambs. Section by Willis in 1843 of the now-demolished thirteenth-century aisled barn showing timber posts of arcades and method of roofing. Height to apex 11.9 m

had an incomparably longer life than the wooden wall posts or aisle posts of a structure like the one at Yeavering.

At Yeavering, then, we are dealing with a palace of the Northumbrian kings, at the time of their conversion to Christianity, with frequently renewable timber buildings, giving some substance indeed to the world of Bede. The palace was quite unfortified; there is no question of a castle.

In Somerset the royal palace of Cheddar, belonging to a monarchy of a more or less united kingdom was revealed by excavations in 1960–2 to have structures belonging to the ninth to thirteenth centuries, spanning the years of the Norman Conquest.[17] The ancillary buildings now included a chapel, although one must wonder whether such a small number of buildings constituted the whole palace, or if others await discovery. The dominant halls at once attract notice: the oldest (c. 800) measured roughly 24 by 6 m and was trench-built with upright timber planks. It was more elongated than anything at Yeavering and, although it had opposed doorways in the long sides, it was not aisled. The convex sides recall Viking houses. The excavator thought it had been two-storeyed, but this is hardly compatible with what appeared

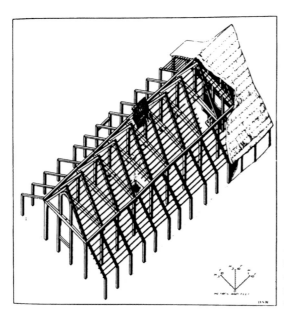

4 Cheddar, Somerset. Reconstruction of the second east hall (*c.* 1100) in the royal palace, showing aisle posts, central hearth and the divisions at the end

to be an open hearth. There then followed a dramatic change in construction method to post-framing in three consecutive unaisled west halls, which measured roughly 19 by 9 m. The next two (east) halls, which were erected after the Norman Conquest, measured up to 33 by 15 m, framed (stone footings in the second case) but now with very definite aisle posts, the arcades forming up to ten bays (fig. 4). The building was subdivided at either end. The west halls had entries in the gable ends, in the east halls the position is less clear. The interesting point about Cheddar is that aisle posts which seem to have disappeared or to be less common after Yeavering suddenly re-appear at the Norman Conquest, perhaps to give the building dignity and possibly owing something to contemporary events in ecclesiatical architecture.

Recent years have seen a number of Saxon halls brought to light. At Northampton a sequence of two halls, probably royal, first in timber and then in stone, have been uncovered by St Peter's church near the castle.[18] The wooden hall, trench-built for timber uprights, measured about 30 by 8.5 m and consisted of a central block with small annexes at either end. It had opposed entries in the long sides and was unaisled. It dated perhaps from *c.* 800 and was succeeded in *c.* 820 by a stone hall measuring 37.6 by 11.4 m. The foundation trenches were 1.2–1.3 m wide and 0.6 m deep, implying a stone rather than a timber-framed superstructure. Asser's *Life of Alfred* says he erected stone buildings,[19] and so this first discovery of a Saxon secular stone building need cause no surprise. It was probably a residential hall of the normal type and comparison with the throne rooms and palaces of Charlemagne by an enthusiastic excavator may be a little optimistic.

Other halls of less than royal status have been uncovered, but we must limit ourselves to describing one where a new element is introduced – defence. Viking raids from the end of the eighth century led to a need for defensive works, the example best known to us being the site at Goltho, Lincolnshire, so skilfully excavated by Guy Beresford a few years ago, and dated to the period 850–1150.[20]

It is not easy to summarise an excavation of such complexity, so only the salient points relevant to our discussion can be mentioned. Excavation of the castle site, adjoining the parish church, at the deserted village, revealed (ignoring Romano-British and a Middle Saxon periods) five periods of occupation, in each case dominated by a hall 15–25 m long. Although the stave-built halls had internal divisions in the first two periods (850–1000AD), they had no aisle posts for supporting the roof. In the next two periods (1000–1150), the hall in each case had posts down one side creating a single narrow aisle (fig. 5). Possibly such single aisles are a Danish feature (we are very much in the area of Scandinavian settlement), since they have been found by the present

5 Goltho, Lincs. View from above the motte showing sockets for post-holes of a single-aisled hall (*c.* 1100) in the bailey. The contrast with Cheddar is perhaps due to Scandinavian influence

writer in Yorkshire in post-Conquest contexts at Huttons Ambo with
wooden posts[21] and at a Conisbrough with stone columns.[22] It is, however, the nature of the defences that is most interesting: in the three
periods from 850–1080 this took the form of a ditch and bank, considerably enlarged by the last period, although subsequently virtually
obliterated by later changes. In 1080–1150 the creation of an earthen
motte or mound turned the work into a motte and bailey castle with a
tower on the motte and a hall in the bailey. In 1150 the motte was
spread over the bailey and the hall built on top. This whole sequence at
Goltho by which strengthened defences were turned into a motte and
bailey castle, the hall retaining all the time a separate identity and
eventually ending up on top of a raised bailey, is surely highly suggestive as to the circumstances that produced castles, epitomising the story
we are going to tell; it will be necessary to return to this sequence at
Goltho.

At Sulgrave in Northamptonshire a trench-built timber hall (unaisled) of interesting form with a kitchen in tandem at one end was
overlain by a stone hall at the same time as the site was enclosed by a
massive rampart.[23] The timber hall was perhaps tenth century in date,
the stone hall and defences being perhaps just post-Conquest.

Briefly looking back, then, after the disintegration of Roman society
immigrants from across the North Sea arrived who, to judge by their
remains at Mucking, were peasant communities without an aristocratic top hamper. In the early kingdoms that arose, leading to the Hep-
tarchy, the hall became the central element of the royal palaces,
wooden but probably deriving some features from Roman Britain. In
Middle and Late Saxon times the hall moves down the social scale,
although still of course aristocratic, and apparently dispenses with
aisle posts. At the time of the Norman Conquest aisle arcades come
back in a very marked way, possibly with church architecture as a
model. No doubt there were marked regional variations, single aisles
on one side perhaps being characteristic of the Danelaw.

To judge by Goltho, defensive works were common by the ninth
century. It is possible, indeed likely, that some of the 'ringworks', circular earthwork enclosures that have so preoccupied archaeologists
in recent years, belong to this class, although those that have been
explored seem to be post-Conquest in date.[24] In Ireland, small round,
or squarish, earthen or stone-revetted enclosures, 'raths' as they are
called, exist in thousands over the island and evidently had long usage,
from iron age to medieval times. They were apparently protected farm-

steads rather than aristocratic seats. Some were converted into mottes by filling in the interior of the rath[25] after the Anglo-Norman invasion of 1169; this is the opposite sequence to Goltho where the motte was destroyed to fill in the bailey.

In England quite a number of Saxon halls have been uncovered, all wooden with the exception of Northampton, and all single storey. At Cheddar, the open hearth makes suggestions of a storey above improbable. No doubt the height of the building when open to the roof conferred dignity on it and on whatever took place there. The famous picture of Harold at Bosham in the Bayeux tapestry (fig. 6) may well be an anachronism: most of the accompanying scenes on the embroidery are in France and if the cartoonist was French, likely enough even if the needlewomen were English (uncertain enough in any case), then a

6 Bayeux tapestry: Harold shown feasting at Bosham in a perhaps anachronistically drawn form of French hall

French form of first-floor hall may well be depicted (see p. 28). Some of the ancillary buildings of the palaces, especially the lord's bower or solar, were two-storeyed; the well-known entry under 978 in the *Anglo-Saxon Chronicle* describing how everyone except St Dunstan fell from the first floor in a building at Calne, Wiltshire, is translated as *in uno solario* in the 'Bilingual Canterbury Epitome'.[26] The writer evidently thought that it must have been a solar if it was two-storeyed. Whether the derivation of 'solar' be from the Classical Latin *solarium* (a sunny balcony or place in contrast to the smoky hall) or from the early French *solive* (joist) it was by definition always on the first floor.

There are five instances, three in Herefordshire (Richards Castle, Hereford and Ewyas Harold) one in Essex (Clavering) and lastly at Dover in Kent where the documentary evidence allows us to infer that a castle existed before the Norman Conquest.[27] In four cases there are or were mottes and baileys on the site, structures entirely different from what we have been describing in Saxon England, and which it has been reasonably argued are evidence of the introduction of this alien form from France by Norman favourites of Edward the Confessor. This seems the most sensible explanation, to which it will be necessary to return in chapter 4.

Aristocratic culture from 500 to 1500 was a culture of the hall, where its chief achievements manifested themselves. The castle might be regarded as either a temporary aberration or the culmination of this culture, depending on how you look at it. No doubt the boon companionship, the camaraderie of the Old English hall did not survive the introduction of feudalism, the more hierarchical society based on strongly agnatic (inheritance by the eldest son) relationship.[28] Protocol and formality became overriding matters, but new functions were introduced and a new French culture which strengthened rather than weakened its importance. Our attention will have to be concentrated largely on castles in the following chapters but let us not lose sight of this background. The undefended halls of the later period, notably in bishops' palaces, which will not be ignored, should help to keep the matter in the forefront of our minds.

Chapter 2

Germany

Germany presents three main difficulties for the student of the castle, differences, indeed, which make its study so fascinating. The first is the language itself: a leading archaeologist tells us that the two great periods of castle-building, *Burgenbau*, in Germany were the Bronze–Iron Age and the early–high middle ages.[1] Where we speak of hill-forts and castles the German-speaker calls all earthworks, stone castles and even towns *Burgen*. The boundaries so clear in English and French are lost, and it undoubtedly leads to much confusion of thought. Secondly, and related, over much of Germany there was no intervening period of Roman civilisation, as in France or Britain, interposed between prehistoric and medieval times; the continuity of earthwork construction over the whole period blurs the conceptual boundaries that we are accustomed to.

The third difficulty, and by far the most important, is the great contrast in the political situation in Germany compared to France at the time when castles came into existence and in their flourishing in the twelfth and thirteenth centuries. Feudalism and castles are in large measure products of disorder, of the lack of central control, born under the French monarchy when it was at its lowest ebb, almost defunct. This was precisely the time when the German kingdom and the German empire, refounded by Otto the Great (936-62), reached its peak of power under Henry III (1034–56). Feudalism and castles entered as a cultural wind from the west, from across the Rhine, and were modified and never indeed fully accepted in Germany.[2] The model to which the German emperors looked was Charlemagne or the Roman or Byzantine emperors. Not surprisingly it was the palace, rather than the castle, that symbolised their authority and when they or their *ministeriales* (civil servants), or the independent nobility built castles the palace derivation is very evident.

The idea of the royal palace as the seat of royal authority continued also in the west: contrast the Palace of Westminster and the Tower of London, for instance. The subject will crop up again. During the

Merovingian period the kings lived in vills, large undefended ranch-like establishments. This was continued by the Carolingians until the time when Viking marauders made such a style of living difficult to maintain. The famous description in a *capitularium* of Charlemagne of 810 of a royal fisc or seat at Annapes, near Lille, although obscure in some respects, gives a general idea of such a centre. Its main hall block (*sala*, Old English *sele*, French *salle*) built of dressed stone was divided into three rooms (or aisles), completely encircled by eleven solars (presumably bedrooms) in galleries, a cellar below, two porches (perhaps opposed doors), seventeen wooden buildings, a stable, a kitchen, a bakehouse, two wheat barns, three hay barns, with a strong enclosure with a stone gatehouse and an office (dispensing solar) over it.[3]

The new-found imperial status of Charlemagne no doubt required the establishment of something grander, which took the form of three great palaces deliberately erected in the eastern part of the empire near the Rhine at Aachen, Ingelheim and Nymwegen.[4] None of them survive, although the ground plans have been worked out.[5] They were what the Germans call monastery or cloister palaces (*Klosterpfalzen*), because the rather widely scattered buildings were arranged in courtyards linked by covered alleys.[6] The two essential elements in the palace were the church, the famous surviving *Kapelle* (now the cathedral) at Aachen, modelled on the octagonal church of San Vitale at Ravenna, and a vast hall with apses in the middle and at either end. None of Charlemagne's halls survives (that at Aachen is under the town hall), but the one at Ingelheim was evidently aisled, while the one at Aachen, built over an earlier Merovingian hall, had a single row of columns down the centre to support the roof. They were clearly throne rooms, where the sovereign sat in state to give audience, rather than Germanic feasting halls and owed more to late Roman imperial palaces than to native tradition. Probably as with the church at Aachen there was an Italian model, although today our knowledge of such buildings is mainly derived from the great hall of Constantine at Trier or from Diocletian's place at Spoleto (now Split) in Yugoslavia.[7] In the latter case, the throne room is at first-floor level over a vaulted basement, but the normal Roman and Carolingian preference was for a ground-floor hall.

The only surviving major secular building of the period of Germanic origin, preserved because it was converted into a church, Santa Maria de Naranco, surprisingly comes from the Visigothic kingdom of northwest Spain and lies 4 km from Oviedo.[8] It is a rectangular, two-storeyed building measuring 21 by 6 m, attributed to Ramiro I (early ninth century). It is vaulted at both levels, the first floor being entered by external steps in the middle of one side, and possibly originally on both sides (fig. 7). The interior walls on the first floor are decorated with arcading and, at either end, the most remarkable feature, there are open verandas with triple arches supported on shafts with sculpted capitals. It is not possible to do justice to the sculpture and other details of the building in this brief mention. Although called a hall, the verandas almost suggest a literal 'solarium'.

7 Santa Maria de Naranco, near Oviedo. An early ninth-century Visigothic royal hall (or perhaps solar) surviving as a church. Vaulted over both storeys, it has verandas at either end and external steps in the centre giving access to the first floor

We are not well informed about palaces of the tenth and eleventh centuries, although it is fairly clear that a major change took place at that time, revealed by the excavations at Paderborn (Minden, Westphalia).[9] On the north side of the cathedral the foundations of an Ottonian hall (40 by 20 m) with spinal columns to support a vault overlay extensive traces of the Carolingian palace. The bishop's palace hall lay to the south-west of the cathedral. The raising of the hall to the first floor seems to have taken place in France about the same time, and from now on this is almost universal in aristocratic halls in castles and palaces on the Continent.

The earliest of these great German hall blocks surviving is that built by the Salian emperors at Goslar, central Germany, south of Hanover.[10] Started by Henry II (1002–14) and rebuilt by Henry III (1034–56) it has undergone so many alterations and such massive restoration in the last century that its original appearance is by no means clear (fig. 8). It measured 57 by 17 m and had a projecting wing at one

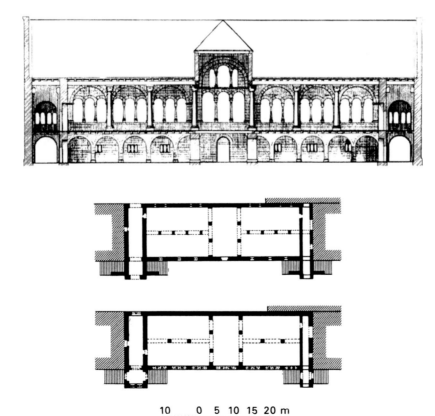

10   0 5 10 15 20 m

8 Goslar, Hanover. The eleventh-century imperial hall is freely restored in this drawing; note spinal columns at both levels, central division, and external stair on the left

end for an external staircase leading to a lobby on the first floor. A kind of transept rises in the middle and there is little doubt that there was a central division separating the building into two halves. The vaulted ground floor had spinal columns and on the first floor there were spinal wooden posts to support the roof. The windows, very heavily restored, were apparently of three lights on both floors but exceptionally grand, with decorated capitals, on the first floor.

Goslar illustrates several features of the typical residential block, the *Palas* as it is called in German, characteristic of the Romanesque period. The reader should not confuse the German word for an imperial palace, *Pfalz*, with *Palas*, which is used for a residential block regardless of whether it was a castle or palace, royal or not. There is no question of it being isolated, in strong contrast to the English hall; it is always a composite block with the main rooms on the first floor, or occasionally on the second floor if it is three-storeyed. Often it is transversely divided in the middle, as if recalling the early central entry, perhaps retained for husband and wife, king and queen – we can only guess the purpose. The ground floor is usually vaulted with spinal columns for support, and if there are not spinal posts on the first floor, a king post rose from the tie beam to the apex of the roof. These structures clearly have an affinity with the French halls that we shall meet in the next chapter which appear at the same time, or indeed those of Spain[11] or Italy.

The function of these blocks was quite independent of the façade, since it has been convincingly argued that the veranda-style of arcades at ground or first-floor level is a conscious imitation of open arcades of Roman villas and palaces.[12] The *Palas* at the castle of Wartburg (near Erfurt, E. Germany), although heavily restored, shows the feature to the most marked degree. This passion for arcades, albeit blank and ornamental, became a general feature of Romanesque architecture, appearing in an impressive form on the keep of Norwich castle (fig. 46). The point is an interesting and important one, but best left to the art historians to pursue.

The distinction between palace and castle in Germany was a legal one: the palace had imperial, administrative status and was probably situated in or near a town, but its physical components were virtually identical to those of a castle. Possibly some buildings were more elaborate, like the two-storeyed chapels[13] yet we are dealing with essentially the same form of structure. But before turning to castles there is still another matter that deserves attention.

Vernacular epic poetry of the style intended to be sung or recited in the hall, the genuine culture of the hall, among which we may include Beowulf, is associated from about 1100 with the French *chansons*, starting with the *Chanson de Roland*. Growing in volume, and altering in character due to Celtic influences to the romantic Arthurian style by the end of the century, it was followed in the late twelfth and early thirteenth centuries by a vigorous German vernacular poetry. In the German poetry the hall tends to play a much larger part than in the French verse. There is one section in a great work by an anonymous poet, written in about 1200, that must provide food for thought for any student of the hall or castle.

In the *Nibelungenlied* the Burgundians were invited to Hungary, but during the feast in the hall after their arrival the treachery of the Huns, stirred up by Queen Kriemhild, led to a great battle in the hall, or, it would be fairer to say, a great slaughter of the Huns by the Burgundians.[14] The key to the success of the latter was that Dancwart held the door controlling access from the hall's external staircase (*sales stiegen*). The Huns could therefore obtain no assistance as they were massacred; indeed, it was control of the staircase that allowed the Burgundians to hold out against an enemy that was vastly superior in numbers. They threw out the bodies of 7,000 Huns from the steps of the staircase, some, still alive, being killed by the height from which they fell. Queen Kriemhild then ordered the hall to be fired at its four corners. The roof apparently fell in, although the Burgundians, by standing with their backs to the wall and protecting themselves with their shields, were not hurt. The floor evidently did not fall in; it may be that the poet takes it for granted that we understand they were standing on top of a stone vault. The whole episode illustrates in a dramatic way the defensive advantages of a first-floor hall, particularly one vaulted at ground level; it is well worth bearing in mind when keeps and halls are discussed in the pages following.

In a very valuable study of castles in south Germany the author has suggested a useful classification and sequence of castles in that area: the refuge castle (*Fluchtburg*), eighth to tenth centuries, motte tower (*Turmhügelburg*), tenth to twelfth centuries, residential keep (*Wohnturm*), tenth to twelfth centuries, real military castle (*Wehrburg*), twelfth to thirteenth centuries.[15] We will look at these four categories one by one.

There are some not very distinctive earthworks from the fifth to the eighth centuries, but it is only after this date that earthworks suddenly begin to proliferate, particularly in Saxony and Lower Germany.[16] The most characteristic are circular works (*Rundwälle*), fairly regular in shape and varying internally from 30 m–150 m in diameter, but most commonly about 60 m (fig. 9). Excavation has shown they contain traces of post-built rectangular buildings, some perhaps qualifying as halls. They had elaborate funnel-shaped entrances, flanked by large posts, presumably sometimes forming a wooden gatetower.[17] On higher ground the shape is much more variable, adapting itself to the contours, so that *Rundwälle* are more readily recognisable on low ground.

The historical context of these earthworks is not open to doubt. In the ninth and tenth centuries Europe was assailed from all directions: Magyar nomads from the east, Arabs from the south, Vikings from the north. Henry the Fowler in 926 ordered fortified refuges (*munitionibus firmis, murisque*) to be built for protection in the face of the ravages of the Hungarians.[18] There is an analogy with English burhs, although the German works were not urban, at least in origin, although they might become so as appears to have been the case at Werla in Lower Saxony.[19]

The precise status of these earthworks is not easy to decide. They were not tribal like hill-forts, but evidently pre-feudal and communal, and not associated with individual land-holding, so far as one can judge. Mottes, when they can be related to them, are always later. The

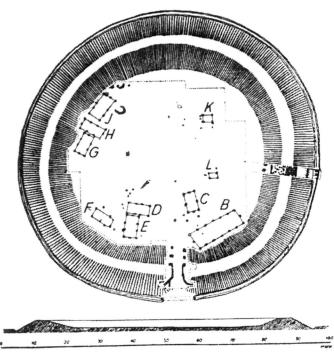

9 Hünenburg, Graftshaft Hoya, Lower Saxony. A German *Rundwall*, a circular earthwork of the tenth to eleventh centuries with traces of rectangular wooden buildings exposed by excavation inside. Internal diameter *c.* 60 m.

great circular forts or barracks of the Vikings in Denmark, belonging to the eleventh century, like Fyrkat,[20] are presumably a final expression of this type of fortification. Whether such structures really qualify for the title of castle must be open to doubt; as the word is normally understood they probably do not.

About the second and third categories there can be no doubt for they bear the hall-mark of feudalism, a tower, in wood in the case of the motte, and of stone in the case of the keep. We are beginning to feel the results of cultural currents wafting across the Rhine. Both mottes and keeps will be discussed more fully in the next chapter and so the subject will only be touched on here.

Mottes occur in many parts of Germany, but have been particularly well studied in the North Rhineland.[21] In this *Land*, nearly 150 mottes have been identified, perhaps significantly densely concentrated on the Dutch border. From 5 m to 10 m is the usual height of the mound, although there are tall examples of more than 10 m and others of less than 5 m. About the very low mounds, there must be doubts as to their defensive character. The majority of mottes in this area have an attached earthwork enclosure, a bailey (*Vorburg*), and are evidently the same sort of structures as one finds in France and England. In at least one case there was evidence for a wooden tower, and from the end of the twelfth and thirteenth centuries stone buildings were erected on the mound.[22]

The rising sea-levels of the North Sea which raised such problems for the saltworkers on the north Kent marshes[23] must have influenced the gradient of the bed of the Rhine, exacerbating the problems and risks of flooding a long way up it. Some of the early raising of mounds in the Rhine valley may have been to counter this risk, a matter that has given rise to discussion. In the well-known excavations at Husterknupp, south-west of Düsseldorf, an original flat settlement with rectangular buildings, the lower parts of which were remarkably well preserved, was superseded in stages by a low and then a high mound.[24] The settlement was a defended one from the beginning, protected by ditches filled with water from the adjoining stream, the Erst. The earlier mound, the *Kernmotte*, can hardly have had a defensive purpose and must surely have been a response to the threat of flooding. The final mound, the base of which covered the whole area of the original settlement, must certainly be a real motte. The buildings were of great interest (built of vertical planks with tongue-and-groove joints held at intervals by posts and at their base by horizontal planks), because of the survival of the wood in the waterlogged conditions, but none seem to have been of sufficient size to constitute a hall. The original settlement was a roughly square moated enclosure about 48 by 42 m with seven internal buildings; at the second stage a bailey (*Vorburg*) was added which was greatly enlarged at the third stage. Surprisingly, houses found in the first and second stages seem to have been absent in the third, although a tower-like structure was inferred on top of the mound. The dating, which depended on pottery, allows wide margins of error, but fell within the range of between the tenth and twelfth centuries.

Mottes are fairly widespread in Germany, albeit they are usually associated with low ground. Their use apparently had a long life, for they were constructed in the later settlements of the eastward drive into the Slav areas.

What is regarded as the stone version of the wooden tower on the motte, the residential keep (*Wohnturm*) is known in Germany only from a small and rather miscellaneous collection of towers.[25] Nothing like the great French or English keeps are represented in Germany, although from the later middle ages isolated towers, recalling the Irish and Scottish tower-houses, occur.[26]

According to Antonow, the reign of the Emperor Henry III (1039–46) saw the initial transition from the motte to the high castle (*Hohenburg*), away from the low ground up into the mountains for the ideal type of fortification.[27] From the middle of the twelfth century castle construction accelerated, culminating in a boom period (*Burgen-Bauboom*) under Frederick II in the first half of the thirteenth century. Antonow's graph shows a falling-off after 1300 and a dramatic collapse after 1450. This certainly differs very markedly from the course of events in England, where the falling-off started much earlier.

In German-speaking areas a castle had three functions: first as a fortified seat of a lord, often an imperial *ministerial* or civil servant, second as a record or legal centre and thirdly as a status symbol.[28] As there was an element of central imperial control there is a much higher degree of uniformity in the form and disposition of the castles than in England, assisted by the fact that they were usually laid out on a fresh site without the constraint of works that were already there. Even when alterations took place, as in the sixteenth century, to take account of artillery, it was done fairly regularly by adding another enclosure equipped with bastions, along the spur.

The castle was placed on a spur with the ground falling steeply, if not

precipitously, on three sides and the main defences on the flat part of
the spur. There were four essential elements which could be varied according to the particular function of the castle. There was an enclosing
curtain wall which, to judge by the measurements of Antonow, was
always wide enough to carry a wall walk and parapet along the top.
The absence of flanking towers along it must have reduced its defensi-
bility. Similarly the gatehouse, the second element, did not develop the
great projecting towers on either side, normal in an English gatehouse,
which must have reduced its effectiveness. The chapel was generally
over the gate, and so readily available to those arriving or leaving.

Within were those two features which are so peculiar to the German
castle: the *Palas* and the *Bergfried*. Of the first we have already spoken
(p. 17): the residential and ceremonial block, always at least two-
storeyed, with the principal 'hall' on the first floor. In the imperial
palace the ceremonial and administrative functions of the *Palas* were of
overriding importance. The main accommodation being undefended,
that is, the principal residence not being in the keep as in England or
France, the need for a curtain wall from an early date can be well
understood.

This brings us to the most remarkable feature of the German castle,
the *Bergfried*. One might translate the word as 'keep' since it was a tall
tower, square or round, that dominated the whole site (fig. 10); but this
would give an English reader an entirely misleading idea of its function.
According to Antonow, the cost of its erection represented about half

10 Münzenberg, Hessen. View of
the castle from below the hill
showing the two *Bergfried* towers
and the windows of the *Palas*

the total outlay on building the castle,[29] for it was solidly built and from 18 to 30 m high. It could be square or round and was entered at first- or second-floor level by wooden steps or a retractable ladder or bridge. There was no spiral staircase inside, the upper floors being reached by wooden steps or ladder, as in a windmill. Normally there were no fireplaces and scarcely any windows, so it was clearly not intended for habitation. Often the tower was so placed on the approach side of the castle that a defensive function was clearly intended: a platform from which missiles could be hurled at the enemy. It could also be used as a look-out and was possibly occupied by a watchman who lived on the lower floors. The tower is often spoken of as a refuge of last resort. However, one must suspect that not its least importance was symbolic; the tall, slender tower, so characteristic of the German castle, and giving it a dramatic aspect; 'nailing the valley', in the expressive German phrase.

The etymology of *Bergfried* has caused much discussion.[30] It was used also to describe the belfry, the wooden tower wheeled up to the outside of the wall during an assault in a medieval siege (fig. 26) to bring the attackers on to the same level as the defenders. Possibly the word originally meant a bell-tower at a cemetery. From our point of view, the fascinating aspect of this type of Hohenstaufen castle is that it seems to represent an attempt to combine on one site the old imperial Carolingian palace and the new French feudal tower, which, not being serviceable for accommodation, became necessarily something of a supernumerary symbol.

One very curious and distinctive feature of Hohenstaufen castles may be mentioned here: the peculiar dressing of the stone used on the military parts of the castle, curtain wall and *Bergfried*. It is a sort of rustication, the stones being squared round the sides and coursed normally, but the surface of each left projecting, half dressed but with sharp edges where it had been flaked (fig. 11). It gives a most distinctive

11 Münzenberg, Hessen. Inner and outer faces of the walls showing the 'rustication' (*Buckelquädar*) on the latter

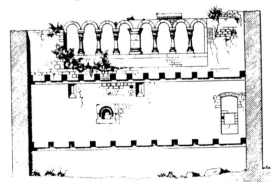

appearance to the building. This *Buckelquädar*, as it is called, is found over the Hohenstaufen area, Germany and Italy, but hardly in France and not in England. As it is not found on the inner faces of domestic buildings it can be interpreted as functional, to render scaling of the walls more difficult, but another school of thought regards it as purely decorative.

To put a little flesh on the bones this chapter may be concluded with brief descriptions of two of the best known of the Hohenstaufen castles, in one case called a castle and in the other, a palace.

The castle of Münzenberg in Hessen lies in the valley of the river Wetter, a tributary of the Main which itself flows into the Rhine. It was erected by a *ministerial* of Barbarossa (Frederick I, emperor from 1155), Conrad von Hagen, and work on it had apparently begun by 1153.[31] There was further building in the late thirteenth century. The plan shows two concentric enclosures, the outer one with towers being from the later periods (fig. 12). Entry was from the east outer curtain

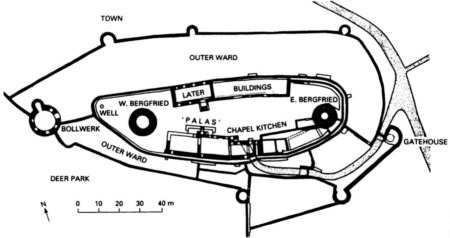

12 Münzenberg, Hessen. Plan of the castle (compare fig. 10)

leading to a fairly modest gatehouse containing the chapel. Beyond was the original oval enclosure, unusual in that it contained two *Bergfriede*, the original twelfth-century one at the east end and a thirteenth-century example at the west end. Both were circular, but there is a very marked difference in wall thickness, so that the eastern tower had an interior diameter of 3.9 m, and the western, 6.45 m. The eastern tower had a rock-cut basement with cupola vault and three storeys above, its entry being 9.9 m above the present ground surface. The west tower also had three storeys with a vaulted basement.

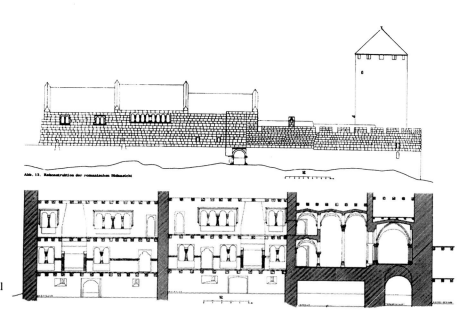

Abb. 13. Rekonstruktion der romanischen Südansicht

13 Münzenberg, Hessen. Elevation and section of the residential buildings and chapel

The *Palas* block standing against the south side of the enclosure measured 29.7 by 11.5 m (fig. 13). It had two storeys over a semi-basement, the first floor being reached by external steps, although how the door of the second was reached from outside is not clear. The block was divided into two, each part measuring roughly 13 by 8 m internally, and a fireplace in the eastern half has led one to infer a similar one in the more ruinous west half. Using *Parzifal* and other vernacular sources there has been an attempt to define the functions of the different rooms: an ordinary hall (*Sal*) on the first floor and a special-occasion hall (*Festsaal*) on the second floor. Both this and the suggestion of the use of the semi-basement as stables are best regarded as matters for discussion. The three-bay chapel, twelfth century in origin, over the gate was accessible from the *Palas*.

Some interesting calculations have been done which suggest that if the buildings were erected in sequence they would have taken about ten years to build: *Bergfried* two years, curtain wall two to three years, *Palas* two to three years, chapel and gate one year and other buildings one year. This does not agree with earlier suggestions that the *Bergfried* would absorb half the cost of construction (p. 22) and should be regarded as a matter for discussion. Medieval building-accounts in any case leave little doubt that several buildings would be erected simultaneously.

The second example, which lies east of Frankfurt, is known as Palace (*Pfalz*) Gelnhausen, because it was erected by Barbarossa a few years later. The palace was constructed in the 1160s and the accompanying town in 1170; both were part of the same design. The palace was largely an imperial administrative centre, 'an expression of the decentralised condition of this mobile kingship'.[32] In this case the earliest stone structure to be erected was a square tower at the gate, acting as a sort of protective *Bergfried*; the construction of a round tower at the other end of the site was never completed. The enclosure took the shape of a very irregular polygon situated on an island (not a *Hohenburg*) and there was a large outer bailey, or *Vorburg*. The *Palas* lay on the north side of the enclosure, so placed that it adjoined the gate chapel (fig. 14). It was of two storeys over a semi-basement, and divided internally into two sections, 12 by 12 m on the west and 13 by 12 m internally on the east.

14 Gelnhausen, Hessen. Elevation of the *Palas*; note the multi-storey construction, and central division in the block

The western part was divided so as to have a passage on the side facing the courtyard. There was a double row of columns in the eastern part, evidently to support a vanished vault. External steps led to a door on the first floor in the eastern section and a doorway from there led into the passage in the western part.

As at Münzenberg, there were elaborate windows with shafts with sculptured capitals, five-light on the second floor and three-light on the first floor. The sculpture at Gelnhausen was of a very high order as befits an imperial seat. The question of the veranda style and its remoter Classical antecedents has already been discussed (p. 17). It may be remarked that in Germany Romanesque styles and motifs continued later than in France, the veranda style persisting until the end of the century.

The most remarkable of the Hohenstaufen emperors was perhaps the last, Frederick II (1212–50), who was more Italian than German, ruling of course at a time when Italy was part of the Holy Roman Empire. South Italy was then an extraordinary mixture of Greek, Norman and Arab cultures. Not surprisingly, the string of castles associated with Frederick's name have a refinement that is quite unknown in Germany itself.[33] It would go well beyond the subject of this book to describe any of these fascinating buildings here, but one exception must be made.

Castel del Monte, near Andria, west of Bari (fig. 15), should be mentioned not only because it is one of the finest of all European castles, but also because it represents something of a departure from what we see in northern Europe (although it is thought to have had some influence there). The first thing that strikes one is the symmetry of the design;

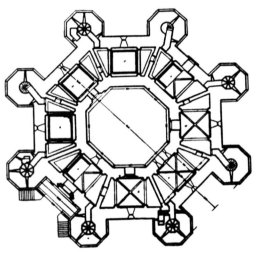

15 Castel del Monte, Apulia. Plan of the remarkable octagonal castle of Emperor Frederick II, with a small tower on each corner and continuous two-storey ranges within, vaulted at both levels (cf. figs. 70 and 71). Scale *c.* 1:1,000

defences and buildings within are conceived as a unity. It is more like a Renaissance palace, and there is certainly a palace feel about it, yet the scale of construction and the towers at the angles leave no doubt that it is a castle. The regular ranges of buildings around the inside of the octagon, two-storeyed and vaulted, are entirely different from the rather scattered nature of medieval buildings in a castle in northern Europe. The castles of Boulogne-sur-mer (fig. 71) in France and Bolingbroke (fig. 70) in England have decided affinities with Castel del Monte, although as they seem earlier, 1220s rather than 1240s, it may be a matter of common ancestry in the Mediterranean (p. 105).

At this point we must take leave of German castles, fascinating as their later history may be, since it is only the earlier stages up to maturity that form part of the background to the subject of the present book.

Chapter 3

France

The castle is perhaps the most striking symbol of feudal society
and of its ideal. In it is reflected the situation, political, social
and economic of the baron . . . But it is the capital of a small
state, since it holds all the essential political organs of the
district that it dominates: army, court of justice, administration . . . It testifies to the complete civil liberty of its master . . .
It shows the human unity of feudal society in its superb
isolation, withdrawn from daily contact with the street or
public place, entirely sunk into the solitude that demands
strong wills, burning imaginations, sharp sensibilities.[1]

The passage above is even more dramatic in the original French of
Louis Reynaud. The sentiments are decidedly French, Reynaud here of
course intending to contrast France with imperial Germany. The
English reader who has not been taught to look at castles in this light
may well ponder the points made. However, before turning to castles
we must give some attention to palaces, since whereas in Germany
castle and palace merged to produce the same form of structure, in
France (and England) palace and castle remained quite distinct.

The palaces of the early middle ages, of the ninth to twelfth centuries, and the extent to which they can be derived from Carolingian, or
ultimately late Roman imperial palaces, is a subject that has attracted a
great deal of interest.[2] In Flanders the palaces of the count (Bruges,
Ghent, Douai) covered a bigger area (1–5 hectares, 2.5–12.5 acres) than
a castle, and included a number of ancillaries among which a collegiate
church was regarded as essential. Such palaces also existed in France at
Troyes, Paris, Laon, Senlis, Etampes, Poitiers and Angers. At Paris the
palace that had existed there since Merovingian times became the
Palais Royal in the Ile de la Cité in the high middle ages.

A distinctive feature of these palaces was a grand hall (*salle*), almost
invariably on the first floor, as at Bruges, Troyes, Paris, Laon, Senlis,
Angers, and Etampes. The exception was the *salle* at Poitiers which,
although on the ground floor, was not aisled. At Bruges the written

evidence suggests some kind of gallery.[3] So far as one can judge there was no very fixed plan: the buildings did not form a courtyard. A keep or donjon of stone was sometimes added. The chapel served by secular canons could be two-storeyed, as at Sainte Chapelle at Paris.[4]

As in Germany (p. 17) there is general agreement that these palaces can trace their origins back to Roman villas,[5] but the links from the intervening period are much more tenuous, mainly because none of the buildings survive, and it is essentially on the decorative features of the facade that the veranda style can be identified. In Germany not only do impressive buildings from the period survive but there was a more conscious and deliberate seeking after imperial grandeur. In France the ubiquitous arcading of the Romanesque is our chief reminder of these remote antecedents.

A 'palace' that may remind us of these links and deserves mention stood in the castle of Lillebonne, near Le Havre, Seine Inférieure, a specially favoured seat of the Dukes of Normandy at the time of William the Conqueror. Today a splendid cylindrical keep built by Philippe Auguste in c. 1204 is all that survives of the castle,[6] but prior to their demolition in the 1830s very substantial remains of the ducal palace survived, including a roofed building which was drawn by John Cotman in c. 1820 (fig. 16). An eighteenth-century plan shows that the

16 Lillebonne castle (Seine Inférieure). Cotman's drawing (c. 1820) of the now-demolished hall of the eleventh-century ducal palace shows a blocked arcade on the ground floor continued round the courtyard on the right. Note the two-light windows of the hall that stood on the vault above and the later Renaissance cornice at roof level

building in the drawing was oriented north–south and was part of an L-shaped group in the south-east corner of the castle bailey (Cotman was facing south-east). The east curtain broken away can be seen at the left-hand corner of the gable.

The blocked arcade below and the windows above remind one of the arcade in the south transept of Winchester cathedral, but this building is clearly not ecclesiastical and there is no question of a triforium. There appears to be a doorway in the gable end with two tiers of windows above. At the right-hand corner of the building three remaining arches form the return of the arcade, which is shown running along the south side of the court in the nineteenth-century view. The cornice on the upper part of the building must be a post-Renaissance alteration. A broken-off return at the north-west corner gable perhaps represents a closing wall to form a court. English visitors before the demolition were greatly impressed by the building, which they described as a great hall that had formerly stood over a ground-floor vault, so it must be assumed that behind the blocked arcade there was a vault supporting the first floor. The surface of the wall seems to be rendered or plastered to just below the gable. The windows have largely lost their heads, but the decorated capitals of the shafts are clear: two lights beneath an enclosing arch. The arches of the arcade, plain and undecorated, do not spring from columns but from an abacus on a plain respond in sections of wall. No doubt when the openings were blocked the small doorway with pointed head was inserted at this end to convert the ground floor into a closed room.

If the building may be interpreted as a first-floor hall forming one side of a courtyard arcaded on at least two sides it is of great interest, whether we date it to the eleventh or the twelfth century. It recalls German halls, but perhaps rather more strongly north Italian urban buildings, like the Badia at Orvieto. Perhaps the cartoonist had something like this mind in the two-storeyed building represented at Bosham in the Bayeux tapestry.

The bishop's palace at Laon, more than a century later, has an elegant open arcade on the ground floor (fig. 17). As very few domestic buildings survive from French castles earlier than the thirteenth century it is to bishops' palaces that we must turn to find out what these buildings looked like in the twelfth century. Owing to their continuity of use, both in England and France, episcopal palaces are one of the most valuable collections of medieval domestic buildings at aristocratic level.

The archiepiscopal palace at Paris lay between the cathedral and the

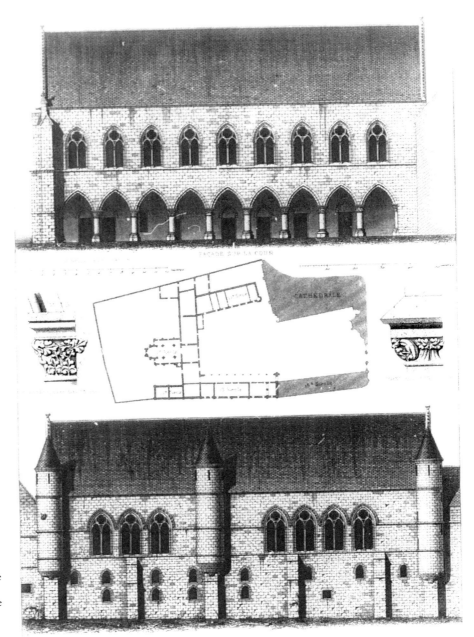

17 Laon (Aisne). Nineteenth-century plan and elevations of the bishop's palace of the thirteenth century after restoration; note the open arcade at ground level. The length of the building is 34 m

river Seine on its south side.[7] There was reference to a *grande salle* from the ninth century among the buildings. The two or three separate churches that lay in an extended line to form the cathedral were replaced by the present cathedral of Notre Dame by Archbishop Maurice de Sully (1160–96) who, as part of the general reconstruction constructed the archbishop's palace that was demolished only early in the nineteenth

18 Paris. Viollet-le-duc's reconstruction of the twelfth-century archbishop's palace (now destroyed) between the cathedral of Notre Dame and the Seine, showing its single block construction with a two-storeyed hall in the middle

century. Sufficient knowledge of it survived for Viollet-le-duc to make the reconstruction drawing reproduced in figure 18. There are five elements: the two-storeyed hall block in the middle, the two-storeyed chapel on the right, a tower, a gallery linking the palace with the cathedral and a fifteenth-century westward extension.

This type of two-storeyed hall was in universal use at the aristocratic level in France throughout the middle ages and beyond. The lower hall, *salle basse*, could serve a variety of functions, including service, as the hall proper, the *grande salle*, was on the first floor. In a bishop's palace this was the synodal hall, used for its meetings. As with the German hall, the ground floor frequently had a vault resting on a spinal row of columns, and there was an external staircase. There could be spinal support on the first floor and Viollet certainly assumes a king-post roof (a central post rising from tie beam to apex of roof, unlike the crown post that only rose to a collar, normal in English roofs). It differed from the German hall in that it was not transversely divided into two halves. Even in the Renaissance, Rabelais tells us how Gargantua led his pursuers a dance 'through the second hall', eventually returning 'to the lower hall where the company was'.[8] When considering keeps in castles it is an important background point to bear in mind.

Information on a number of French bishops' palaces will be found in appendix 1. The earliest halls at Angers and Meaux, both twelfth century, had vaults supported on a spinal row of columns on the ground floor, the normal later practice. The hall at Laon, which is of interest because of the open arcade on the ground floor, belongs to the thirteenth century. It has been heavily restored: de Caumont showed it without tracery in the windows, the turrets finishing at the eaves and the roof of low pitch. So in its present form it should not be regarded as accurate in detail.

It is time to turn back to the origins of the castle. In France as in Germany, the ninth-century invasions certainly caused a large number of defensive works to be thrown up; in 864 Charles the Bald issued the famous Edict of Pîtres ordering the destruction of fortifications constructed by private individuals in defiance of the need for royal licence.[9] It was like King Canute ordering back the tide: in the face of a monarchy that was fast losing all authority there was no alternative to self-help. Charles was no doubt right to see this multiplication of private fortifications as a challenge and a menace to royal authority. Given then that there was a proliferation of privately constructed earthworks, at what point can one speak of these fortifications as castles? This is the central and most contentious area in the study of castles.

At the time of these events profound social changes were taking place of which we are only made aware from written and archaeological sources long after they had happened. The subject of 'feudalism' has caused historians to spill so much ink over so long a period of time that one is loath to raise it again, but it is so central to the subject of castles that it cannot be avoided. In a society where land was held as a fief by doing homage as a vassal, and where tenure of land was by military service, where the principal occupation of aristocratic males was to enhance the martial spirit by practising at arms and using them in earnest, a pride was generated that found expression in an aggressive sort of dwelling, the castle. This dwelling took the form of either a stone tower or a conical mound with a wooden tower-like structure on top.

The word 'motte' is Celtic in origin,[10] meaning a clod of earth, and in early instances of its use could be applied to any heap of soil, for example, the dam to create a mill pond. Later its use was restricted to the mound of a Norman castle, to which other names were also applied: donjon, *arx* and so on. In English it is now the normal word for the castle mound, although it has the same origin as the differentiated form, moat, applied to a water-filled ditch. It may be doubted whether the very restricted area on top of a conical mound like a motte had any military advantage over a level area surrounded by a substantial bank, which permitted much greater freedom of movement within. It may be suspected that the motive behind the construction of such a mound owed more to a crude instinct analogous to that of the child climbing on to a high place and shouting 'I am king of the castle' than to military considerations.

Although a good many Norman earthworks did not have mottes it is very difficult to decide on the status of an earthwork enclosure lacking one, unless there is masonry or some other indication to corroborate that it was a castle. The example of Goltho (p. 9) must come to mind, where the pre-Conquest defences did not constitute a castle, but the addition of a motte in *c*. 1070 did. Inevitably, therefore, the discussion about the origin of the castle has turned into a search for the origin of the motte. There seems to be fair degree of consensus that this place of origin lay between the Garonne and the lower Rhine and that emergence took place between the early tenth and early eleventh centuries.[11] A recent survey concluded that it was an imitation in wood, its base protected by soil, of a stone tower, perhaps a Roman signal tower.[12] Such a theory seems too contrived for the present writer; as a working hypothesis the following might be offered.

If a group of scattered buildings dominated by a hall, such as was described at the beginning of this book (p. 2), was threatened by attack the natural reaction would be to form a bank with stockade and ditch around it, or at least around the main buildings. The lord did not live in the hall but in his two-storeyed solar; to prevent this being fired by the enemy what more natural than to bury its ground floor in soil, dug from a surrounding ditch. The mid-eleventh-century wooden tower at Court-Marigny (nr Montargis, Loiret) was occupied by the family in its upper part who lived, entertained and slept in the solar (*solarium*) with its mortared floor over the cellar.[13] It would soon be apparent that rather than cover the base of an existing building a framework of four posts, set upright, could be buried that would support a structure that mushroomed out from the top. The very odd constructions on the top of the mottes in the Bayeux tapestry might be intelligible on that basis, while the man shovelling at the bottom of the Hastings motte might be covering up something that had already been buried (fig. 19). Wace's *Roman de Rou*, a poem written a hundred years after the invasion of England in 1066, is not history, but its author presumably understood how mottes were constructed.[14] The carpenters arrived at Hastings,

9 Bayeux tapestry: shovelling soil at Hastings perhaps to cover the supports of a superstructure on the motte

unloaded the timbers from the boats and, using the ample supply of pegs in barrels, constructed the castle, the diggers only working afterwards to make the ditch and presumably covering the framework supporting the superstructure. It may be remarked that the very puzzling flanges projecting from the foundation of the keep at Farnham Castle, Surrey (p. 56), which might be explained as a skeuomorph in stone of just such a construction in wood, cannot be readily explained in any other way.[15]

The main attraction of such a theory, apart from rendering superfluous a *deus ex machina* like a Roman signal tower, is the social one: by singling out the lord for special recognition it chimed in with the position already conferred by social changes. Not surprisingly, this gave such a construction an appeal that spread the idea across Europe like wildfire. When translated into stone the mound became superfluous, leaving a simple tower; too small for a hall but large enough for a solar. The majority of the keeps of western France are too small to have contained a hall (p. 39). At Farnham the original square tower seems to have been in this kind of relationship to the great hall, accessible from its upper end, a place of private retreat for the bishop throughout the middle ages and afterwards.

At this point reference must be made to the remarkable discoveries of the late Michel de Bouard, doyen of French 'castellogistes', at Doué la Fontaine, Maine et Loire, near Angers.[16] It was known that there had been a Carolingian palace in the area. From 1967 to 1970 excavation of walls exposed by a bulldozer revealed a rectangular building measuring 16.5 by 23.5 m externally, 13.5 by 20 m internally, masonry walls 1.6 to 1.7 m thick and standing to a height of 5.3 to 6.1 m. The walls were of rubble masonry with some parts of herringbone work, the stones laid on edge. The building had a central hearth with doors in two walls, and a window in the north wall. It had been destroyed by fire somewhere between 925 and 950, dating being provided by a conveniently placed coin and radiocarbon readings on charcoal. The walls were reddened by burning. The excavator identified the structure as a ceremonial hall (*salle d'apparat*). After the fire the whole building was raised, spinal posts put in on the ground floor to support a first floor, new doors made at first-floor level and those at ground-floor level blocked. Two mid-tenth-century coins gave a date for these changes. Entry was now by an external staircase. In the final stage, which was appreciably later, the whole base of the structure was buried by material cast up from an encircling ditch 15 m wide and 5.6 m deep. The creation of the motte, for this is clearly what the mound was, is to be referred to the eleventh century, and the site was abandoned in the following century.

The importance of the discovery cannot be exaggerated: at one stroke the motive for raising the hall to the first floor becomes apparent, a general feature on the Continent as we have seen (p. 34). Burying the base of the structure in a motte lends weight to the hypothesis just put forward for motte origins. It was no doubt easier with a smaller building like a solar, especially if made of wood; it must be doubted whether Doué la Fontaine can be regarded as the normal line of development, however suggestive it may be. The problem of hoisting a large building like a hall on to the top of a freshly made mound, even with internal supports, is virtually insoluble; either time, many years, had to be allowed for the mound to consolidate, or the mound was left out and a large masonry tower was constructed. The latter required quite a lot of experiment before the huge keeps of northern France and England proved to be the solution.

A valuable analysis of the castles of Fulk Nerra in Touraine, close to Doué, has much influenced our views on this subject.[17] Fulk the Black, Count of Anjou, who lived *c.* 970–1040 and was Count from 987, was credited with having built at least thirteen castles. He is a major figure in the history of both feudalism and castles, dominating central France for fifty years, in ceaseless conflict with his neighbours, a great founder of castles and abbeys, four times a pilgrim to Jerusalem; he was the quintessential medieval baron. Deyres sees a pattern in Fulk's castles: set on a spur they were guarded at the level end by a motte, no doubt originally with a wooden tower on top. Within the defended area behind the motte was a residential block, the *domicilium*, in effect a first-floor hall such as we find at Langeais (Indre-et-Loire). This famous building is usually regarded as the first keep, built by Fulk in 994, which would put it into the same sort of category as Doué la Fontaine, essentially a first-floor hall. Montbazon (Indre-et-Loire) would fall into the same category, a rare survival from this early period. Originally these *domicilia* would have been more common and have some analogy with the German *Palas*. At Langeais (fig. 20) there were three floors in the rectangular block. Deyres would see three elements in Fulk's castles, apart from the enclosing earthwork: the motte or donjon in earth and timber, the stone *domicilium* or residential block and a stone gatetower. The three elements can vary on different sites, but are well worth bearing in mind when considering later castles.

20 Langeais (Indre-et-Loire). The interior of the three-storeyed *domicilium*, or hall, of *c*. 1000 AD, probably built by Fulk Nerra

Apart from the somewhat enigmatic representations of superstructures on the French mottes in the Bayeux tapestry, which clearly show a peripheral stockade, central structure and a sort of flying bridge over the ditch, there are a number of references from the twelfth century which leave no doubt that a large central superstructure was an integral part of the work. Since these superstructures never survive on existing mottes, it is worth quoting two of the references to remind ourselves that the earthen mound we see was essentially a pedestal for a wooden superstructure, and that we are really looking at a left-over stump. In Suger's Life of Louis the Fat (Louis VI 1108–37) the phrase is met, 'in the motte that is the upper wooden tower' (*in mota scilicet turre lignea superiori*).[18] In Gautier's Life of John, Bishop of Thérouanne (Somme), 'the richest and noblest men are accustomed to devote a large part of their time to provoking conflict and committing murders. They have a practice also, in order to protect themselves from their enemies and overawe by their greater power their equals or subdue those weaker, of raising from collected soil an earthen motte (*agger*) of the greatest height possible, cutting a wide and very deep ditch around it, fortifying its upper edge with squared timbers tied together as in a wall, creating towers around it and of building inside a house or citadel that dominates the whole structure.'[19]

This is probably as far as the question of mottes can be taken, for their origin will always be a matter for discussion. In the next chapter the question of mottes will come up again, but so far as Continental Europe is concerned it seems that by the early twelfth century they were virtually ubiquitous over much of Europe, or the feudalised part of it. We hear much less about castles in the Cid's struggles with the Arabs in Spain, for the Arabs were not of course feudalised. A point that has recently emerged is that a good many earthwork castles did not have mottes, even in Normandy, or perhaps especially in Normandy.[20] The explanation for this is not clear, but the subject is best postponed until 'ringworks' in England are discussed (p. 49).

Contemporary with mottes, the stone equivalent of the wooden towers, the obverse of the coin so to speak, were stone keeps or towers. Found all over France, the 108 square or rectangular examples found in western France between the Somme and the Garonne have been the subject of study.[21] These keeps are not the only type in the area, but they form a reasonably uniform group, especially distinguishable by the 'pilaster buttresses' which run up the sides of the majority; these may be curved or square in section, but are called 'pilaster' because they project only a few centimetres from the wall face. They are usually evenly spaced along the wall surface, with two clasping the corner or enveloping it. As the floor levels were not vaulted over there was no outward thrust to be counteracted by an external buttress, so it seems they were ornamental. Some scholars regard the pilasters as skeuomorphs of wooden posts when such structures were made of wood. The interesting aspect from an English point of view is that, ecclesiastical architecture apart, they are not found on other Continental keeps further east, but are normal on English towers, a fair indication of where the links lay.

The greater number of these keeps are found in the south between the Loire and Garonne, although denser occupation in the north may have led to greater destruction. On the whole the smaller keeps are in the south, and the larger keeps in the north are more comparable to English examples.

The normal French tower was some three storeys high, with the ground floor acting as a sort of basement, since the entry doorway was about 6 m above outside ground level. Unlike English keeps, there is only very rarely a forebuilding to contain the entry stairs to the door, which must have been reached by a retractable ladder or bridge of wood, as with the German *Bergfried*. Like the latter, communication between floors seems to have been by wooden steps, a spiral staircase being unusual. Window openings are small, giving the towers a decidedly grim appearance. The towers were probably usually on the enclosing defences of some kind of bailey, although we are less well informed on this point. Wall thicknesses vary from about 1.4 to 3.8 m, but the average seems rather less than that in English keeps. The wall surface is sometimes rubble but finely dressed stone is much more common here than in England.

Measurements of M. Chatelaine's plans suggest that about a third have an internal space that could contain a room of 10 or 11 m more in length, or, in other words, at least a small hall. Hall-keeps, if the term will be allowed, seem therefore to be in a minority. The other two-thirds, which vary in size are usually square and may be very small; perhaps we can speak of solar-keeps. The former presumably derive from first-floor halls like Langeais or Doué la Fontaine, the latter having more affinity to the wooden towers of mottes. Square hall-keeps sometimes have a central dividing wall, no doubt carried up to assist in spanning the roof, and possibly pierced below by an arcade acting like the spinal columns of a Continental hall.

So far as dating goes, the series presumably begins with Doué la Fontaine or Langeais, but the real development must have been at the end of the eleventh and during the twelfth centuries. If the Norman invaders of England had had more experience and knowledge of stone keeps when they arrived, the virtual absence of these keeps in this country, before experimental forms like the White Tower and Castle Acre appeared, would be quite inexplicable. Indeed it is beyond doubt that the majority of the large French hall-keeps were erected in the twelfth century, the greatest builder of them being the English king, Henry I. Space will only allow the briefest reference to a few examples.

Figure 21 gives ground plans, all at the same scale, from the publication cited in note 21 of seven examples in Touraine: Langeais, Montbazon and Loches down the right-hand side of the panel, and four smaller keeps down the left-hand side. Grand Pressigny, an extremely

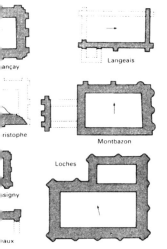

Ground plans of French Romanesque keeps in Touraine. Note the difference between 'solar-keeps' on the left and *domilia*, or first-floor halls, on the right. Scale *c.* 1:1,000

small example, measuring only 5.9 by 5.5 m internally, would qualify as a solar-keep. Langeais and Montbazon, the two early *domicilia*, need no further mention. Loches is a formidable structure dated to around 1100, its lower part being an earlier *domicilium*, or so it has been suggested, subsequently raised to its impressive height of 37 m (fig. 22). None of the floors are vaulted. The forebuilding on the north is a later and unusual feature, as are the remarkable pilaster buttresses, round on a square base. Loches is built of dressed and coursed stone, and is one of the finest of French keeps. It is given a specially forbidding air by the scarcity of window openings.

Moving further north to Normandy there are some splendid keeps, the foundations of a mighty example at Caen having recently been revealed by de Bouard. Cotman's dramatic view of the keep at Falaise (fig. 23) shows its square shape and pilaster buttresses contrasting with the cylindrical shape of Philippe Auguste's round tower, added seventy years later. The keeps at Falaise, Caen and Arques la Bataille are the work of Henry I, so at Falaise there is a dramatic contrast between the work of the English king and the French king who later conquered Normandy.

Not all the keeps were square or rectangular; they could be round or lobed, like the curious mid-twelfth-century example from Etampes (Seine-et-Oise). Even later is the fine cylindrical keep at Châteaudun (Eure-et-Loir) shown in figures 24 and 25 in elevation and section. It is

22 Loches (Indre-et-Loire). Nineteenth-century drawing of the keep: note the unusual pilaster buttresses and annexe

23 Falaise (Calvados). Cotman's drawing of *c.* 1820 showing Henry I's keep of the 1120s with pilaster buttresses, and Philippe Auguste's round tower of *c.* 1200

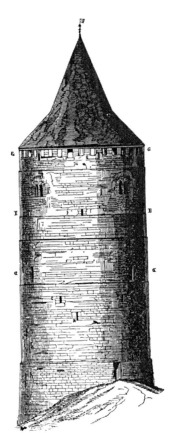

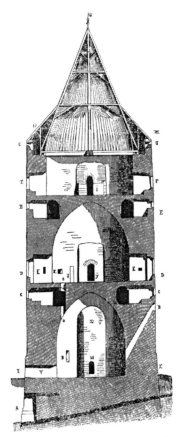

24 Châteaudun (Eure-et-Loir).
Elevation of the late twelfth-
century round keep with fifteenth-
century roof

25 Châteaudun (Eure-et-Loir).
Section of keep showing vaulting
at the two lower levels and entry
door on the first floor

vaulted at both levels and surmounted by a fine fifteenth-century roof.
Whatever the shape, the keeps had several common traits: great height,
several storeys, thick walls, few and small windows, but interior accommodation improving in quality as one went up the tower.

In Germany from an early date the large residential block had required
an enclosing or curtain wall to protect it, and this took an irregular
shape following the hill. In France, as in England where the keep was
the main residence, a protective wall is found less often. In England the
curtain wall remained irregular in shape until the late thirteenth century, but in France a rectangular shape seems to have been preferred
from an early date.[22] It was not that the idea of the keep was abandoned, on the Continent at any rate, for it was regarded as indispens-
able for another hundred years and highly desirable until the close of
the middle ages. The motive for erecting a strong encircling wall was
similar to that in Germany, that is, to allow large and splendid residential buildings to be erected in the bailey, but it tended to take a much
more aggressive form than the German one, with large flanking towers
and a gate thrust forward from it.

The pivotal structure in the development of the European castle was built by the English king Richard I with incredible speed and equally unbelievable cost between 1197 and 1198 at Château Gaillard (Eure) to protect his dukedom from the formidable French king Philippe Auguste (Philippe II, 1180–1223), but lost by Richard's brother in the famous and successful siege of 1204.[23] Viollet-le-duc's drawing shows the siege in progress (fig. 26), with the castle on the chalk ridge overlooking the river Seine. The besiegers face a triangular outwork with stone curtain and large round corner towers blocking the course of the ridge, itself separated from the outer bailey of the castle by a huge ditch. The curtain wall of the latter was itself fortified with large round towers along its course. The inner bailey, instead of towers, made use of slight rounded projections joined by arches projecting the wall walk forward, so that missiles could be dropped through the openings

26 Château Gaillard (Eure). Viollet-le-duc's reconstruction of the siege in 1204. Note the belfry and trebuchets used by the French attackers

behind to richochet off the sloping base on to the enemy. These remarkable machicolations, as they are called, apparently the earliest in western Europe, are thought to have been learnt about from the Crusades in Arab lands. The keep, which has the same type of protection (fig. 27), is chiefly remarkable for its shape, rounded on one side and pointed on the other, or *donjon en bec* to use the French term.

27 Château Gaillard (Eure). View of beaked keep and machicolations on the inner curtain of Richard I's castle erected in 1197–8

There is little doubt that a larger and more determined garrison could have held out successfully against the French. There are contemporary accounts of the siege, on which Viollet-le-duc based his drawing, of the attack being prepared with a 'belfry' to bring up to the wall and trebuchets or great slings for hurling missiles at the enemy.

Just as Henry II was the great castle-building king in this country, so in France a few years later Philippe Auguste was the great royal castle-builder.[24] In that short period of time there had been a profound change in building design in two important respects: the keep was invariably cylindrical, possibly the better to deflect missiles, and vaulted at each level (as a fire precaution) (fig. 25); secondly, a regular rectangular form of enclosure was preferred. The most impressive example was the Louvre in Paris, rectangular with flanking towers and a great freestanding cylindrical keep in the middle. The king built round keeps elsewhere (Dourdan, Lillebonne, Chinon, Gisors, Falaise, Laon), especially on territory that he had just taken in Normandy and elsewhere. Unfortunately, although there is not much doubt about what he did, the wealth of documentation that is available in England from the annual accounts of the sheriff, the Pipe Rolls, is lacking. There was now a clear and growing difference between England and France in castle design: in England irregular polygons were the rule for the shape, with round keeps (without vaults) only popular in Wales and Marches, and quite a different type of aisled ground-floor hall increasingly held centre stage.

A convenient point at which to end this brief account of French castles is reached at what might be regarded as its climax in the second quarter of the thirteenth century: the construction of the great castle of Coucy (Aisne) not by the king but by one of his richest vassals, Enguerrand III.[25] Situated at the extremity of a spur there was a vast defended outer enclosure on the level ground preceding the castle proper. The latter took the form of an irregular quadrilateral with large round towers at the angles (fig. 28). Facing the approach was the immense circular keep (fig. 29), one of the wonders of medieval secular architecture before its tragic destruction by the Germans in the first World War. There were buildings all the way round, some being additions of the fourteenth century, covering the continuous series of arches along the inner face of the curtain wall that carried the wall walk above. One of the later buildings behind the keep was a range 60 m long, with a vault over the ground floor supported on a spinal row of columns, the hall being on its first floor. The keep had its own moat and was entered across a bridge within the inner bailey. Viollet-le-duc's section shows that below the wall walk the great cylinder contained three storeys, each with its own vault. The rooms, or halls one might call them for they were 15 m in diameter internally, were painted. The tower was over 40 m high and the walls 8–9 m thick. In one of his reconstructions, Viollet shows a multitude of figures standing on the floor and in a gallery of the main upper hall, which gives some conception of the scale of this prodigious structure.

Some idea of how English and French domestic arrangements differed by the thirteenth, or even by the late twelfth century is vividly illustrated by Joinville's description of the great feast held by St Louis (Louis IX, 1226–70) in 1241 at Saumur (Maine et Loire).[26] The English king Henry II was also Count of Anjou, where he spent much time, passing Christmas at Saumur in 1188, and he was also there just before his death in 1189. It is therefore quite feasible that the attribution of the building to him is well-founded, and if so it must be assumed he employed English craftsmen, or at all events an English master mason, for the work. The account of the protocol and ceremony associated with the feast is of great interest, quite apart from the building that the feast was held in. The account may be summarised as follows:

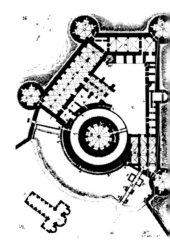

28 Coucy (Aisne). Viollet-le-duc's plan of the castle; note the large corner towers and huge isolated keep of about 1230, and the later domestic range with the hall raised over a vault. Scale *c*. 1:2,750

29 Coucy (Aisne). Photograph of the great keep at Coucy of *c*. 1230 the climax of keep construction, before its demolition in the First World War

King Louis held court at Saumur. Next to him at the high table sat the comte de Poitiers whom he had knighted on St John's day, next to him the comte de Dreux who had just been knighted, then the comte de la Marche, and then the comte Pierre de Bretagne. The King of Navarre sat opposite the king's table. The king's brother, the comte d'Artois, stood facing his majesty ready to serve the meat, while comte Jean de Soissons acted as carver. Imbert de Beaujeu, later high constable, with Enguerrand de Coucy and Archimbaud de Bourbon were on guard at the king's table; behind them were thirty knights in tunics of silk and behind them a large company of sergeants. The king wore a tunic of blue satin and a bright red surcoat.

The king held his banquet in the hall (*hales*) of Saumur which it is said was built by the great King Henry of England so he could hold feasts there. And the hall is made in the form of a Cistercian cloister, but I think none is so big. There was room for a table for twenty bishops and archbishops. The queen mother sat at another table at the side of the 'cloister'. She was served by the comte de Boulogne, the comte Hughes de St-Pol and a young German of 18 years.

At the far end of the 'cloister' were the kitchens, the wine cellars, the pantries and the butteries, from where the king and queen mother were served. Down either side and in the middle so many knights were dining that I could not count them. Many said that they had never seen so many surcoats; it is said that no less than 3,000 knights were present.

Joinville was a youth of 17 at the time of the feast and, although an eye-witness, was recalling events some years later, which no doubt accounts for the exaggerated numbers and size of the hall. The building was evidently in the (pre-fourteenth century) castle and the triple division longitudinally, the service end with buttery, etc., can leave no doubt that it was a large aisled hall of English style. The unusual word used by Joinville is the French for the pillared market-place in Paris or other French towns – *les Halles*. The Cistercian cloister refers to the multi-columned (double or triple aisled) chapter house favoured by that order,[27] and the idea of rows of columns in the hall was clearly quite unfamiliar to a French aristocrat; unlike the English hall, the French one was either free of columns or (very rarely) had a single line. The pillars in the Saumur hall could have been of stone, as in the Angers hospital of the same date, or, as suggested by *les Halles*, of wood, which we now know was used in late twelfth-century English halls.[28] The matter must be left open. The description of the knights in the middle and on either side of the hall is at once intelligible in the triple division of an aisled building. More significant is the concentration of services, buttery, pantry, kitchen at one end; this is clearly the lower end of an English style of hall. The French hall, with external stair in the middle, did not have a screens passage and services were outside or underneath, which profoundly affected seating and serving arrangements.

The hall at Saumur evidently left a deep impression on Joinville, since nowhere else in the life of St Louis does he give a detailed description of a feast of this kind. He was slightly contemptuous but also puzzled, as indeed were many of his modern fellow-countrymen (like Caumont), who have had St Louis eating in the market-place at Saumur. Ground-floor halls without aisles were not unknown in French castles, like the splendid structure at Lucheux (Somme),[29] although the well-known example at Blois with spinal columns over a double basement level is hardly a relevant case. At the aristocratic level with which we are concerned there were, so far as I know, no aisled halls, so that Joinville's puzzlement can be well understood.[30]

G. I. Meirion-Jones, who has done a great deal of reconnaissance on the vernacular architecture of France, tells me that in certain parts aisled halls occur in some numbers at vernacular level.[31] In France, as in Germany, the aisled hall in domestic architecture had been relegated to peasant culture, for aristocratic taste made a two-storeyed structure obligatory. In England, on the other hand, the intrusive first-floor hall existed side by side with the native aisled one, enjoying social prestige throughout the middle ages, although at the time St Louis was at Saumur aisles were having a marked revival under Henry III at Winchester Castle and elsewhere.

The question of whether there was a functional or social difference between the two types of hall is one that will have to be discussed further (p. 91) but what is quite beyond doubt is that the two types of structure looked entirely different. The point may be made by comparing the vast hall erected by Philippe le Bel (Philippe IV, 1284–1314) at the Palais Royal in the Ile de la Cité in Paris with what it is thought Westminster Hall may have looked like before the arcades were taken out and the present roof put in at the end of the fourteenth century. Viollet-le-duc's section (fig. 30) shows the French royal hall (its upper part was burnt in the seventeenth century but drawings then existed of it) had a double gable (double pile in modern jargon) but like the Norman dorter at Christchurch monastery, Canterbury, the wall joining

30 Paris. Section by Viollet-le-duc of the great hall of Philippe le Bel (built *c.* 1300) in the Palais Royal (only the lower part survives); note the vaulting and spinal divisions with a double gable

the two parts was in fact an open arcade at both levels to give two gigantic sections on both floors.[32] The ground floor was further sub-divided by spinal columns to support vaults. The building was 70.5 m long and 27.5 m wide and so was larger than Westminster Hall. Although probably very different in construction, the two buildings served rather similar ceremonial purposes, the French parlement holding its meetings in this hall in Paris.

Chapter 4

Wooden castles

'While these events were happening in Desmond, Hugh de Lacy, like a wise and prudent man, was building strong castles throughout Leinster and Meath.'[1]

Giraldus Cambrensis was speaking of the Norman conquest of Ireland, which failed in his view because castles were not planted 'from sea to sea'.[2] The successful conquest of England a hundred years earlier was attributed by Orderic Vitalis, born at Shrewsbury in 1070 and so virtually an eye-witness, to the skilful use of castles with which the native inhabitants had been unfamiliar.[3] The Normans also erected mottes in southern Italy, but in the Crusader kingdoms of the Levant only stone keeps,[4] the treeless landscape failing to provide the material for erecting the wooden structures for which the motte merely acted as a pedestal. If the Bayeux tapestry may be regarded as a contemporary (or even perhaps 'official') record, then castles and mottes in France appear to be one and the same thing, to judge by the four representations of castles (fig. 31).[5] The predominant French locale, the details of preparation and embarcation and so on must imply surely at least a French cartoonist, albeit with the embroidery done by the ladies of Kent; if it were wholly English in manufacture its value as historical

31 Bayeux tapestry: the motte at Bayeux; note the huge superstructure with flying bridge and mounted knights wearing mail

evidence would be very seriously reduced. The fortifications or fortified residences that the invaders erected in this country from 1066 and
in Ireland from 1169 were principally of this type.

One of the most interesting facts that has emerged since the 1950s is
that not only conical mottes with attendant baileys were constructed
after the Norman Conquest, but also small earthwork enclosures without a large mound, which have been given the name of 'ringworks'.[6]
They are not like the German *Rundwälle* which enclose several acres,
but are normally small, less than 10 m across internally, and sometimes
indeed raised mounds embanked wholly or partially along the edge. A
good example of this is at Long Buckby, Northants, where a bank some
3 m high encloses an oval area roughly 25 by 15 m[7] It was certainly
intended to act as a motte, for it has one or probably two attendant
bailey enclosures on either side. This type of quasi-motte has to be distinguished from a larger, single enclosure with the proportions of a
normal bailey.

The earthwork excavated in 1953–4 by the author at Huttons Ambo
on the edge of a steep slope overlooking the river Derwent, near Malton, Yorkshire, helps us to understand this kind of site.[8] An enclosure
measuring roughly 35 m by 55 m internally, protected by bank and
ditch, was entered at the north-eastern corner across a solid causeway
(fig. 32). Two pairs of large post-holes (up to a metre across) flanked the
entry, interpreted at the time as pairs of sockets for gateposts, but in the

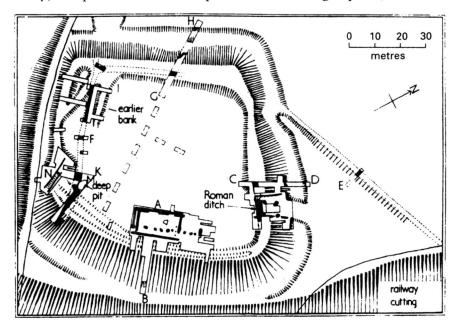

32 Huttons Ambo, N. Yorkshire.
Plan of the fortified hall of the
Dane Colswain, who held it by
keeping the gate of the royal castle
at York; note the gatetower and
the timber hall replaced by a stone
one

light of further work probably best explained as holding uprights for an overhead gatetower. On the escarpment edge there had been two successive halls: a trench-built structure, 13 by 7 m, evidently formed of timber uprights, with opposed entries in the gable ends; followed by a stone building, roughly 18 by 10 m, with an aisle down one side created by wooden posts let into the ground. It was very crudely built, the stone being laid directly upon the turf without a foundation trench. The timber buildings recall Viking discoveries at York, while the single-aisled hall may also have Scandinavian connotations (see p. 9). The pottery was probably dated too late and should be twelfth and late eleventh centuries. There was no motte, although a large section of masonry in the south-west corner may have belonged to a crude tower with its base laid directly on the ground surface.

The interest of this site is that the original grantee of the manor, Colswain, who gave his name to the manor of Hutton Colswain,[9] was evidently a Scandinavian and presumably a native. He held the manor by sergeanty of keeping the gate of the king's castle at York. A sergeant was no doubt too low in feudal status to be entitled to have a motte at his residence, and would indeed be laying claim to something above his station in the hierarchy if he had one. The best he could hope for would be an earthwork of the style we see at Huttons Ambo; this may indeed be the origin of a number of 'ringworks', an earthwork enclosing a hall of wood or stone, as have been described at Sulgrave, Northants, or Penmaen, Glamorgan,[10] where the occupant was not entitled to a castle.

To judge by Continental sources, the constricted area of a motte top encumbered by a large residential structure was not a suitable place for a substantial garrison in an alien country; a strongly defended enclosure would serve much better. William of Poitiers tells us in his contemporary account that William the Conqueror withdrew deliberately from London to allow a defensive work (*firmamenta*) to be constructed for fear of the volatility (*mobilitas*) of the fierce native population of the town.[11] Excavation has confirmed that this was created by a defensive bank and ditch cutting off the south-east corner of the Roman town, making use of its wall on the east side;[12] there was evidently no motte. Mottes were perhaps omitted for similar reasons at other places, or only added when they came into full residential use (the military use was secondary for a motte); no dramatic conclusion need necessarily be drawn from this. In London, the White Tower of the Tower of London proved to be a very good substitute only a few years later.

Another explanation has been put forward for the omission of mottes in 'ringworks'; the geological subsoil was too hard to allow the necessary digging out of the ground to form them.[13] It is true, that in Germany, for example, mottes are particularly associated with low-lying or alluvial ground, as in the Rhineland (p. 20). However, it is not a very convincing argument, since rocky ground usually has plenty of suitable humps and bumps, often of morainic material, to give a good head-start to such an operation. Many other more plausible explanations come to mind: a pre-existing hall or chapel needed to be retained; the local people did not understand the carpentry in the motte needed to support the superstructure; or simply that the native, non-feudalised population did not grasp what a motte was all about.

Figures 33 and 34 show the distribution of mottes and ringworks in England and Wales plotted by the late David King. Although we know that there were earthwork enclosures in pre-Norman England, as at Goltho, Lincolnshire (p. 9), there seems little doubt that the two different types of earthwork shown on the map are contemporary. There are definite concentrations of mottes in the Midlands, Welsh border and Dyfed. In the last two cases, ethnic hostilities no doubt encouraged their proliferation. In Wales, mottes and ringworks seem to be associated one with each other, but in England there is no such correlation. A good many have been destroyed by agriculture and building, so that we are dealing with two types of earthwork that were constructed in large numbers over a relatively short period, mainly from 1050 to 1150. There seems little doubt that the parent earthwork was the motte and bailey from which the ringwork was derived, so it is that original earthwork which must be our main object of study.

Somewhere around one thousand mottes are known from the British Isles, varying in height from a little over a metre to 20 m. Similarly, the diameters vary from about 50–150 m at the base, excluding the encircling ditch, to 5–50 m across the flat top, for they are shaped like a truncated cone or plum pudding. The outward appearance can be highly deceptive: at Richards Castle, Herefordshire, the motte which was famous for its height proved on excavation to contain, in its upper five metres, the basement and part of the first floor of a buried octagonal tower (fig. 35), the original mound being of fairly standard size and height. The optimum size for a motte, here as in the Rhineland (p. 9) seems to have been 5–10 m with a top diameter of say 20–40 m. The base of the motte was encircled by a ditch, say 3–6 m deep and 10–20 m wide, the digging of which provided the material for the mound itself, and which was normally continuous, uninterrupted by a solid cause-

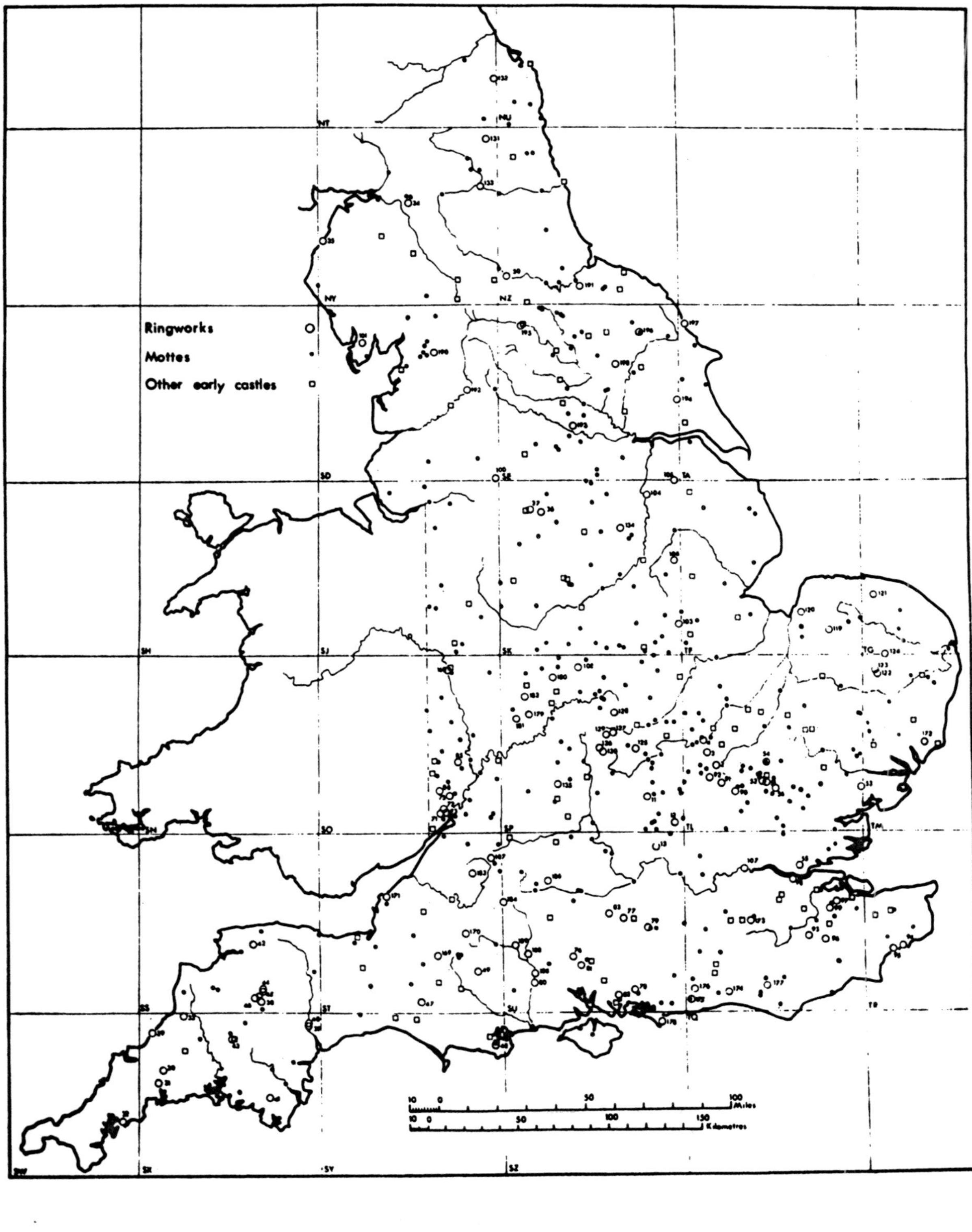

Ringworks   ○

Mottes   ●

Other early castles   □

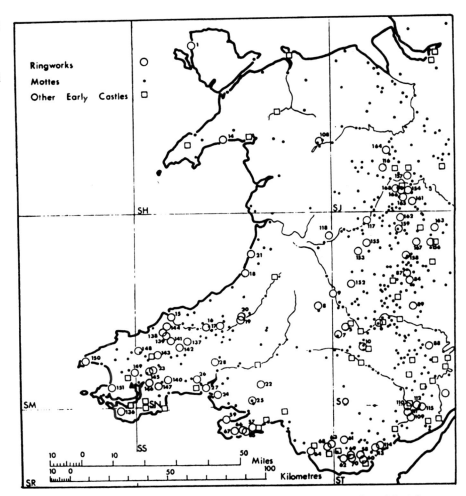

way, since access to the top was by a horizontal or inclined bridge, as shown in the Bayeux tapestry.

It is the traces left by the vanished wooden superstructure on the motte that are of main interest, for the obvious reason that they give a clue as to how it was used. Their study presents great difficulty. Sockets made to hold uprights for wooden buildings can usually be clearly distinguished in the undisturbed geological subsoil, but the whole mound of a motte is made-up ground, so the definition of such earlier disturbances may be difficult, indeed impossible, in such a matrix. Furthermore, the raised surface of the motte often proved to be a tempting site for planting ornamental trees, follies, Home Guard slit trenches, summer-houses and the like, thus destroying all traces of earlier use. Perhaps, even more usual, a building or great tower was erected on top in later medieval times, as at Richards Castle, rendering it inaccessible.

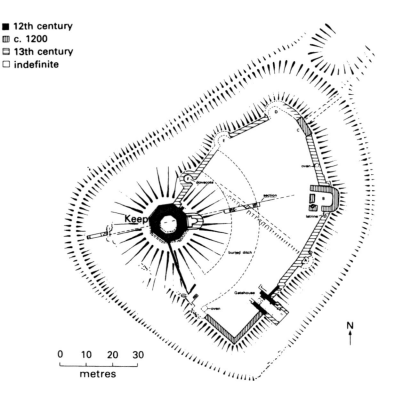

■ 12th century
▥ c. 1200
⊟ 13th century
□ indefinite

Keep

dovecote

oven

section

latrine

buried ditch

Gatehouse

oven

N

0   10   20   30
metres

35 Richards Castle, near Ludlow, Hereford and Worcester. Plan of the motte (c. 1050) and bailey with later octagonal keep (c. 1175), and the town bank (c. 1200) at the top

Mottes are usually protected ancient monuments and so are rarely accessible for the excavator who wants to see the inside. In any case, the sheer bulk of the mound makes detailed inner investigation costly and difficult. The use of modern earth-moving machinery would probably make it impossible to detect traces of internal wooden supports for the superstructure, and it is noteworthy that the discoveries that have been made, such as the one at Farnham, have been of stone which could hardly be missed. Although where the material of the mound had been continually dampened and beaten hard during construction, as at Farnham, a light structure could have been erected on the surface, it is a fair assumption that in most cases a fresh mound required internal support for any large superstructure. I described some of the tantalising evidence on this subject a few years ago.[14]

Interest was first aroused in the superstructures of mottes by the skilful exposure of the sockets of the stockade encircling a square central structure at Abinger, Surrey, in 1949.[15] The motte was small, 6 m high and 11 m across the top, and if there had been an attendant bailey it had been destroyed. An earlier set of structures had been replaced by more clearly defined ones, apparently all in the mid-twelfth century (fig. 36).

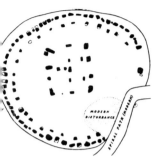

Abinger, Surrey. Plan of traces
a central structure and stockade
top of the motte. Diameter
1 m

The body of the mound was not explored. A line of smaller post-holes behind the main stockade indicated supports for a walkway or fighting-platform. The central structure was small, 3 by 3.5 m internally, but apparently reached a height of more than one storey. The excavator thought it was open at the bottom, but analogies with the Bayeux tapestry must be treated with great caution. The walls between the uprights were formed of horizontal planks. Although the excavator did not think the top of the motte was permanently occupied, the small ditch encircling it, 4 m deep and 8 m wide, contained 'an abundance of large fragments of cooking-pots'. Access was by steps up the side of the mound and not by the kind of flying bridge depicted in the Bayeux tapestry. In view of the very small size of the mound it would be unwise to draw too many general conclusions about mottes from these interesting discoveries.

A few years later an even more suggestive discovery was made in a motte at South Mimms, Middlesex, although we are still very ill-informed about the details.[16] The structure, which was again attributed to the anarchy period of Stephen's reign (1135–54), was surrounded by a ditch 10 m wide and 5 m deep. In the middle of the mound, but on the old ground surface, was a foundation of flints forming a square of 11 m, and clearly intended to support timber uprights, some of which had survived. Even more puzzling was a passage within the mound leading from the central structure to its perimeter. The outside of the mound was faced with wood.

The addition of mounds to stone towers (*gemotten* in the expressive German phrase), sometimes covering windows and doors, has been reported from time to time; one of these was so remarkable and seems to throw such a flood of light on the basic purpose of a motte that it deserves description here, even though the tower was of stone. The bishops of Winchester had had a seat at Farnham, Surrey, since long before the Norman Conquest, but the castle-building activities of Bishop Roger in the adjoining diocese of Salisbury set off repercussions that were felt in several other dioceses.[17] The bishop of Winchester, Henry of Blois, is recorded by the annalist to have started six castles in 1138, Farnham being among them. The triangular inner ward of the castle consists of hall, chapel and bishop's quarters along the south side with a huge shell keep at its apex (fig. 37). The hall contains the wooden capital of a post that evidently formed part of the arcade of an aisled hall, such as occur at the bishop's palace at Hereford and in Leicester castle. However as the south face of the castle bears chiselled-off ornamental Romanesque arcading from the wall of a taller building (fig.

37 Farnham, Surrey. Aerial view of the castle; note the motte with base of square tower, the hall range and outer curtain with gatehouse and towers

38), it seems likely that an earlier first-floor hall was succeeded by an aisled ground-floor hall, as happened in other bishop's palaces (see appendix 1). Probably the earlier first-floor hall is the one to be associated with the motte. The close association of the hall, whichever it was, and the motte is of special significance, for it was reached by a bridge connected to the upper end of the hall, and the function it performed from medieval times up until this century of being a private retreat for the bishop makes the name solar-keep particularly appropriate in this case.

The excavation in 1958, undertaken to ease pressure outward on the shell, had an astonishing result: an enormous foundation, 15.5 m square, was exposed, scarcely half a metre below the surface in the middle of the shell (fig. 39). It soon became clear that this was at the centre of a motte, 28 m in diameter at the top, and almost unbelievably the masonry, which started on the old ground surface, originally 11.5 m square, had been expanded by a flange 2.2 m wide all round the motte top. The marl of which the mound was made up had evidently been dampened and beaten hard as it was laid, so as to bear the weight of the extension. The outer face of the masonry was heavily mortared; 5.5 m thick at the bottom, it was expanded to 7.7 m wide by the flange at the top. The internal shaft dimension was 4.5 m square with an offset to

38 Farnham, Surrey. Fifteenth-century gatetower and planed-off arcading, perhaps from the earliest first-floor hall of the castle

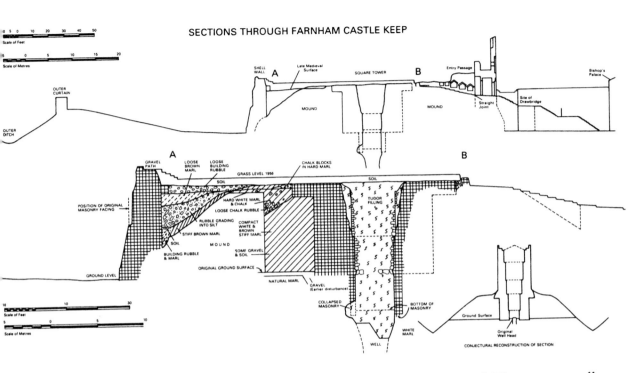

SECTIONS THROUGH FARNHAM CASTLE KEEP

39 Farnham, Surrey. Section of the motte showing the buried base of the tower enlarged with a flange at the surface. The tower itself was probably demolished by Henry II

carry joists for a floor about 4 m above the ground. There was a well at the bottom, but the collapse of the soft chalk made it too dangerous to explore or even to decide if the shaft was round or square. There were no openings, windows or doors, in the masonry and no plinth or pilaster buttresses on the outside, and as the masonry passed continuously into the flange with no joint above the first few centimetres, it is quite clear that masonry and mound were designed as one structure and put up in one operation. The tower that rose above may have had a further three storeys, but it was demolished, perhaps as early as 1155, by Henry II (fig. 39). At a later date the enclosing shell was erected, and subsequently the gusset-shaped void between it and the motte slope filled in to produce the flat ground surface that we see today.

Placing masonry on made-up ground is contrary to all common sense, so there must be a strong suspicion that we are dealing with a 'skeuomorph', something constructed in a different and unsuitable material because it was made habitually in a suitable material, which in this case means wood. This peculiar structure has been described at some length, since although it may owe its existence to the well-recorded vanity and ingenuity of Bishop Henry it can perhaps give an insight into normal methods of motte construction which, in the nature of things, have left only very elusive traces. Erected in wood, such a structure would not cause surprise, since our knowledge of motte superstructures might lead us reasonably to expect it.

Hitherto we have been discussing mottes, but we must not forget the partner, the bailey, the adjoining enclosure. This was, after all, the place where most of the people spent most of their time. We are indeed very ill-informed about baileys, with one exception, that at Hen Domen ('Old Mound' in Welsh) in Powys, right on the Welsh border. Erected before 1086 by Roger de Montgomery, it was superseded by the royal establishment of Montgomery Castle in the 1220s. Its excavation, which began in 1960, has been executed with meticulous care for thirty years and is still in progress.[18] About half the bailey has been studied, but the results of the excavation of the remainder, as well as the motte which is still to be carried out will be awaited with keen interest. It would be discourteous to the excavators and in any case hardly feasible in this book to enter into details of the work; only a few salient points may be mentioned.

Five main periods of occupation in the period from 1071 to 1300 have been defined. All construction was in timber, massive framed construction in the first phase, and subsequently vertical posts inserted into the ground. The buildings in the bailey were not set neatly against the bank or fortified platform that enclosed it, but spread out over the enclosed area. There was a flying bridge to the top of the motte in Bayeux-tapestry style, renewed several times, which took off in at least one period from the first floor of a two-storeyed hall adjoining the bridge by the motte ditch. The interpretation of the two-storeyed character of the building depended on the size and depth of the post-holes that had held its uprights. The relationship of the building on the motte, a solar presumably, is distinctly reminiscent of Farnham, while the two-storeyed hall, following Continental fashion, points to the place of origin of the occupants. The very surprising scatter of buildings over the whole area may have something to do with the constructional material; stone buildings in the later castle ward could make use of the curtain wall for one side of the building, but with an earthen bank there was no such advantage. The reconstruction drawings one sees frequently published with buildings around the perimeter of the bailey are quite misleading, to judge by the evidence from Hen Domen. The progress of the excavations will be watched with the keenest of interest by students of the castle.

At Sandal, Yorkshire, the earliest form of superstructure on the motte was not identified in the excavations because of later disturbance.[19] No substructure was located. A fine five-bay hall with sockets for timber uprights and central hearth was uncovered in the bailey with its attendant external kitchen. This structure was set against the bank and not, as at Hen Domen, by the motte ditch. Service from the kitchen seems to have been through the main door, as at Ludlow.

The disappearance of the essential wooden elements of mottes has left them curiously enigmatic and puzzling objects. Most published reconstruction drawings are quite unconvincing and none takes account of the new evidence from Hen Domen. The embroidered threads of the Bayeux tapestry show vivid glimpses of structures that it is hard to translate into reality (fig. 31). Without excavation, the surviving earthworks are not a rewarding subject of study. Nevertheless, the shape of the wooden castle has imposed its form permanently on the majority of later castles, so the rest of this chapter will be devoted to looking at the subsequent fate of some mottes and baileys.

The sheer discomfort of living on top of a mound and the frequent replacement of the timber structures, for wood that is partly buried, like a modern gatepost, has a relatively short life of, say, twenty years, encouraged either abandonment or alternatively replacement of wood by stone. There is little doubt that of the large number of mottes known in England and Wales, approaching a thousand, a majority were abandoned and had been abandoned by 1300. This was not always a voluntary event.

How many motte castles were deliberately pulled down and never reoccupied as a result of Henry II's policy of demolition of unauthorised castles of the Anarchy period of Stephen's reign, or at other times, it is impossible to say; but it was probably a higher proportion than one might at first suppose, as a glance at Allen Brown's list of castles from 1154 to 1216 reveals.[20] The stone tower at Farnham may well have been picked down level to the present horizontal surface at that time. The Pipe Rolls refer to expenditure on picks, hooks and ropes,[21] so it is fair to assume that with wooden castles a team of oxen or horses were attached by ropes to the superstructure and the whole work was torn down. Unusable timber could be heaped up and burnt, usable timber, which had a value even then, sold for reuse in roofs, houses and so on. If the edge of the motte top was then thrown down the slope it would not be easy to bring the castle back into use.

With the passage of time the material of the mound would have consolidated sufficiently to risk masonry construction on it. No modern builder would dream of building on such a base without first putting down a concrete raft at least a metre thick, but our ancestors were

braver. There were three or perhaps four ways in which the mound
could be retained as the citadel of a stone castle.

In the first method masonry was built up on the original ground surface all round the skirt of the mound, following the slope up and then
turned into a vertical wall at the top, so that the motte was encased in a
vast stone plinth. It reduced the risk of subsidence to a minimum and
was probably essential where a large structure was to be erected above,
as in the case of the vanished keep at Pontefract, Yorkshire, or the existing one at Berkeley castle, Gloucestershire. It is likely that the great
keep at Kenilworth, Warwickshire, enclosed a mound in this way, and
even more likely that this was the case at Taunton, Somerset. At Farnham, the inner face of the shell was vertical at some distance from the
motte top, so a gusset-like void was created that had to be filled in. At
Sandal, Yorkshire, there was a compromise solution in which the wall
was raised from a shelf dug into the side of the mound.

The first method was the safest, but very costly because of the volume of masonry required, so that by far the most common device was
simply to build a defensive wall around the periphery of the motte summit, not a parapet but a proper wall with sufficient thickness for a wall
walk around its top. The central area was open and unroofed, but usually contained small buildings. There could be arrow slits at ground
level, as at Pickering castle, Yorkshire.[22] Heavy masonry on the lip of a
made-up mound was precariously placed so no doubt there was a serious casualty rate. Some of the most dramatic examples that have survived are at Restormel, Cornwall (fig. 40), Lincoln (fig. 41) and Arundel, Sussex.

40 Restormel castle, Cornwall.
The shell keep or unroofed
enclosure on top of the motte,
from the air

41 Lincoln castle: the shell keep with its pilaster buttresses and gateway at the top of steps up the motte

Such unroofed keeps could serve as solars or places of retreat. At Farnham, for instance, by the later middle ages the bishop had a suite of timber-framed buildings behind the gate, with a garden, in what must have been an extremely pleasant private retreat, away from the public bustle of the hall but with a commanding view of all that was going on in the castle.[23] In the event of siege, the keep could revert to its military function. For men of the middle ages there was no incongruity in such a dual role for a building, strange as it appears to modern usage.

The third and fourth forms of adaptation of the early wooden castle were to erect a stone tower on or against the mound, and trust that with the passage of a hundred years or so consolidation would allow it to bear the weight. In some cases the eye is certainly deceived, for it has been found at Bungay, Suffolk, and Skenfrith, Gwent[24] for instance, that the towers were erected on the ground surface and mounds added afterwards, creating false mottes. At Richards Castle, Hereford and Worcester, the base of an octagonal tower with pilaster buttresses and an eastward apsidal projection, perhaps for a chapel at a higher level, had been erected c. 1175 on the mound which may itself date from 1050, since this is one of the handful of reasonably documented pre-Conquest castles. Two fine cylindrical towers that come to mind, perhaps a generation or so later in date, rest on large mounds at Bronllys, Powys, and Longtown, Hereford and Worcester. The most dramatic of such structures, erected between 1240 and 1260, is the quatrefoil, lobed tower on the mound at Clifford's Tower, York, looking like a shell keep with a roof supported on a central column (fig. 42). It contained a full domestic suite for the use of the king or his constable.

42 York castle. Clifford's Tower, the petal-shaped tower erected on the eleventh-century motte between 1245 and 1255

The last category comprises two rectangular towers built against the side of the mound at Guildford, Surrey, and Clun, Shropshire. In the latter case the upper floor of the elongated structure is on a level with the top of the motte suggesting, as it were, that the object was to bring the hall up to the same level as the solar, if that was on the motte.

Stone keeps are the subject of the next chapter, so this is a convenient point at which to end. Although the wood has long since vanished, the ancillary earthworks of most Norman castles have permanently moulded their shape as distant views of Windsor, Durham, Lincoln, Oxford, Cambridge (fig. 43), Arundel, Cardiff and others constantly remind us.

43 Cambridge. The castle motte in front of the Shire Hall, from which a later tower has been removed

Chapter 5

Stone towers

All the French castles represented in the Bayeux tapestry were of earth with a wooden superstructure, but there is a curious stone building, the stone shown as a sort of chequer pattern, beside Duke William seated on his throne (fig. 44). No designation is given – although the suggestion by Allen Brown that it is the tower of Duke Richard of Rouen mentioned in contemporary sources is possible – but it is clearly a gate-tower with central opening. Perspective was difficult, but the floating building above could be a palace hall of the Lillebonne type in the background, with the two figures inadvertently shown by the English semp-stress behind instead of in front of it. That aside, the building in the foreground is clearly a gatetower, not a keep, and this is perhaps all Duke Richard knew about.

On their arrival in England the Normans built stone gatehouses at Ludlow, Richmond (later converted to keeps) and Exeter, which might resemble that in the tapestry, and first-floor halls or *domicilia* (Chep-stow and Richmond) of the Langeais type, and stone curtain walls, but there appears to have been a considerable lapse of time before large residential towers were built by them. The likely inference surely is that before they came they had had no experience, or at all events very

44 Bayeux tapestry: Duke William seated beside the stone gateway, perhaps that built at Rouen by Duke Richard, with what may be the palace hall in the background

Keep details

	Internal dimensions	Storeys	Cross-wall Central	Off-centre	Other divisions	Galleries	Vaulting Basements	Higher level	Buttresses Pilaster	Large	Forebuildings	Chapels	Latrines	Fireplaces	Wells
	1	2	3	4	5	6	7	8	9	10	11	12	13	14	15
Hall-keeps															
Appleby, Cumbria	11 × 11 m	3							•			•			
Bamburgh, Northumberland	16 × 13 m	4	•	•		•			•			•			
Benington, Herts.	10 × 9 m								•		?•				
Berkhamsted, Herts.	14 × 9 m								•						
Bowes, Yorkshire	17 × 11 m	3	•				•		•			•			
Bungay, Suffolk	11 × 10 m						•				•	•			
Canterbury, Kent	21 × 16 m	2	•	•					•					•	•
Carlisle, Cumbria	13 × 10 m	4							•					•	•
Carrickfergus, Antrim	11 × 11 m						•						•	•	•
Castle Acre, Norfolk: Proto-keep	19 × 19 m	2	•										•	•	
Castle Acre, Keep 1	16 × 16 m	?3	•												
Castle Acre, Keep 2	6 × 16 m	?3													
Castle Rising, Norfolk	17 × 15 m	3	•	•	•	•			•		•	•	•		•
Chepstow, Gwent	26 × 9 m	2							•						
Clun, Shropshire	12 × 7 m	3							•						
Corfe, Dorset	? × 12 m								•		•			•	
Craigie, Strathclyde	14 × 7 m	2							•						
Dover, Kent	18 × 16 m	4	•						•		•	2		•	•
Duffield, Derbyshire	20 × 19 m			•					•						•
Grosmont, Gwent	23 × 8 m	2													
Hedingham, Essex	12 × 10 m	5							•		•		•		
Helmsley, Yorkshire	12 × 11 m	3				•			•		•				
Kenilworth, Warwicks.	14 × 10 m	2							•		•		•		
Lancaster	18 × 18 m		•	•					•						
Ludlow, Shropshire (originally gatehouse)	12 × 6 m	4	•												
Lydford, Devon	11 × 10 m	4	•											•	•
Maynooth, Kildare	16 × 13 m	2							•		•				
Middleham, Yorkshire	25 × 16 m	3	•			•			•				o		
Monmouth, Gwent	17 × 8 m	2							•						
Norham, Northumberland	18 × 12 m	3	•	•		•			•					•	
Norwich, Norfolk	23 × 12 m	3	•		•				•				•	•	
Ogmore, Glamorgan	11 × 6 m	3	•											•	
Old Sarum, Wilts.	12 × 11 m		•											•	
Pendragon, Cumbria	13 × 12 m								•						
Portchester, Hants.	14 × 12 m	5	•						•		•		•	•	
Rochester, Kent	13 × 12 m	4	•		•				•		•	•	•	•	
Rushen, Isle of Man	12 × 12 m									•	•				
Saffron Walden, Essex	11 × 11 m								•		•				•
Scarborough, Yorkshire	10 × 8 m	3							•		•		•	•	
Sherborne, Dorset	12 × 8 m			•									•		
South Mimms, Middx. (wood)	?10 × 10 m														
Taunton, Somerset															
Tower of London	27 × 22 m	3	•	•					•			•	•	•	
Trim, Meath	12 × 12 m	4								•		•	•	•	
Wareham, Dorset	11 × 11 m								•		•				•
*Wolvesey, Winchester, Hants.	12 × 12 m	2	•						•						

	Internal dimensions	Storeys	Cross-wall				Vaulting		Buttresses						
			Central	Off-centre	Other divisions	Galleries	Basements	Higher level	Pilaster	Large	Forebuildings	Chapels	Latrines	Fireplaces	Wells
	1	2	3	4	5	6	7	8	9	10	11	12	13	14	15
Solar-keeps															
Abinger, Surrey (wood)	3.5 × 2.5 m								•						
Adare, Limerick	9 × 8 m	•							•						
Aldingbourne, Sussex	7 × 7 m								•		•				
Ascot d'Oilly, Oxon.	7 × 7 m														
Brandon, Warwicks	8 × 5 m						?•		•						
Bridgnorth, Shropshire	6 × 6 m	3							•					•	
Brough, Cumbria	9 × 7 m	3							•						
Brougham, Cumbria	7 × 7 m	3						•	•			•		•	
Clitheroe, Lancs.	6 × 6 m								•						
Dolwyddelan, Gwynedd	9 × 7 m	2											•		
Farnham, Surrey	5 × 5 m														•
Goodrich, Hereford and Worcester	5.5 × 4.5 m	3							•						
Guildford, Surrey	8 × 7 m	3							•				•	•	
Kenfig, Glamorgan	8 × 7 m							•	•						
Lydney, Glos.	9 × 7 m														
Newcastle, Tyne and Wear	9 × 6.5 m	5				•			•		•	•	•	•	•
Oxford	5.5 × 5	4													
Peveril, Derbyshire	7 × 7 m	2							•						
Prudhoe, Northumberland	8 × 7 m								•		•				
Richmond, Yorkshire (original gatehouse)	9 × 6.5 m	3							•						
Sutton Valence, Kent	6 × 6 m								•						
Totnes, Devon	5 × 4 m														
West Malling, Kent	7 × 6 m	4							•						
White Castle, Gwent	4 × ?4 m														
Round and polygonal keeps															
Athlone, Westmeath	15 m d														
Barnard Castle, Durham	6.5 m d	3											•	•	
Bronllys, Powys	6 m d	3											•		
Caldicot, Gwent	6 m d	3				•							•		
Chilham, Kent	6.5 m d							•							
Conisbrough, Yorkshire	8 m d	4					•				•	•	•	•	•
Dolbadarn, Gwynedd	9 m d	3										•		•	
Dundrum, Down	9 m d													•	
Inchiquin, Cork	9 m d	3											•		
Longtown, Hereford and Worcester	8.5 m d	3								•				•	
Lyonshall, Hereford and Worcester	6 m d														
Nenagh, Tipperary	9 m d	3									•		•		
Odiham, Hants.	11 m d									•					
Orford, Suffolk	8.5 m d	4				•				•	•	•	•	•	•
Pembroke, Dyfed	8 m d	4					•						•		
Richards Castle, Herefordshire	7 m d									•		?•			
Skenfrith, Gwent	7 m d	3											•		
Tickhill, Yorkshire	10.5 m d									•					•
Tretower, Powys	6.5 m d	3												•	•

* No medieval kitchen has a transverse dividing wall of the keep type; the Wolvesey tower must surely have been designed as a keep, possibly at the apex of a triangle facing the W. Hall, like Farnham, Surrey. The wall thickness is comparable to Chepstow. I fear that I must disagree here with Martin Biddle in the *English Heritage Guide* (1986).

limited experience, of anything of this kind. These vast structures are particularly associated with England, and the case for believing that special conditions in this country either gave rise to the idea, or perhaps stimulated one that was fairly embryonic, is a strong one. An English king, Henry I, Beauclerc, perhaps took the idea back with him to the Duchy, where he erected many of the largest keeps, such as Falaise, Arques la Bataille and Caen.

The table of keep details in England and to a lesser extent in Wales, Scotland and Ireland (making use of D. F. Renn's invaluable list, guidebooks and so on) will help the discussion.[1] Measurements have been converted to metres and must be regarded as definitely approximate, for published scales are not always compatible. The dimensions are all internal, representing the accommodation area available at each floor level, which, because of the beam offsets, increased slightly as one went up. Some keeps merely survive as stumps of masonry or fragmentary ruins and this, together with lack of information on details, means the columns for chapels, latrines, fireplaces and wells are certainly incomplete. Unroofed shell keeps are not included, nor are buildings later than the end of John's reign in 1216. With these limitations, the table should be reliable for the discussion that follows.

The keeps have been divided into three categories: rectangular keeps with an internal dimension of more than 10 m, called hall-keeps, rectangular keeps with no internal measurement reaching 10 m, called solar-keeps, and round and polygonal keeps. Within these three categories the towers are arranged alphabetically. Starting with the dimensions on the left, followed by the number of storeys (including basement) fifteen columns record the occurrence of special characteristics within the towers.

The first point that must strike one is that there are forty-four hall-keeps against twenty-four solar-keeps, almost exactly the opposite to what we found in France (p. 39). In this country the hall-keep is the rule while in western France, where the keeps are closely linked by the use of pilaster buttresses to those in this country, the solar-keep is the rule and the hall-keep the exception. The latter grows common as one goes further north, that is, approaches England. The significance of this hardly needs emphasising.

The 10 m adopted arbitrarily as a boundary between hall and solar-keeps is nevertheless presumed to imply a difference in function: the former were for the private use of the lord and his family and a few servants, while the latter had a public function for the whole household and guests, with a capacity to house them at least for meals. It is more difficult to make such a distinction with the polygonal and round keeps which are chronologically later. Possibly a diameter of 8 m or more and certainly 10 m and more could qualify as hall-keeps, but one has a distinct impression that they are mainly solar-keeps, especially those on mottes.

Columns nos. 12, 13, 14 and 15, show constructions that are all related to everyday occupation, for it is most important to remember that these buildings were not refuges like the German *Bergfried*, but full-time dwellings, the principal ones in the castle at the time of their construction. At Farnham the whole structure, motte and keep, was erected around the well and, although apparently not universal in keeps, the well was certainly more general than our table suggests. Clearly the well took on special importance in the event of siege; its huge depth in the keep of Dover Castle, Kent, above the white chalk cliffs is a reminder of this. The great open fire in the centre of a ground-floor hall was not practicable in a multi-storeyed building where it had to be set with a flue in the wall, although probably much wider use was made of portable braziers burning charcoal, as in Mediterranean countries today. Two of the finest wall fireplaces are the great hooded examples in the second- and third-floor rooms at Conisbrough, Yorkshire, where all the stonework in the keep is of the highest quality (fig. 45). Latrines were not water-flushed, of course, but consisted of a stone or wooden seat with aperture, usually set in a recess in the thickness of the wall, suspended over a chute running down through the thickness of the wall and discharging into the ditch at the bottom. Structural latrines, as opposed to portable receptacles, were normal until early Tudor times, when the suppression of moats and ditches made disposal a necessity. In a few cases there were stone wash-basins, like a church piscina, as at Conisbrough. Window apertures were small and the amount of daylight that could enter the rooms was reduced by the thickness of the walls, and in some cases light was lost in wall passages. Flame-torches and oil lights or candles must have been in use a great deal of the time. Chapels and little oratories were certainly more numerous than the table suggests, perhaps universal, although none can have achieved the scale and beauty of the apsidal chapel with aisles and gallery of St John's chapel in the Tower of London (fig. 87).

Almost without exception the keeps were entered at first- or second-floor level. Round and solar-keeps were probably entered by wooden steps with a retractable bridge at the door, the normal Continental

45 Conisbrough, S. Yorkshire. The fireplace overmantel with joggled head on the second floor of the castle keep

method, but a forebuilding (see col. 11), erected as an integral part of the structure housing the steps which rose by the side of the keep wall, became a normal feature of the hall-keep. The forebuilding itself could be decorated with carving, and the doorway itself more frequently had its head and jambs decorated with Norman carving, as at Norwich. There could be rooms above and below the entry only accessible from within the keep, the chapel being placed here, for instance at Newcastle upon Tyne. The keep's exterior was usually undecorated, Norwich, covered with blank arcading being an exception.

46 Norwich castle, showing the arcaded decoration on the keep, remade in the last century by Salvin following the original pattern

As in Norman ecclesiastical architecture, the strength of the walls derived from their massive thickness, 2.5–6 m, and for the same reason there were opportunities to create recesses, chambers, passages and galleries within the thickness of the wall. Some of the grandest keeps had rooms filling two storey levels with a gallery in the wall thickness that had openings looking down to the floor level below. Such an arrangement has a decidedly ecclesiastical feel, recalling as it does clerestory passages, or in Continental terms triforium passages. Such thick walls should have made external buttressing unnecessary, especially as there were no vaults above basement level whose outward thrust had to be resisted. Yet pilaster buttresses are practically universal, evenly spaced along the walls and clasping the corners. It is difficult to see what purpose they served, other than an ornamental one. Possibly they acted as anchors in walls that were usually constructed of undressed stone, ashlar only being used for doors, windows and other detail. There must be a suspicion that they were skeuomorphs, representing the timber posts of earlier wooden structures which could have been carved. Plinths and sloping bases are normal. Original parapets were no doubt crenellated for it was from roof level that the main defence took place; the buildings were there four or five storeys high, so gravity was on the side of the defenders.

Columns 3 and 4 are perhaps the most important for the light they throw on the nature of hall-keeps, since this feature is not found in solar-keeps, nor in round and polygonal ones. Nineteen out of forty-four hall-keeps have a cross-wall and in every case the wall is off-centre dividing the tower into two compartments of different sizes at each level. The wall normally rose from ground to roof level, dividing the area to be spanned at the roof level into two unequal parts. Although in a few early cases the roof sloped inwards to form a valley (Richmond, Portchester) from which the rainwater was drained, in most cases the roof had a double gable, 'double-pile' in the jargon. The two gables would be, of course, of unequal size, not the symmetrical double gable of the great dorter built by Archbishop Lanfranc in the monastery of Christchurch, Canterbury.[2] The asymmetry was clearly intentional, since the external door from the outside steps always led into the larger compartment. We may presume that the public room, the hall, was entered directly from outside, while the private room was behind, away from the door. A Frenchman coming up the steps would have felt the first-floor hall arrangement to be very familiar. Although the cross-wall was primarily to assist in spanning the roof, it had an almost equally important function of creating an unequal division of rooms at each level. Both sections could be united if an open arcade was made in the wall at one level, as at Rochester, recalling Lanfranc's dorter or indeed Philippe le Bel's great double-pile hall in the Palais Royal two hundred years later (p. 47). If roof support only was required then one gigantic transverse arch could supply it, as at Hedingham, leaving the space unobstructed below (figs. 47, 48). The enormously thick side walls clearly did not need lateral strengthening, so the common name 'diaphragm' wall is decidedly misleading.

If we exclude the elongated structures which are halls rather than keeps, Chepstow, Monmouth, Christchurch, there is plainly a tendency for the hall-keeps to be square, or squarish, and even more so with the solar-keeps. On the face of it, the explanation that seems most sustainable is that the latter are earlier, but by enlarging the square and dividing it unequally, an internal elongated shape for a hall could be accommodated within it.

Our starting-point must be the castle ruin at Castle Acre, Norfolk, where the excavations in the 1970s have not only transformed our knowledge of the structural history of the monument, but also provided a wealth of small finds, some like arrowheads and horseshoes vividly revealing aspects of social life, others, like bones of animals, birds and fish, demonstrating the nature of the food eaten by the occupants of the castle.[3] The Warenne family, earls of Surrey, to whom the land had been granted by the Conqueror just after the Conquest, had their main seat at Lewes, Sussex, where they had built a castle and founded a Cluniac priory; the family did the same at Castle Acre. The site consists of two enclosures formed by massive earthworks, upper and lower wards, set in a motte-and-bailey relationship, with a town enclosure beyond, and finally the priory ruins further to the west. It is with the square ruin at the centre of the huge earthwork of the upper ward, which has a diameter (c. 60 m without ditch) roughly corresponding to the ground diameter of the largest standard motte that we are concerned with here (fig. 49).

47 Castle Hedingham, Essex. An eighteenth-century view of the keep showing pilaster buttresses and entry

48 Castle Hedingham, Essex. Section of the keep showing the two great spanning arches and the gallery in the hall

Castle Acre, Norfolk. Aerial
view of excavation of the keep,
showing a larger outer compartment (the hall, now demolished)
separated from a smaller inner
compartment that is still standing.
Note the apparent foundations of
a later aisled hall in the outer
bailey, perhaps superseding the
hall within the keep

The excavation revealed that the square structure had undergone
three transformations. In its first phase (soon after the Conquest in
date) it measured roughly 19 by 19 m internally with a cross-wall dividing it into two unequal compartments, 8 m and 9.3 m wide respectively.
The building had been two-storeyed with a ground-floor door on the
south side leading into a wider compartment, with the masonry still
surviving sufficiently high to be sure that there was no vault, and that
there was an intercommunicating door with the smaller northern section. There was evidence for windows at both floor levels, a fireplace
and a latrine. There was no internal staircase and the first-floor was
evidently reached by an external stair. From the front, the south, it
must have looked like a normal French *salle basse* and *grande salle*
above, but it was of course double pile with a slightly smaller part
behind. It was defended by a bank 3.2 m high at the back and a stone
gatehouse was added a little later. The excavations at Hen Domen (p.
58) make one hesitate about the scale of wooden defences the bank may
have supported. Before discussing this remarkable building, further
mention should be made of the subsequent stages of development.

The walls of the first building were fairly thin, 2 m, like that of a hall (cf. Chepstow) and the second stage consisted of a massive thickening of the walls by building more masonry against them on the inside, including the cross-wall, and at the same time blocking the apertures at ground level. Then the structure was evidently raised, giving what the excavators called a keep and resembling in its general dimensions the keep at Castle Rising, Norfolk. The alteration perhaps took place at a not very different date to the construction of the latter in the twelfth century. At the same time there was a very substantial increase in the size of the encircling earthwork, which was crowned with a stone wall. Clearly, defence was the motive behind all the work. The third stage was a remarkable one: the whole of the larger southern compartment was taken down, leaving the narrower compartment standing as a tall elongated tower. As the foundations of an as-yet-unexcavated hall, which by its width, 15 m, seems to have been an aisled building, are visible in the lower ward this demolition may indicate a transfer of function such as we see in bishops' palaces (see appendix 1) or other castles (chapter 6). The narrower surviving part would represent a solar-keep in function, even if one dimension exceeded 10 m, equivalent to the bishop's *camera*.

Returning now to the first stage, the absence of plinth and pilaster buttresses, more or less *de rigueur* in the buildings of the period, together with the suggestive dimensions of the earthwork (i.e. diameter of a motte base) must suggest that burying the base, that is, the lower storey, was not far from the builders' minds, as a contingency measure at all events, doors and windows notwithstanding. The square shape surely points fairly clearly to its antecedents – the square flint base at South Mimms comes to mind – as a tentative effort to make a motte tower base a free-standing building. In general features it corresponds in dimensions and design, with its cross-wall off-centre, to a normal large hall-keep. The differences are in the thinness of the walls and ground-floor apertures, and these were quickly eliminated in stage 2 to bring it into line with normal keeps. We are surely dealing with an early experimental stage in the attempt to pack the hall into an enlarged motte tower, a proto-keep. Country houses of the period, as at Cheddar, Clarendon, or the bishops' palaces consisted of a dispersed group of buildings; only one motive was strong enough to put everything under one roof (albeit with two gables) – defence. I would prefer therefore the use of the designation 'proto-keep', rather than 'country house', used by the excavators, which I think is quite misleading as to the nature of the structure, and to the sort of social conditions obtain-

50 Chepstow, Gwent. The castle
across the river Wye with the
domicilium (first-floor hall) later
raised, in silhouette, with the
original door (*c.* 1070) just visible
in the left gable end

ing at the time it was erected. Whether William de Warenne built the
castle with the single motte or the one with two at Lewes, Sussex, this is
the social background into which the structure at Castle Acre must be
fitted and interpreted. The troubles with Hereward the Wake hardly
suggest a peaceful East Anglia at this date.

Three other kinds of experimental hall-keep that are assignable to the
eleventh century can now be mentioned: a real hall serving as a keep
(Chepstow, Gwent), gatehouses later turned into keeps (Ludlow,
Shropshire, and Richmond, Yorkshire) and the two huge structures in
southern England (the White Tower in the Tower of London and Colchester castle keep, Essex). They can be taken in that order (fig. 50).

The castle at Chepstow occupies a splendid position overlooking the
river Wye not far above its junction with the river Severn.[4] The castle
was founded by William Fitz Osborn in 1067–71, immediately after the
Conquest, and the large rectangular structure from which the castle
developed has some claim to be the earliest stone building in a castle in
the country. It was two-storeyed before later additions, over a very low
cellar with a doorway decorated with carving at the gable end. The
whole of the inside wall on the first floor on the west side as well as the
northern gable end were decorated with ornamental blank arcading.
There was no vaulting, as the floors were of wood. The walls, which
varied in thickness from 2 to 4 m, unlike those of the proto-keep at
Castle Acre, bore pilaster buttresses. The structure is clearly a two-
storeyed hall serving as a keep, related to the *domicilium* of Langeais-
type (p. 37), not to the future hall-keeps in the way that the structure at
Castle Acre was.

The two gatehouses at Ludlow and Richmond go back to the early years after the Conquest,[5] but both were converted into hall-keeps in the following century by blocking the gate passage and extending or raising the building (fig. 51). In the two cases the curtain wall abutting the gatehouse on either side is original, and at Richmond the castle retains its original first-floor hall, Scolland's Hall (fig. 52). The implication seems to be in both cases that the builders were unfamiliar with stone hall-keeps, although they made use of stone halls, gatehouses and curtain walls.

This brings us to the two most spectacular structures, undoubted hall-keeps, that were built in the last quarter of the eleventh century, no greater precision being possible: the White Tower, the great rectangular block in the middle of the Tower of London (figs. 53, 54), believed to have been designed for the king by Gundulph (originally from Lanfranc's Norman monastery at Bec, and Bishop of Rochester from 1077) and the keep at Colchester castle, Essex. Both keeps, it is thought, had the same designer.[6] The plan is indeed very simple, rectangular with longitudinal cross-wall resting on the chapel in the south-east corner, so oriented that its eastern apse projects like a round corner turret. A westward extension of the chapel at Colchester was probably linked by an arcade to the north wall of the keep, forming a sort of single aisle to the large compartment. The chapel itself was on the first and second floor. St John's chapel at the White Tower, a beautiful little Roman-

51 Richmond castle, N. Yorkshire. View from inside the eleventh-century gatehouse raised to form a keep with pilaster buttresses

52 Richmond castle, N. Yorkshire. The eleventh-century first-floor hall shown from inside, with a ground-floor door and a window altered to a door on the first floor

esque building, has vaulted aisles supporting galleries. It rose through two storeys in the adjoining rooms of the tower, which had a wall gallery at the corresponding upper level (fig. 87). The White Tower is better preserved and was always more refined work than the Essex structure. The latter's larger corner turrets with their spiral staircases belong to what was the largest of the hall-keeps in this country. The place seemed to have had special status before the Conquest and it was erected over a Roman temple. [7] The external doors, on the first floor at the Tower and above ground level at Colchester, were evidently en-

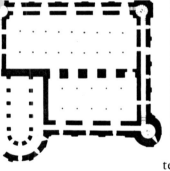

London: the White Tower. View from the SE showing the apsidal projection for the east end of the chapel, the pilaster buttresses and the first-floor door on extreme left

London: plan of the upper storey of the White Tower, showing the wall galleries and chapel aisles

tered by wooden steps, and led in both cases into the larger compartment, following the general rule.

The origins of these two huge structures have been a matter of much discussion. No building of this kind survives from this date on the Continent. When Duke William arrived at London he found the Confessor's palace already in existence at Westminster, a normal palace of separate buildings. As William of Poitiers tells us, there was considerable doubt about the trustworthiness of the city's population and the new king stayed outside the city until a fortification had been erected. So when he came to erect the Tower defence, which was clearly a primary consideration, this was achieved by packing the necessary buildings and services within a more or less square envelope and taking it up two or three storeys to provide additional space. It was a fairly crude solution, with elements like the chapel hardly absorbed.

Although more explicitly defensive than Castle Acre, with thicker walls of church-like size and suppression of ground-floor apertures, it is surely the same device: an expanded square motte tower to enclose the hall and private apartments. I doubt whether we need go back to the Continent for antecedents; more likely the Tower, and then Colchester castle, were a response to the particular circumstances of the time.

Very few stone solar-keeps can be assigned with confidence to the eleventh century, although there must have been a large number of wooden ones. The tower at Oxford, with crudely stepped outside, is both defensive and acts as a bell tower for a vanished church: it may have been erected just after the Conquest[8] and its base looks suspiciously as if it was intended to be buried. The fine tower at West Malling, Kent, with Romanesque arcading at first-floor level, was probably erected at the turn of the century by the same Gundulph, Bishop of Rochester, who is thought to have designed the White Tower.[9]

The pattern having been created in the late eleventh century the first half of the twelfth century saw an outburst of keep-building all over the country. It is unfortunate that virtually none of these keeps have firm construction dates, and sometimes we have to fall back on tenuous resemblances to keeps in Normandy built by Henry I: Norwich and Falaise, Canterbury and Domfront. Although precise dates are lacking, some of the finest hall-keeps belong to this period: Canterbury, Castle Rising, Hedingham, Kenilworth, Lancaster, Middleham, Norwich, Old Sarum, Portchester, Rochester and Sherborne. Construction was mainly by the nobility, less by the Crown, in marked contrast to the second half of the century. It would need many pages of text, as well as scores of figures and plates, to describe these great buildings so it will be possible only to say a few words about some of them.

The keep at Canterbury, Kent, is a substantial structure with its entry at first-floor level leading into a central compartment between two cross-walls, an unusual variation. There is a standard motte hard by with the name of Dane John (an amusing corruption of donjon). In a rural setting the keep at Castle Rising, Norfolk, recalls Castle Acre by its massive encircling earthwork, which has partly overriden a Romanesque church with apsidal end that was contemporary with the keep (fig. 55). Although the dimensions of this keep recall the one at Castle Acre, it is a far more mature and sophisticated structure.[10] The forebuilding has ornamental arcading on it. The door led into the larger of the compartments created by a cross-wall, with spinal columns in the basement supporting at one end a vault under the service rooms of the

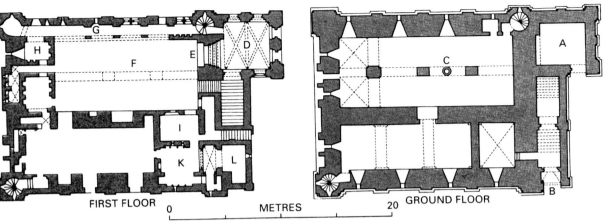

FIRST FLOOR   0   METRES   20   GROUND FLOOR

55 Castle Rising, Norfolk. Plans
of the keep at ground- and first-
floor levels showing the unequal
division. Entry was into the larger
compartment (the hall), which
had spinal columns
supporting its ground-floor vault

A   Prison
B   Later main entrance
C   Well
D   Vestibule
E   Entrance
F   Hall
G   Gallery
H   Kitchen
I   Ante-chapel
K   Chapel
L   Upper part of forebuilding

hall. It is unusual to have the hall so unmistakably defined, even if the
entry door and spinal columns in the *salle basse* give a decidedly French
feel.

The keep at Hedingham, Essex, is one of the most impressive in the
series, due largely to the extra height given it by an additional storey, no
doubt as a compensation for the loss of rooms due to the absence of a
cross-wall division, the floors being of 'open plan' (figs. 47, 48). An
unusual and dramatic feature is the pair of great arches spanning the
width of the tower at first floor level to support the second and third
floors, which form one great tall hall with a gallery in the wall thickness
looking down into it, and another arch in this to support the topmost
floor. Doubling the height of the room and giving it a gallery in the
thickness of the wall, which we find in a number of the major keeps (the
Tower, Norwich, Rochester, Dover, Castle Rising) not only gave additional light but created a room of great splendour. As explained
above (p. 68) the idea probably comes from the clerestory galleries in
cathedrals and churches.

At Kenilworth, Warwickshire,[11] the keep (fig. 56) is remarkable for
its enormous corner turrets and the raised ground surface inside (p. 60).
The entry led into a large hall or room on the first floor, perhaps divided
before the Elizabethan alteration and Parliamentary destruction. The
kitchen adjoined the keep, as at Conisbrough, presumably allowing
food to be brought in more easily. At Middleham, Yorkshire, the date
of construction as well as the name of the builder are not known, but
since the keep resembles Castle Rising it may be mentioned here.[12] The
external steps along one of the long sides, which lead straight into the
first floor of the larger compartment with the spinal columns in the
basement below, give a decidedly French atmosphere to the arrangement (fig. 109).

56 Kenilworth castle, Warwick-shire. The keep from the court-yard side showing the great plinth perhaps enclosing the motte, the forebuilding on the left and Elizabethan alterations to windows

Norwich, a royal castle, was in some ways the most impressive of all the keeps (fig. 46). It was originally covered by arcaded decoration, which was retained in the restoration by Salvin in the last century, but without using Caen stone, which has no doubt altered the colour and made the decoration look strangely fresh. The keep dominates the city from the top of a hill, part of which is certainly artificial. The forebuild-ing leads up to a carved Norman doorway which gives access to an impressive interior, the volume given greater emphasis by the removal of the cross-wall and its replacement by an open arcade in the last cen-tury. There are galleries at first-floor level. Long use as a prison seems to have imparted to the interior a drab, sinister appearance.

Portchester castle, Hampshire, occupies one corner of a well-preserved Saxon Shore fort (fig. 92), the red tile courses of the Roman walls and bastions providing a bold setting for its fine keep.[13] Its date of construction is quite uncertain, but as the pilaster buttresses do not reach the top it is clear that it has been raised by one storey some time after its original erection. The keep is almost exactly square, with a cross-wall well off-centre, the larger compartment thus formed being entered from a forebuilding at first-floor level.

The last keep to which allusion need be made here is at Rochester, Kent, where the castle was originally created by Gundulph, although the beginning of construction of the keep can be dated with some de-

Rochester castle, Kent. The
ep from the forebuilding side
owing corner turrets and rubble
alling

gree of confidence by a charter reference to after 1127.[14] It has a highly
interesting design, and its height, like that of Hedingham, gives it a
boldness lacking in the more squat keeps (fig. 57). There is a cross-wall
set slightly off-centre with a well in the middle, which was encased in a
cylindrical well-pipe so arranged that water could be drawn, at each
floor level, through the building. The forebuilding led to a first-floor
door giving access to the large compartment. The clasping pilaster
buttresses at the corners create turrets usable for the spiral staircase in
the normal way. The turret has been rebuilt with a round projection at
one corner, since this is a reconstruction after it had been brought
down by mining during the successful siege in 1215. The most remarkable feature in the interior is the arcade of two bays on each side of
the central well on the second floor, removing thus the division between the two compartments and creating one large hall, on the same
principle as the spinal arcade in Lanfranc's dorter at Canterbury. The
wall gallery at the higher level adds to the splendour; if plastered and
painted, as was no doubt the case in many keeps, a very impressive hall
could have been produced. The forebuilding was carried up two levels
higher and had a chapel at the topmost storey, reached from the second
floor of the main keep. The spinal arcade, albeit a little off-centre, is a
normal Continental device, but is very unusual in this country above
basement level.

Some of the solar-keeps certainly belong to this period, but firm links
with written sources are not easy to establish. The tendency towards a
square interior, characteristic of hall-keeps, is even more marked with
solar-keeps. The most obvious difference, the absence of a cross-wall,
is also common with hall-keeps, where the diminished span did not
require it and where subdivision into separate rectangular compartments was not made. Entry steps normally must have been of wood,
since forebuildings are rare, as also are chapels and wells. Pilaster
buttresses are universal as they were with hall-keeps up to about 1200.
By modern house standards the rooms of 6 by 8 m square are fairly
generous.

The second half of the twelfth century is lit for us by the surviving Pipe
Rolls that run virtually without interruption from 1155 to the last century. These were annual accounts made by the sheriff of each county
to the Exchequer giving details of income and expenditure, the latter
including costs of maintenance and construction on castles. From the
volume of expenditure and rather laconic references to the nature of
the work carried out it has been possible to define the pattern of royal

castle-building in the period from 1154 to 1216, as well as the names of some of the master masons or 'engineers' in charge of the work, Alnoth, Maurice, Elyas and so on.[15] The scale of work was impressive, some £46,000 (multiply by perhaps 1,000 for a modern equivalent), mainly for the reconstruction of existing castles, although also for a few entirely new ones. Keeps gave rise to the major outlay in all the castles for 'specifically residential or administrative buildings within the castle seldom amount to more than a fraction of the whole'.[16] A number of keeps from this period, 1155–1216, can therefore be firmly dated: Dover, Peveril, Chilham, Scarborough, Newcastle upon Tyne, Orford, Bridgnorth, Tickhill, Odiham, Bowes.

They are a quite a mixed bag. Only the keeps at Dover, Kent, and Bowes, Yorkshire, fit comfortably into the same category as the great keeps of the first half of the century. On the 10 m rule Scarborough just qualifies, but Newcastle upon Tyne, in spite of its very elaborate construction, does not. Peveril, Derbyshire, on its summit in the Peak, and the leaning tower at Bridgnorth, Shropshire, fall firmly into the solar category. A new category, the polygonal or 'transitional' keep, now appears at Orford, Suffolk, Chilham, Kent, Tickhill, Yorkshire and Odiham, Hampshire, the first built between 1170 and 1180, and the last by King John between 1207 and 1212. The term 'transitional' is used for polygonal towers on an assumed transition from rectangular to round towers. It is noteworthy that the Crown built no round towers if we exclude Orford, which is polygonal on the outside, in marked contrast to the buildings ordered by the French king, Philippe Auguste, who is famous for his erection of round towers (p. 43). The crop of round towers in the early thirteenth century owe their erection to Marcher lords in Wales and the Marches.

After one hundred years of settlement, the summit of a motte was more or less ready to receive a tower built on top of it, and both its shape, as well as the greater ability of a round or polygonal form to resist irregular subsidence, made it an obvious choice. The earlier polygonal keeps (Richards Castle and Tickhill) or the somewhat later round ones (Bronllys and Longtown) are set on mottes. However, many of these towers are firmly set on the ground or indeed have a false motte, as at Skenfrith, Gwent.[17] There is little doubt that the change in shape was also stimulated by the improvement in defence it effected by deflecting missiles and making mining more difficult; the spectacular success of the mining of the corner of the keep at Rochester castle in 1215 was a lesson not to be forgotten, a demonstration of the weakness of a rectangular shape.

Was the change in shape also connected with a change in function? There was presumably only one room at each level, since there is no cross-wall in any of these keeps, nor indeed does a round or polygonal shape divide easily into usable rooms. A glance at the table shows that the diameters would allow these buildings to be used only as solar-keeps, with the exception of a few with diameters of 8 or 9 m, giving floor areas at each level of 50 square metres or so. They were clearly single residential units, that is, keeps not lodgings. They had the normal services: latrines, fireplaces, wells and occasionally chapels (Conisbrough). Forebuildings are rare, although entry at first-floor level remained the rule; in France the entry was lowered to ground level, allegedly to facilitate surprise counter-attack. The floors are rarely vaulted above basement level, and often not even there, again unlike the French round towers, and only Pembroke, Dyfed, has a vault at roof level.

Only four keeps can be briefly mentioned here, two of the traditional rectangular form and two of the new shape. Dover by its size and cost of construction clearly must come first, situated on its chalk hill overlooking the Dover Straits (fig. 58). It was perhaps something of an anachronism when it was erected at immense cost in the 1180s in the last years of the reign of Henry II.[18] Whereas the keeps of the earlier twelfth century were usually encircled by a hefty earthwork, at Dover an en-

58 Dover, Kent, from the air. The Roman lighthouse and church of St Mary de Castro in the foreground and behind them the castle with keep and inner curtain with square towers built by Henry II in the 1180s

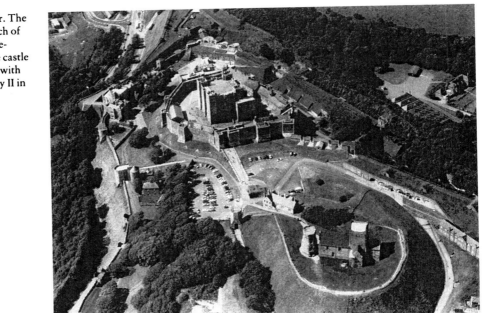

closing curtain wall of stone fortified with square-wall towers was part of the original work carried out simultaneously with the erection of the keep. The curtain wall seems almost to render such a massive keep superfluous, a point that will be discussed in chapter 6. Although its interior is smaller than that at Norwich or Middleham, the great thickness of the walls allowed a large number of chambers to be constructed within them. A highly elaborate forebuilding along one of the longer sides led into the wider compartment (7.5 m wide) connected to the narrower compartment (6.5 m wide) by a doorway. At a higher stage there is the familiar gallery in the wall thickness. The corner turrets are well developed and the normal services were available, including a well of great depth and two chapels.

The keep at Newcastle upon Tyne was the northernmost erected by Henry II between 1167 and 1178. By its internal dimensions it falls just within the solar-keep category.[19] It had an impressive forebuilding that gave access to the second floor, the lowest level having a central column to support a vault. The chapel was below the forebuilding. There was space for chambers and a gallery within the thickness of the walls. It is one of the most compact in this style of keep.

The keep at Orford, Suffolk, built between 1165 and 1178 is the earliest of the 'transitional' keeps, polygonal on the outside and round inside with three great projecting buttresses that rise above the roof (fig. 59). Built on the coast partly, no doubt, with coastal defence as one of its main functions, it is thought to have had political significance, a counterpoise to the Bigods at Framlingham Castle, Suffolk.[20] It had a central well, wooden floors throughout, wall passages of gallery scale and a chapel over the forebuilding that abutted one of the buttresses.

The keep at Conisbrough castle, near Doncaster in South Yorkshire, was not of royal construction so that we have no documentary evidence as to when building took place, but it is likely to have been only a few years later than that at Orford.[21] It was almost royal in that the likely builder was Hamelin Plantagenet, half-brother of the king. Like Orford it has huge buttresses, six this time, that rise above the roof line, but in this case the tower was round both inside and outside (figs. 60, 61). The most striking feature of the building is the finely dressed ashlar of which it is constructed, so that it would look more in place in France than in England. Most of the keeps that we have referred to have dressed stone in the details, windows and doors, string courses and quoins, but the main wall face is of an undressed rubble, local stone. The first floor was probably originally reached by wooden steps, replaced a century later by stone steps with a void to be bridged in front of

59 Orford castle, Suffolk. The circular keep with three great buttresses built by Henry II between 1165 and 1170

Conisbrough castle, S. Yorkshire. Aerial view showing the
cylindrical keep with six
buttresses of *c*. 1180, and the curtain wall with solid towers and
dog-leg barbican

Conisbrough castle, S. Yorkshire. The keep in close-up to
show the fine masonry, plinth,
buttresses and absence of window
openings

84   The rise of the castle

the door. Inside, a vaulted lower chamber containing a well could be reached only by ladder. A fairly grand staircase (not spiral) led to an impressive room with a great hooded fireplace on the second floor, and there was a similar grand room on the third floor. From this room a door led into a fine little chapel contrived in one of the buttresses. At roof level the buttresses were ingeniously pressed into service for dovecot, oven and cistern – all valuable amenities in the event of siege.

It may be useful to summarise the sort of picture that emerges from this fairly lengthy discussion of keeps. The subject is fundamental to castle studies, because the creation of the keep was also the creation of the castle; the motives and causes that lay behind the creation were those that sustained the castle throughout its history.

In the early stages of the castle the use of a tower of wood or stone as a residence by the lord seems to have been very general, the former probably preceding the latter. What is peculiar to England is the exaggerated degree to which it was carried: a group of buildings that would have been dispersed in a normal palace or aristocratic establishment were crammed together to create a structure of elephantine proportions. Such buildings are unknown over most of Europe except across the Channel in northern France and Belgium, and even in Normandy it is possible that Henry I, Beauclerc, introduced the fashion from England.[22] Two questions must come to mind, even if we cannot answer them with full confidence: what was the origin of these enormous hall-keeps and, secondly, what was the motive for their construction?

It seems most unlikely that they were known to the Normans when they arrived in 1066 or we would have expected them to have sprung up immediately after the Conquest. The stone building depicted in the Bayeux tapestry looks like a gatehouse with the arcaded hall of the palace in the background; we know the first arrivals knew about stone gatehouses because they built them at Ludlow and Richmond. The origin probably has to be sought in this country.

The essence of these hall-keeps is that the interior is rectangular, but with a decided tendency to be almost square. A cross-wall (or cross-walls) created two unequal portions and the door on the first floor always led into the large compartment. The impression that we are dealing with a Continental first-floor hall crammed into a small square defended enclosure with massive walls is irresistible. A chapel or church was an essential element in any important establishment, so Romanesque churches were ingeniously incorporated into the design at the Tower and Colchester castle. Current church architecture suggested galleries and passages. The design for the White Tower was surely a skilful but *ad hoc* one, to suit special needs, and has no resemblance to a Carolingian palace.

At Castle Acre, Norfolk, the proto-keep (the excavator's 'country house') is surely fumbling towards the same thing, only betraying its motte ancestry rather more clearly than at the Tower. The initial idea in both cases is the same, a square motte tower expanded so as to contain as many of the normally dispersed buildings as possible. At Chepstow, which is earlier, the idea had not yet been thought of, so a plain Continental-type hall, or *domicilium*, was erected. At Castle Acre we are seeing the moth, as it were, coming out of its chrysalis.

The second question for which we need an answer, another working hypothesis, is closely related: why extend the notion of the keep beyond the solar-keep, why try and cram everything under one roof? This must surely bring us back to the *mobilitas* of William of Poitiers, the untrustworthiness of the native population that caused the Conqueror to withdraw from London until a fortification had been built (p. 75). The invaders were entirely alien in speech and culture; something of the mutual hostility can be detected in the *Anglo-Saxon Chronicle* in the Peterborough version or indeed in Orderic Vitalis, who was born of an English mother and proud of it. There was not the incessant fighting that took place in Wales, but common prudence would not allow the matter to be ignored. The donjon is no doubt feudal but non-feudal factors may well have played a part in the form it took in this country. The subject will come up again later in this book.

Once the keep developed this form it took on a life of its own and probably had some influence on the Continent, certainly in Normandy. The subsequent development of polygonal and round keeps is well documented in the Pipe Rolls, and although the round keeps of Wales and the March clearly are contemporary with those of Philippe-Auguste in France they are a pretty poor relation. The change in the form of residence that rendered the keep a luxury, if not unnecessary, probably started earlier in England, so the French round keep was too late to be adopted by the English Crown. The architectural element that formed a common bond between western France and England, the pilaster buttress, was not used on round keeps and was being superseded or omitted by the time of John's reign on polygonal keeps (Odiham) and even rectangular ones (Carrickfergus). Castles in the two kingdoms took different paths (p. 43), at least until Savoyards, introduced by Edward I towards the end of the century, brought the two countries more back into line.

Chapter 6

Dwelling and defence divided

The dilemma that runs through the whole history of the castle was whether the chief defence should be the inhabited building itself, or whether this should be left undefended and reliance should be placed on a strongly fortified perimeter. In the German castle the *Palas* was what was important, as the 'keep' or *Bergfried* was uninhabited, so perimeter defence was the main consideration, but in the Gallic castle the dwelling itself was constructed for defence and display in the form of the keep or motte. The dwelling flaunted itself as a challenge to the attacker. Perhaps there was an element of this in the late medieval tower-house, a very evident fortified dwelling. The conflict of interest was always there, but the shift in predominance from one to the other, from fortified dwelling to fortified perimeter, that took place in about 1200 is a fundamental one. Disentangling the inhabited buildings from the fortification is the first step towards putting the two in different places, the process that was accelerated by the introduction of artillery in the later middle ages.[1]

The perimeter's defence was by no means overlooked in the eleventh and twelfth centuries. The exposed wooden buildings within a ring-work were presumably defended by the work itself, and even in a motte and bailey, while the lord may have inhabited the former, most people living in the exposed timber buildings of the bailey had to rely on the perimeter defence. The excavations at Hen Domen have shown that these could be formidable: a fighting platform behind a palisade set on the bank, even with towers projecting from it, overlooking a substantial ditch.[2] If the defences on ringworks resembled those at Hen Domen then perhaps we can understand why the motte or keep was omitted, the lord preferring the comfort of living at ground level and trusting to the defences of the perimeter for security.

The defensive circuit could be of stone, of course, a curtain wall as it is called. Where this already existed in the form of a Roman fort it could be re-utilised, as at Portchester, Hampshire, where the castle and its attendant Augustinian priory were planted within the walls of the

Saxon shore fort (fig. 92).[3] Something rather similar was done at Cardiff, substituting an earthen motte for a stone keep, and elsewhere. On the whole, however, Roman enclosures were too large, their perimeters too extended to be properly manned, for the more modest requirements of the medieval castle-builder, so that as a rule the castle was set in a corner of the Roman *enceinte*, its walls giving protection to the castle on only two sides. The Tower of London or Lincoln castle are examples of this.

The alternative was to construct a walled enclosure on a fresh site. This was done, as we have seen (p. 74), at Ludlow, Shropshire, and Richmond, Yorkshire, where the gatehouses on the circuit were later converted into keeps. Scolland's hall at Richmond is not apparently defensible (there are apparent suggestions of defence on the outside), while the famous round chapel in the inner ward at Ludlow of *c.* 1100 suggests its builders were equally confident about the efficacy of the perimeter defence (figs. 89–90). At Eynsford, Kent, a wall of *c.* 1100 forms an oval enclosure around a small hall set over a vaulted undercroft with a solar at one end, entered by an external staircase, very skilfully described by the late Stuart Rigold.[4] The dramatically situated castle at Corfe, Dorset, started off as an eleventh-century enclosure, into which a twelfth-century keep was inserted; two later enclosures further down the hill followed, one of which had an eleventh-century first-floor hall on the line of the original earthwork.[5] It is a fascinating sequence to which there are several parallels that we shall meet, but nevertheless we must certainly regard early curtain walls as unusual so long as the keep was the main interest, as the great enclosing earthworks at Castle Rising, Castle Acre or Castle Hedingham in East Anglia remind us.

Dover castle, perched above the white cliffs, the construction of which is so splendidly documented in the annual Pipe Rolls, shows us how things had changed.[6] It not only had an enormous keep but a massive curtain wall, also fortified with projecting square towers, encircling it (fig. 58). This is a 'belt and braces' solution: why compress the living accommodation into so confined a space when adequate defences allowed much less constraint? The answer no doubt is that the builders were bound to a great extent by tradition and saw nothing incompatible between the two.

A closer insight into the paradox may be provided by the very fine castle at Framlingham, Suffolk, erected by the Bigods, not the king, and so much less securely dated (fig. 62). It has a curtain wall furnished with no less than twelve open-backed, projecting rectangular towers and a

similar gateway.[7] This curtain wall (with very remarkable coupled arrow slits in it at ground level), although probably contemporary with the one at Dover, had no stone keep associated with it. There was evidently an earlier earthen motte or ringwork, for some 7 m depth of made-up ground was revealed in recent excavation on the west side, assumed to have its origin in the spread from this earlier earthwork.[8] On the lower ground to the west is an earthwork enclosure and another large one embracing the south and east sides. Of great interest is the fact that the curtain wall on the east side was built around two pre-existing buildings, a two-storeyed hall with its axis parallel to the wall, and at its southern end at right angles to the wall a chapel that had had pilaster buttresses in its east gable wall. The hall had fireplaces in both storeys, the chimneys remaining, recalling the *salle basse* and *grande salle* in France. At the time the curtain wall was erected in the late twelfth century a new and larger ground-floor hall was built on the west side with its windows perforating the curtain. The earlier first-floor hall was retained, perhaps to become the solar of the new one, albeit not adjoining. It is a sequence that we shall meet in the bishops' palaces (p. 90), and is not unknown at other castles, for example, at Arundel.[9]

62 Framlingham, Suffolk. Aerial view of the castle, showing the square mural towers and gate-house, and the absence of a keep

Two examples from Wales may illustrate this point.[10] At Monmouth castle, Gwent, the twelfth-century first-floor hall survives, set at right angles to the thirteenth-century ground-floor hall tacked on to its upper end for which it clearly served as solar or chamber. These two ruinous buildings which are virtually the only medieval ones still surviving on the site, form a neat, almost dramatic, demonstration of the point to be made about the bishops' palaces.

At Manorbier castle, Dyfed, in west Wales, the fine first-floor hall and adjoining chapel, both over vaulted undercrofts and both with fine external steps, are a prominent feature of the site. Adjoining the entry is a square tower of the same date, superseded by one of the next century through which the gate passage actually passed. It formed part of the thirteenth-century circuit which has two round towers on its corners; in this case there is no visible later hall, unless it lies under the modern house within the enclosure.

The question posed by Framlingham and to a lesser extent the other cases is: was the construction of the curtain wall prompted by the desire to build a new hall or did it just provide the opportunity for that? Put in another way as a more general question: did the desire for accommodation outside a keep lead to the construction of an enclosing curtain wall, or was it the construction of the latter that led to the former? Textbooks on castles tend to assume the second, but it may be that the first was the more important of the two. As in all questions of this kind, there was no doubt a reciprocating action, as with a piston. In this chapter there are then two subjects for discussion: the emergent domestic buildings on the one hand and the formidable defensive walls with towers and gatehouses, which in the popular mind are the distinctive features of a castle, on the other.

The domestic buildings can be treated first. From the Migration period to Tudor times the hall was the dominant building outside or inside the castle enclosure, all other buildings being in some degree subservient to it, the relationship now, indeed, finding formal expression in their disposition. This will have to be discussed, but first let us turn our attention to the hall itself. The word 'hall' is used for three types of structure: a long building with two rows of columns dividing it into a broad central 'vessel' and two side aisles on either side; a similar building but, narrower and without the columns; a two-storeyed structure with the main 'hall' over a vault or wooden floor on the first storey. The latter, with a central row of columns supporting the vault, was the almost invariable form at an aristocratic level in France and the Continent;

as we have seen, a thirteenth-century Frenchman found an apparently English style of aisled hall at Saumur quite alien (p. 45).

Domestic lay-outs from the middle ages survive much better in bishops' palaces than in castles because of the continuity of use, and for this reason I have assembled information (in appendix 1) on halls in them for the period from 1100 to 1350. In contrast to French bishops' palaces, where the hall remained of the same first-floor type until the Renaissance and beyond, there is a striking sequence in England. As a rule an aisled or ground-floor hall supersedes a first-floor hall. Sometimes the earlier hall was demolished and replaced as at Taunton or Newark, but more often it was still retained as at Wells, Lincoln, Winchester, Norwich, Durham (over a vault). There are exceptions of course: Old Sarum has an early aisled hall, while at St Davids, Dyfed, both older and newer halls extend above transverse vaults at first-floor level. The earlier first-floor hall sometimes became the bishop's private hall or chamber, as at Lincoln (fig. 63) or Durham, giving rise to a very

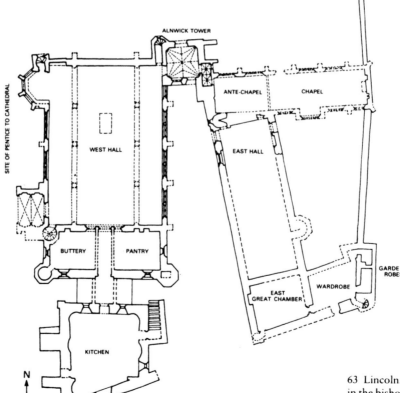

63 Lincoln. Plan of the two halls in the bishop's palace: the later W. hall aisled, and the narrow E. hall set over a great vaulted undercroft. Scale *c.* 1:600

confused terminology (like the east and west halls at Lincoln). Possibly earlier first-floor halls existed at other places like Canterbury and Hereford, but are now lost. The change may have some connection with a process of anglicisation if we assume – as we surely must – that the aisled form is the native one and the first-floor form was introduced from France. If this is so then one must wonder whether the time-honoured medieval arrangement in England with the two-storeyed chamber wing at right angles to the hall, and a marked reluctance to put both under the same roof line, may not represent a marriage of Continental and native halls of the type we saw at Monmouth castle (p. 89), and of which one is so distinctly reminded at Durham castle. French in speech and French in outlook until the fourteenth century, the English lord was probably always more at home on the first floor.

We blandly apply the word 'hall' to three structures of very different kinds: did they have different functions? Perhaps a glance at the contemporary monastic lay-out will help. In large monasteries of the twelfth century, apart from the church, the one large aisled building was the infirmary. From the fragmentary remains (at Ely, Fountains, Rievaulx and others) it is quite clear that they were vast buildings with aisles like the twelfth-century hospital at Angers (fig. 1). The bay divisions created by the pillars served as compartments for beds. The frater or refectory at a monastery was never aisled, although it could be two-storeyed, for pillars were surely an encumbrance in a dining-hall. Could it be that it was the side bays that were of real interest in an aisled hall, utilisable during the night as sleeping compartments and during the day for other purposes such as offices for meeting clients? It is very difficult to see where else the large household of a twelfth-century bishop could have slept if it were not in the hall. It is worth reflecting that when cellular, individual lodgings were introduced in the late fourteenth century, aisled halls went out.

Returning now to the monastic plan: guest halls in the outer court were two-storeyed, like the fine examples at Fountains, Yorkshire. Matthew Paris described such a newly constructed hall at St Albans in enthusiastic terms (*nobilissimam aulam ad opus hospitum . . . et sub-aula, quae Palatium Regium dicitur, quia duplex cryptata*) which can leave no doubt that there was a social cachet attached to this style of building.[11] Throughout the middle ages the first-floor hall was always preferred, for private use at any rate, as was so remarkably demonstrated at Kenilworth castle in the late fourteenth century, where John of Gaunt apparently converted the original ground-floor hall into the surviving first-floor one.[12]

A reversal to the sequence described here was found at Sandal castle, near Wakefield in Yorkshire, where the excavators found the aisled timber hall (p. 58) had been replaced behind by a stone hall with undercroft as part of the general reconstruction in stone in the mid-thirteenth century.[13] The spread of the earlier bank had raised the ground level so it may have been a solution to that problem, but may it mean some sort of upgrading socially, of the accommodation perhaps?

The 'ground floor' in a two-storeyed structure is not always easy to distinguish from a basement. Only occasionally can we speak of a *salle basse*, as at Framlingham or St Albans, where there is a room that can be described as a hall at ground level, as is common in France. In England there is usually a basement feel about the lower space, which is sometimes on a 'split-level'. Where there are fireplaces at both levels the situation is usually clear, but fireplaces are unusual. If the lower area acted as a servants' hall, as inferred in France, it must have been heated with braziers. This would increase the fire risk and make a stone vault above highly desirable. The rather limited daylight entering the room must have made artificial lighting by torch essential for much of the time, creating another fire hazard. Where the room was entirely unlighted by windows of any kind storage, especially of liquor, can surely have been the only use.

The central hearth is presumably a survival from Saxon times. It also had important social connotations, implying a hall open to the roof with a louver rising above it to let out the smoke; this could both carry a weather-vane and be painted and decorated. There seems to have been a strong sentimental attachment to the open hall in England, as opposed to the Continent. This was another reason for retaining the ground-floor hall, since the natural and safest place for a central hearth was on the ground, not on top of a floor. It is clear that central fireplaces were sometimes set on top of a vault or even on top of a special column built up from ground level through the basement to bear it, as at Ludlow, but the natural and normal place for a fireplace in a two-storeyed structure is in the wall. When the hall was reconstructed at Kenilworth in the late fourteenth century two enormous fireplaces were made in the opposing walls. The flat ceiling and wall fireplace are what chiefly distinguish the Continental hall from the English one; the huge carved roof timbers were quite alien to the Continent.

It is also in the twelfth century that the polarity of the hall becomes very marked, although there had been hints of it earlier. By 'polarity' is meant a 'lower end' with opposed doorways creating a cross-passage screened from the main hall and with direct access to services through

64 Lincoln. The three service doors in the W. hall of the bishop's palace. The central door led to the kitchen, with a chamber over (perhaps a private dining-room). Note the bases of piers of the aisle arcades, the central hearth and entry door

the end wall (fig. 64), and at the other end a raised dais and direct access to the lord's chamber or solar. There is some analogy to a parish church with its north and south porches and west door, and it may be that the desire to create processional ways played some part in both. The use as a courtroom may also have had something to do with it. It was certainly an arrangement ill-suited to a two-storeyed structure and was not adopted on the Continent, although the familiar three doorways (buttery, kitchen, pantry) left exposed high up in the ruined hall of the palace of the bishops of Winchester at Southwark, London, is a reminder that this arrangement was quite feasible in a first-floor hall.

Kitchens were regarded as separate buildings both in the medieval monastery and castle, no doubt because of the fire risks, the smoke and the smells. One need only think of the monastic kitchens at Glastonbury and Durham. The middle doorway in the screens passage opened into a corridor that led out to the kitchen standing some distance away.

At Conisbrough, Yorkshire, and Kenilworth, Warwickshire, the whole orientation of the hall must have been decided by the kitchen's position, since this had to be placed adjoining the keep so it could serve both it and the hall. The curious position of the kitchen at Ludlow in the middle of the court was due to the same dual function, to serve both hall on the one side and keep (converted gatehouse) on the other.[14]

The castle buildings were now articulated according to their relationship to the hall. The only building whose position fluctuated between the upper end of the hall and the gate was the chapel. The inner face of the curtain wall served as one side for the buildings, their roof timbers resting on corbels in it, and so they formed a sinuous line taking the shape of the curtain. A right-angle in this could be taken advantage of to turn the chamber through the same angle to the hall (Conisbrough) or alternatively the kitchen at the other end (Kenilworth). The curtain wall was the deciding factor, for it had to follow the natural crest at the top of the gradient or cliff on which the castle was built, the buildings in the right sequence being attached like a string of beads. The site of the hall was probably decided on even before the curtain was built. An existing keep could be retained as a chamber block for the lord, like the older hall in a bishop's palace, but it was an anomaly in the new lay-out so that we can readily understand that on new sites it was normally omitted, thus greatly reducing construction costs.

A few examples may be mentioned briefly. Scolland's Hall at Richmond, Yorkshire (fig. 52) has already been mentioned, as have others at Monmouth, Manorbier and Christchurch, Hampshire. As we might expect, halls are rare when keeps were still in use, or when they were constructed predominantly of wood as at Hen Domen (p. 58) and so have vanished. Examples are best studied in monasteries and bishops' palaces.

Henry II may have built a large aisled hall in the castle at Saumur (p. 45) but, although he apparently did not build any in English castles, the foundations of one that was excavated on the site of the royal palace at Clarendon, near Salisbury, Wiltshire, are thought to be his work.[15] Our most striking example is at Oakham castle, Leicestershire, where the aisled building owes its survival to its continued use as a courthouse.[16] It is the single survivor of what must have been a larger group of buildings set in an earthwork, evidently an early ringwork (fig. 65). It originally had doorways at its east end with service buildings beyond. The round columns of the aisles with acanthus capitals and moulded bases are very fine, and if the ingenious suggestion that before the roof was

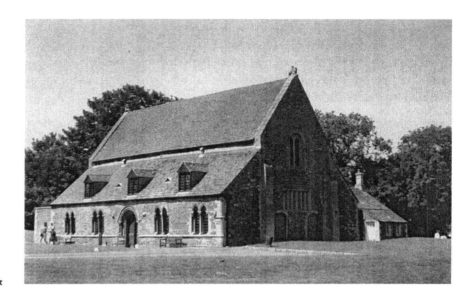

Oakham castle, Leics. Exterior view of the aisled hall of 1180, showing blocked service doors in the gable end. It should be noted that the entry door has been moved one bay to the left

reconstructed there had been a clerestory with windows, as in a church, is sound it must have been a very imposing building with a decidedly ecclesiastical feel (fig. 66). Reference has already been made to possible church influence in the apparent revival of aisles at the time of the Norman Conquest, as shown at Cheddar (p. 8). The hall was probably

Oakham castle, Leics. A nineteenth-century view of the interior of the hall showing stone piers with fine capitals

erected *c.* 1180 by Walkelin de Ferrers, in the 'transitional' period between Norman and the Early English styles. Fragmentary parts of aisled castle halls with wooden arcades from a similar period at Farnham and Leicester have been mentioned, as has the single aisled hall revealed by excavation at Conisbrough Castle (fig. 67).

67 Conisbrough castle, S. Yorkshire. View from the keep-top of the foundations of a single-aisled hall revealed in excavations, two pier bases and a central hearth being visible

From the reigns of Richard I and John very little castle domestic architecture has survived. In the reign of the latter, keeps were still being erected by the Crown (at Odiham, Hants),[17] and major defensive work was carried out at Kenilworth, Scarborough, and elsewhere. One of the most striking and significant features of castle history is the difference in the nature of the constructional work carried out in the second half of the twelfth century by Henry II when compared with work carried out by his grandson, Henry III, in the first half of the thirteenth century. In the first, keeps and curtain walls were very much the order of the day, while in the second, where the written evidence is much fuller, the construction and embellishment of halls and ancillary buildings were the chief activities.[18] The most important work was probably the erection of a new hall by the river wall in the south-east of the Tower of London's inner ward. It was almost certainly aisled, but no trace of any kind survives. The main building of the period that has come down to us is the hall at Winchester castle, Hampshire, a surprising survival because virtually the whole of the rest of the castle was demolished in the Commonwealth.[19] It owed its survival to the fact that, as at Oakham, it was used as a courthouse. It was built from 1222 to 1231. It is a five-bay structure measuring roughly 32 by 16 m, its

68 Winchester castle, hall (c. 1220). Note the Purbeck marble columns, the window seats, and tracery (altered)

arcades formed of Purbeck marble columns, each with four attached shafts and roll-moulded capitals (fig. 68). Although the tall, handsome, two-light windows have been altered and the roof reconstructed, it is a magnificent building, as befitted the castle in the former capital.

Leaving the inside of the castle we turn to the new forms of exterior defence which were often merely a replacement in stone of earthworks and wooden stockades of the Hen Domen type. The outmost defence was still a ditch, usually flat-bottomed, from 4 to 6 m deep and from 15 to 25 m broad. Unlike the V-shaped ditch of the Iron Age hill-fort, which was designed to break a headlong charge on foot, the broad U-shaped medieval ditch was intended to prevent or impede a 'belfry' from being brought up to the wall face. This was a tall wooden structure on wheels or rollers that was dragged and pushed by the attackers up against the wall or near enough to bridge the gap, so that on its top platform the attackers were at the same height as the defenders (see fig. 26). In order to create a firm causeway across the ditch it had to be filled in with brushwood, logs, stones, etc.; the main objective of the defenders was to impede its advance by bombardment and, when it reached the ditch, either to cause it to topple over, or to set it alight (appendix 2).

Most castle ditches were certainly dry, particularly of course where they were situated on top of a hill formed of porous rock. On a low-lying site adjacent to a stream or river its waters could be diverted into the moat, as with the Tower of London. Mining by the attackers, that is, driving an adit in under the wall and then firing the wooden props supporting its roof to bring down the superincumbent masonry, became an increasing menace, as the events at the Rochester siege in 1215 demonstrated (p. 79). The great expansion of the water defences at Kenilworth[20] in John's reign may have been prompted by this fear, as was the movement down from the hill to the valley at Bolingbroke, Lincolnshire, in the 1220s.[21] The water also had other useful purposes: for fish-breeding, watering stock, dowsing fires, and so on.

Unlike a monastery, which had a main drain or culvert, the individual latrines disposed about a castle discharged directly down a vertical chute in the thickness of the wall into the dry ditch or wet moat below. Hygiene made an encircling ditch a necessity for a castle, quite apart from defence.

In the case of a rock-cut ditch its excavation served an additional purpose in that the rock, if suitable, could be employed for constructing the curtain walls. Except for quoins, plinth, window and door details, and coping on the parapet, all built of a finer freestone that might have to be brought from some distance, the wall itself was built of local stone. The topsoil and weathered 'natural' could be spread on the inside of the enclosure to raise the level, either to facilitate drainage or, on low-lying sites, to reduce the risk of flooding. There was always a fear of the inner lip of the ditch crumbling, subsequently causing subsidence and collapse, as happened with catastrophic results at Conisbrough. Usually the wall was set well back from the ditch, with a sloping or battered base or, alternatively, the outer face of the wall could be built upward from the bottom of the ditch to cover over its side.

The dimensions of the wall were variable but had to take account of two factors: sufficient width to allow a crenellated parapet with continuous walk or path behind to allow defence at whatever point was required, say 2–5 m, and sufficient height to deter an attacker's attempt to scale it, say 6–12 m. The wall consisted of coursed stones, usually 'rubble', that is, not dressed although sometimes partially worked, forming the inner and outer faces which retained a great mass of rubble in a matrix of lime mortar in the core of the wall. This type of core, even very thick, was vulnerable to a swung metal-pointed bore; its efficiency was greatly improved if the core itself was coursed, which tended to be done in the thirteenth century onwards (at Bolingbroke, for example). Lime mortar made from quicklime burnt on the site, mixed with several parts of sand and then made viscous with water, was the binding material used in all medieval building.

Some of the earliest curtain walls had one or two projecting square towers, as at Richmond and Ludlow.[22] The surviving walls of Roman towns had solid semi-circular bastions projecting from them which had served as platforms for *ballistae*, so that mural towers were not an innovation requiring much prompting, although the excursions into the Mediterranean in the First and Second Crusades must have impressed the participants with their importance. The purpose of a projecting mural tower was twofold: to keep the face of the adjoining wall under view from in front of it, and of course to assail the enemy from the side if he tried to attack it. The tower had added advantages if it rose above the curtain level, both improving the view and overlooking any attempted use of a belfry. The interval between the towers had to be sufficiently reduced for the wall face to be within range of archers and missiles from one or both towers, say from 20 to 50 m. The rooms in the towers could be fitted with arrow slits facing three directions, forming a tiered defence. Whereas a defender on an ordinary wall walk on the curtain, the only place for the defender hitherto, was very vulnerable when he tried to protect the lower part of the wall, the archers in the towers were all more or less shielded when they attacked the enemy.

Without becoming too involved in the *minutiae* of towers, two further points deserve mention about their development in this period. In the later twelfth century they were built square or rectangular in plan as at Dover, Framlingham, Farnham or Windsor; from the builder's point of view this is the natural way to construct them. However, following the example of keeps they were made round in the thirteenth century: half round or three-quarters round, fully round, segmental or horseshoe-shaped. Presumably the curved surface more readily deflected missiles which, with the introduction of the *trebuchet* (a giant sling operated on a pivoting arm with a great counterweight on the shorter arm) were becoming larger, while the round form gave an extended, less impeded view, as in a cylindrical lighthouse.

Secondly, even when constructed to be open at the back they could be floored, roofed and closed with timber framing behind. If made solid at the back with a wall containing doors and windows, they provided habitable accommodation to supplement courtyard buildings, as at Bolingbroke in the 1220s.[23] Rooms with fireplaces and larger windows in the upper floors particularly lent themselves to this. At Kenilworth, where the outer circuit probably dates from John's reign, there are no interval towers but large keep-like structures at the corners.[24] The two great towers at Cilgerran, Dyfed, in west Wales are even more impressive: two great keep-like cylinders overlooking the Teifi gorge, whose wooded slopes sent admirers of the picturesque into rhapsodies.[25]

For fairly obvious reasons the entrance through the walled circuit was the most vulnerable point, since any obstruction had to be movable so that the occupants of the castle could themselves enter and leave. Height had been a special form of protection in Norman times: one thinks of the flying bridges in the Bayeux tapestry, or the flights of steps in the forebuildings of Norman keeps. Nevertheless, a formal gatetower traces its origins back to Iron Age hill-forts, and saw great development in Roman times. A gate passage through the ground floor of a square tower was certainly familiar to the Normans before 1066: a tenth-century example may be depicted at Rouen on the Bayeux tapestry, as we have said (p. 48), while two of the earliest Norman stone constructions in the country are represented by the original gateways at Richmond and Ludlow. A little later the gate tower at Castle Acre was erected, not on a stone line of defence but interrupting an earthen bank, so vulnerable was this point thought to be.

Entry through a square tower certainly allowed a fair measure of control. It was used at Framlingham in the twelfth century and was the normal device for a back entry (*postern*) or minor gate in castles (or on a grander scale for monasteries) throughout the middle ages. Its weakness was that it left the area immediately in front of the gate indefensible except from the top of the tower: attempts to use a battering-ram or to set fire to the gate could not be readily countered. The solution was apparent once wall towers were introduced: by setting two such towers close together on either side of the entry the defenders overlooked the outside of the gate, making unhindered attack on it virtually impossible. At Dover, the towers were of rectangular form although not of matching size. From soon after 1200 flanking round towers were the form of gateway prevailing for the rest of the middle ages. It was usual to create a three-storey square building at the back with gate passage on the ground floor in the middle, which became one of the most characteristic and distinctive structures of a medieval

69 Beeston castle, Cheshire. The aerial view shows the outer curtain, the inner curtain with early thirteenth-century gatehouse, and the absence of a keep

castle. A notable and early example is at Beeston, Cheshire (fig. 69), while the base of another erected in the 1220s by the same earl of Chester was recently uncovered at Old Bolingbroke castle, Lincolnshire (fig. 70). Numerous examples survive, but surely none more dramatic than the bold shape on the rocky hill dominating the beaches of the town of Criccieth, Gwynedd, in the Lleyn peninsula, even if its attribution to the Welsh or English is in hot dispute.

The upper rooms at the back of the gatehouse provided accommodation of a useful kind, possibly at this date serving as the lodgings of the constable, the lord's permanent representative on the site, who dealt with the considerable administrative and legal business that arose. The ground floor housed the porter on one side of the gate passage and possibly a prison on the other. If the object of the curtain wall was to free the domestic buildings from the necessity of fortification it is surprising how quickly parts of the perimeter fortification began themselves to serve residential purposes.

The two gatetowers were normally set from 2.5 to 3 m apart, the minimum clearance for the passage of a horse and cart or pack animal; life in the castle required a constant flow of food, fuel, household utensils, linen etc. The gate passage could be closed by two-leaf gates pressed by a hefty drawbar at the back that slid out from a deep socket in the wall into brackets on the gates. Of course, there could be more than one set of gates. Another method of closure coming into use in the thirteenth century was the portcullis, a grill sliding up and down in grooves in the wall (usually the only part now surviving) and operated from the chamber over the gate. It was probably just as easy to operate as a gate, and, apart from having no point of weakness at the hinges or central rebate, it allowed the enemies' activities to be kept under surveillance. The vertical movement could be harnessed to act inversely as a counterpoise weight for the bridge in front. The gate passage, for obvious reasons vaulted against fire, could have apertures in the vault ('murder holes') for pouring water on to fires lit by the enemy in front of the gate, or discharging missiles. Outside the gate passage with its series of movable barriers was the bridge over the moat which could be raised, probably pivoting with counterweights in a pit at this date, rather than hinged, as was usual in later medieval times.

If the constriction created by the flanking towers could be projected even further forward with parallel walls it made access more difficult for the enemy who were more bunched and so more vulnerable to attack from the defenders. If the pair of walls could be turned through a right angle it became even more difficult to attack the gate, making the use of a swung ram impossible (fig. 60). Such a device is called a 'barbican' in the modern jargon, although in medieval times the term was applied to any work outside a gate, even outer bailey, as at Pickering. Barbicans were in use from c. 1200 and gained in sophistication during the century.

No clearer demonstration of the above points can be made than in the three large-scale coloured plans of the Tower, Windsor and Dover castles in the box accompanying the first two volumes of the *History of the King's Works* (HMSO, 1963). Unfortunately they are far too large to reproduce here.

At the Tower a small walled enclosure was added, to the south of the great twelfth-century keep, running down towards the river, within which the new great hall was erected by Henry III. The Wakefield tower on the corner, and the Coldharbour gate abutting the keep are of the type just described. The Roman town wall on the eastern side was demolished and a much larger circuit running round to meet Richard I's Bell tower was largely constructed in Henry III's time, although only completed by Edward I (1272–1307) later in the century. This was furnished with round towers with three arrow slits at each level. The later development comes into the next chapter (p. 117).

At Dover (fig. 58), the great keep and the encircling wall with its square towers built simultaneously by Henry II have already been described (p. 81). There is some work of that period on the north-east side but the outer enclosure is for the most part attributable to John (1199–1216). What the plan makes fairly clear is that the curtain wall of John with its round towers lacked the standard gate with flanking towers described above (p. 100). The palace gate and Arthur's gate of Henry II, or the Constable's gate even, reconstructed by Henry III after the siege, all seem to be experimental. Only with Henry III's Fitz-william gate do we have the standard pattern. The whole sequence confirms that mural towers, from which the standard gate derived, come first. Earl Blundeville of Chester in his gates at Beeston, Cheshire (fig. 69) and Bolingbroke, Lincolnshire (fig. 70), built in the 1220s, was possibly even ahead of the king.

Windsor castle, Berkshire, which has remained a principal royal seat and palace since Norman times, presents a dazzling range of colours on its dated plan. Like Arundel castle on the Sussex coast, the original design was very simple, a motte in the middle with two appended enlongated baileys or wards on either side. Unlike Arundel, the main residential buildings have always been in the upper ward. The castle has undergone many reconstructions over the years, but like Dover the essential defensive walling is due to Henry II. He built the original great shell keep on the mound and walled the upper ward, furnishing the curtain with the characteristic rectangular mural towers set at about 20 m intervals. Unfortunately there has been so much reconstruction of the residential buildings on the north side of the upper ward that we cannot say in what form Henry II constructed them, although it may be reasonably supposed that the motive for constructing the wall was to protect something fairly grand. The very interesting later buildings will need further attention.

An early and very remarkable defensive wall is to be seen at Conis-brough, Yorkshire.[26] The fine cylindrical keep with its six great buttresses has been described (p. 82); the curtain wall, a coarse and irregular work, clearly post-dates it, since it abuts on to it on either side. The remarkable feature of the curtain is the solid half-round towers projecting from it at irregular intervals, forming part of the original construction (fig. 60). Two of these conjoined at the gate, although one side has fallen down the hillside. The smallness of the towers (they vary in size) and their solidness, like buttresses, certainly suggest that we are dealing with an experimental structure erected by masons unfamiliar with this sort of work. The single-aisled hall in the north-west corner is also fairly crude – its ancillary buildings have been discussed (p. 94). One has the impression that domestic buildings and curtain were de-signed at the same time.

The dramatically situated castle at Scarborough, on a triangular headland with cliffs on two sides, dominates the modern seaside resort and harbour. On the south-west the headland is cut by a massive ditch with a long wall furnished with round towers behind it. At the northern end is a ditched and walled enclosure, evidently the earliest castle, within which stands the shattered keep, the construction of which has left a record of its costs in the Pipe Rolls of 1157–69.[27] There is a very splendid barbican extending from here down to the entry: a classic of its kind. The curtain wall (and perhaps the barbican) have been assigned to John's reign on the strength of £2,000 expenditure recorded in the Pipe Rolls of that reign. Against this curtain is a two-storeyed hall, Mosdale's hall, containing traces of early work, but mainly that of the 1390s, the time of John Mosdale. Excavations in 1888 revealed the base of an aisled hall a short distance further into the headland. It is tempting to suggest that the early two-storeyed hall stood on a twelfth-century bank and the aisled hall was built a little later when the stone curtain had been erected, but the true sequence of events has not yet been elucidated.

Three castles that were erected or entirely reconstructed in the 1220s by Ralph de Blundeville, earl of Chester, are those at Bolingbroke, Lincolnshire, Chartley, Staffordshire, and of course his main seat at Beeston, Cheshire (fig. 69).[28] The latter is a particularly splendid monument, set on a cliff overlooking the Cheshire plain; it has a tight inner circuit of walls with round towers and an impressive gatehouse with a much longer curtain with smaller towers further down the hillside. The form of the domestic buildings would be of great interest had they survived.[29] At Chartley, Blundeville evidently reconstructed the timber defences of an earthen motte and bailey in stone. Much of it has been pulled down and a folly created on the mound, but two very fine cylindrical towers have been left standing. They have the sombre and forbidding look of thirteenth-century towers, without windows on the outside, only arrow slits. The tower dimensions and form are almost identical with the bases of those revealed by excavation at the very different style of structure on the northern edge of the Fenland at Old Bolingbroke, Lincolnshire.

At Bolingbroke, the site of the castle had evidently been moved south from the earthwork on Dewy hill to the lower ground, where a very substantial water-filled moat could be excavated around it. Even here a bank had to be thrown up on the downhill side to contain the water. The design of the castle was quite simple, an irregular hexagon with round towers on each corner, with the gatehouse formed by two such

70 Bolingbroke castle, Lincs. The polygonal castle of the 1220s, exposed since 1965, with a broad (originally water-filled) moat, towers on the angles and a gate-house facing the church

towers set side by side, constituting one side (fig. 70). By prolonging the lines of the curtain on each side to their points of intersection, one could indeed see how the design had been laid out on the ground. There had been a swivel bridge connecting a causeway across the moat in front of the gatehouse. A sunken chamber in the gate passage may have been a prison. The semi-basements of the horseshoe-shaped interiors of the towers survived up to first-floor level, each with a door and a window at the back. Their floors were much lower than the interior of the castle, which had been raised with made-up ground; they must have been very damp at basement level. The varying lengths of wall between the towers may have been intended to accommodate different build-ings, the hall on the longest side, let us suppose, but unfortunately the wooden structures have vanished without trace, and the later hall was certainly on the other side. The regular octagon at the palatial Castel del Monte in Italy built by Frederick II a few years later (fig. 15), or the more irregular polygon at Boulogne-sur-mer (fig. 71), known from an inscription to be contemporary, had continuous domestic ranges all the way round.[30] As Blundeville had just returned from a Crusade in the Mediterranean it is perhaps not too fanciful to detect foreign influences here. Although strongly defended, the small size of the castle suggests that pleasure played an important part in the motives for its construc-tion; its later use by the widowed Queen Isabella, Henry de Lacy and more especially John of Gaunt – it was the birthplace of his son Henry IV – lends weight to this view.

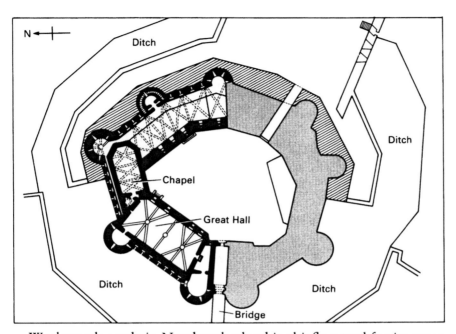

71 Boulogne-sur-mer, Pas-de-Calais. Plan of the castle (dated by inscription) to compare with fig. 70. The continuous ranges within are vaulted at both levels. Scale *c.* 1:1,000

Warkworth castle in Northumberland is chiefly noted for its great late fourteenth-century keep (p. 174) set on top of a motte, but the site has much to interest us from the twelfth and thirteenth centuries.[31] There was at least partial walling of the bailey in Norman times, while a hall on the west side, which was remodelled in the thirteenth century, was given an aisle on the inner side. This recalls Conisbrough, as does the general lay-out with the kitchen serving both hall and early solar on the motte. The development of the full late medieval domestic lay-out, with chapel adjoining the later solar, can be traced in the remains. A fine gatehouse with flanking polygonal towers, and curtain with two polygonal and one square tower, belong to the thirteenth century. If the late collegiate church set transversely across the site is included, the whole sequence is profoundly illustrative of medieval history.

Farnham castle, Surrey, has been frequently mentioned in these pages in connection with its keep, but it has a most interesting albeit badly weathered, outer circuit of walls.[32] This had square towers on its vulnerable north side, presumably corresponding in date with the later keep and the aisled hall, perhaps to protect the latter (fig. 37). The gatehouse with flanking U-shaped towers is evidently to be referred to the early thirteenth century.

The list could be substantially increased, particularly if slightly later structures, like the splendid gateway at Rockingham castle, North-ants, so often reproduced, were included. The very intriguing little rectangular castle at Barnwell in the same county has such towers and a fine gatehouse.[33] However, I would like to close this chapter with a few words about some castles of the Welsh March in this period.

Surprisingly for a land of castles, Wales has few large rectangular keeps, just as it had scarcely any great country houses at a later date and possibly for similar reasons: it was not a land of great seats. It has indeed many round keeps, particularly in the Marcher area (p. 85), the most notable of all being at Pembroke. The keep/hall at Chepstow, Gwent, has been mentioned already; the later twelfth and thirteenth centuries saw very notable extensions of the castle east and westward along the cliff edge over the river Wye, two baileys to the east and another with a barbican to the west.[34] There are one or two round towers on the circuit, and a fine gatehouse at the east end formed of two such towers juxtaposed. The intention was clearly to move the main accommodation out of the Norman hall into a less constricted area where a new lay-out was possible; there is a group of buildings of the late thirteenth century, including two halls in the lower bailey.

The 'Three Castles' in Gwent, given this title because they were usually held together by the same person, consist of Skenfrith, Grosmont and White castles. All three were granted by King John to his justiciar, Hubert de Burgh, who was responsible for much of the construction work at the first two. Skenfrith consists of a simple quadrilateral enclosure with round towers at each corner but, in view of the date, perhaps significantly without a twin-towered gatehouse.[35] There is a free-standing round keep in the enclosure in a motte that excavation has shown – a remarkable fact – was added after the tower had been built. On the west side is a long range of basements, the hall presumably originally forming part of the buildings above. Grosmont is very different, with a long first-floor hall, 29 by 10 m, with a remarkable chimney, of Chepstow style although apparently built by de Burgh, which forms part of a semi-circular enclosure of curtain with round towers of a few years later in date.[36] The gate passage passes through a tower. White castle is the most ambitious of the three, with massive earthworks and wet moats.[37] The inner ward takes a pear shape, apparently walled in the early twelfth century without towers, but having a square keep on the circuit (fig. 72). In the thirteenth century, circular towers were added to the wall, with two juxtaposed at the narrow end for the gatehouse. The most dramatic change was the demolition of the keep, with the new curtain carried across its stump; such was the thirteenth-century contempt for keeps. The outer ward was also walled in this century.

72 White castle, Gwent. The thirteenth-century curtain, with mural towers, passes across the stump of the twelfth-century keep Note also the wet moat and outer enclosure of rather later date

It may be of interest that a few years ago experiments in archery were made in the towers of the inner ward of White castle, at which the author was present. The degree of accuracy of even amateur archers was impressive, so that it was clear that the medieval archer behind his arrow slit was more at risk than one might have supposed. The second point that impressed the writer was the rapidity of fire achievable with the longbow as opposed to the crossbow, a point often overlooked. Only experiments of this kind can bring the dumb masonry to life.

Wales has many other castles of this period to offer, both in the March and independent regions; Pembrokeshire, now part of Dyfed, an English enclave in the Welsh area, has particularly fine ones. The atmosphere of hostility perhaps led to a prolongation of Norman traits – one thinks of first-floor halls. We shall return to this subject in the next chapter. The study of the native Welsh castles forms a subject of its own.[38] Erected for the most part by Llywelyn the Great in the first half of the thirteenth century they often occupy dramatic situations in the landscape, but evidently had somewhat different domestic arrangements.

Chapter 7

Defence paramount

The history of castle construction in Britain in the late thirteenth century is dominated by Edward I's campaigns of conquest in north Wales, his final reckoning with the Welsh princes. The profusion of documentary record in the national archives in the Public Record Office have allowed the whole dramatic course of events, costs and duration of construction, names of designers and numbers and places of origin of the craftsmen and labourers, quantities of material, and so on, to be elucidated. The main story was worked out by the late Goronwy Edwards in a lecture to the British Academy,[1] while A. J. Taylor has spent a lifetime filling in the details and tracking down the antecedents of the main actors in their Continental homes.[2] It was almost certainly the most instructive and informative study of castle construction that medieval history has to offer, both in terms of the actual surviving buildings then erected and in the precise written information with which they could be brought into direct relation. It is not too much to say that it has moulded our views on castle erection and, to a lesser extent, on the buildings themselves into a new form. The present writer, who spent ten years in Wales looking after these castles, has been subject to this influence.

Before turning to the defences of the Welsh castles, which must necessarily occupy a large part of this chapter, the earlier practice will be followed and the residential accommodation of the period will be discussed in relation to the plan of the castle.

There is no fundamental change in the design: the hall is the centre of all, with subservient buildings arranged according to their relationship to it. Normally they are arranged in the same sequence against the inner face of the curtain wall. There is a multiplication of rooms at both ends, particularly at the upper end, and there is a tendency for two wings set transversely to the hall to form at either end. The finest example of this is undoubtedly at Ludlow, where the block at the upper end is a little later than that at the service end. This, after all, was the contemporary

development outside castles in secular domestic architecture in the latter part of the thirteenth century, not in royal or bishop's palaces but in
the great army of 'hall-houses' with one or two wings which largely
make up the vernacular architecture of the later middle ages in this
country. In fact, because of the desire to make use of the curtain wall
on one side, the buildings in castles tended to remain extended, not
set in projecting wings, no more so than in the castles of Edward I, as
at Conwy and Harlech, although, of course, there may be a barrack
element there.

Two buildings in Shropshire (although called 'castles' they cannot
really qualify for the title) belong to the period under discussion, the
late thirteenth century, and must be mentioned here: Acton Burnell and
Stokesay.[3] The first is a fascinating two-storeyed structure with corner
turrets, its hall on the first floor, but really a sort of compact
house, an episcopal rustic retreat, for it was built by the bishop of
Bath and Wells. As it has doors on the ground floor it cannot be said to
be fortified, but its affinities are with fourteenth-century castles, discussed in the final chapter (p. 171). Stokesay was undoubtedly meant to be
fortified, for the buildings lie within a square rock-cut ditch, and deserves fuller discussion.

The outstanding feature of Stokesay is its unaltered state; unused
since the eighteenth century, the hall has never had its windows glazed,
and retains its original shutters (fig. 73). Uncluttered with modern fit-
tings, furniture or carpets, no other building makes one feel quite so
close to the late thirteenth century (fig. 74). The two-light traceried

73 Stokesay, Shropshire. The hall
of c. 1270 within the fortified
manor with flanking wings with
hipped roofs, unglazed windows
closed with shutters and a first-
floor chamber on the left reached
by external steps

Stokesay, Shropshire. Interior
he hall seen in the nineteenth-
tury looking towards the upper
, with cruck-style roof and
ar, and stone seats in the
dows

windows still retain their opposed stone benches, about the only fixed furniture at this period and intended, not for amorous encounters (although eminently suited to that purpose) but for private conversation and business away from the smoke of the hall and with full daylight and some privacy. The hall itself, bare as now except for reeds on the floor and central hearth, could be furnished with trestles with tables on them and benches as and when necessary; like all other medieval rooms it was a multi-functional unit supplied with demountable furniture or hangings as occasion might require. We entirely misunderstand medieval buildings if we introduce the notion of rooms with fixed purposes, as in a modern house. The tower at the lower end may be earlier than the hall itself, while the tower beyond the chamber at the upper end is probably later. The two-storeyed chamber block has its own external steps. Although not aisled, the hall retains its original timber roof. The image of Stokesay is a good one to have at the back of one's mind when dealing with medieval domestic buildings.

The social distinction between ground- and first-floor halls which had its paradigm in the two halls at Westminster Palace, the huge ground-floor structure, probably then aisled, and the private first-floor hall behind (now vanished), appears in castles. At Conwy and probably at Caernarfon the distinct halls were in separate wards, in these cases the first hall evidently designed for the king himself. At Harlech, the transverse halls at the back of the great gatehouses served the latter function. The extraordinary device at the Mortimers' castle at Ludlow of building up a large block of masonry from the ground through the semi-basement to provide a hearth in the midst of the wooden first-floor speaks volumes. The social prestige of a raised hall, not to mention cellarage and servants' hall below, could be combined with open hearth, open roof and no doubt louver over; it was the best of both worlds. On the Continent this would have been regarded as absurd, and surely illustrates English sentimentalism of a familiar kind.

As the construction becomes more complicated, any kind of description without elevations, plans and photographs is quite inadequate. In the case of Ludlow to which we now turn the interested reader must pursue further details in the original publication.[4] The residential block lies on the north side of the inner ward of the castle, facing south, the aspect normally favoured. The hall in the centre is flanked by wings of roughly the same size (fig. 75). It was entered by steps at the west end, the dimension of the room being about 18 by 9 m. The semi-basement over which it was set had four small square-headed windows facing into the court (fig. 76). The hall itself had three fine two-light windows

75 Ludlow castle, Shropshire. The hall range with flanking wings, the hall itself over a grour floor or basement with separate entry

76 Ludlow castle, Shropshire. Interior of the hall showing both levels. The central window has been blocked to form a fireplace

on the inside and three single lights facing outwards. In both cases the window recesses are furnished with the stone seats just mentioned. The normal three service doors are absent from the west end, and the food was evidently brought in through the main door from the kitchen in the court. Both wings were three-storeyed, containing fine chambers on the first and second floors. In both cases, extra toilet facilities required by the building meant alterations to the earlier curtain wall, a tower at the east end and a discharge pit in the angle of tower and curtain at the other.

Another set of domestic buildings that may be mentioned are those in the great castle of Caerphilly, Glamorgan, a few miles north of Cardiff, the erection of which started under Gilbert de Clare, earl of Gloucester in 1268.[5] Its defences will be discussed below, but here we may just mention the domestic buildings on the west side of the inner ward (fig. 78). The hall itself is a rebuild of the early fourteenth century by Edward II. It has internal dimensions of about 20 by 11 m, a common 2 : 1 ratio that we have met elsewhere in ground-floor halls, for first-floor ones are usually narrower. It evidently did not have a central hearth, for there is a contemporary fireplace in the courtyard wall-side. At the northern upper end there is a three-storey block projecting as a wing, but the whole structure is much less integrated than at Ludlow. The lower end only had two doors, because the kitchen, displaced as at Ludlow but for quite different reasons, lay outside the curtain wall on the platform adjoining the moat, being accessible through a passage cut through the curtain wall. It almost became part of the castle's defences like a tower, a most ingenious solution.

Two other groups of domestic buildings in Welsh castles, situated further west in Dyfed, deserve mention, at Llawhaden and Carew. In the former case a thirteenth-century enclosure had been demolished at the bishop of St David's palace in order to erect an irregular polygon with long ranges forming its sides.[6] The hall, 23 by 17 m internally, is set over a vault, as are most of the other buildings. The remarkable feature is that the hall's flanking wings, kitchen at one end and chamber at the other, are reversed so that they project outward as towers on the defensive line of the castle, instead of into the courtyard. It gives a dramatic feel to the design, apart from making the siting of latrines much easier. The remaining towers are polygonal. The other surviving palaces of the same bishop at Lamphey and St David's are not really castles, but both have noteworthy first-floor halls, a sequence in each case of earlier thirteenth-, and later fourteenth-century, structures.[7] The very distinctive arcading supporting the wall-walk (they are distinctly fortified) above the eaves is unknown elsewhere in Britain, although a Continental source has not been precisely identified.

The fine ruin on a tidal inlet at Carew was a castle which had three main periods of construction: thirteenth and fourteenth centuries and Elizabethan.[8] The earliest work is on the south side of a quadrilateral enclosure and consists of the smaller of the two halls with chapel on one side. On the west side is the later hall, measuring 25 by 8 m, its dimensions indicating that it was a two-storeyed structure, for both halls are set over vaulted undercrofts. The larger one has been so laid out that it fills the west side, and the two corner towers of the castle house its chamber at one end and services at the other, recalling the arrangement at Llawhaden. These towers are square at the base but spurred or mitred at the corners, so the main tower becomes round above. This type of tower is a speciality of the March occurring at Goodrich (fig. 77) and Martin's tower at Chepstow. The military need that continued longer in Wales because of the hostility of the native population may have prolonged the use of the first-floor hall; the Caerphilly hall was not built by a man of the March.

At a vernacular level, both in England and Wales, the ground-floor hall was universal, and the lowest level socially at which one might expect a first-floor example in England is represented by the fine hall at Donington-le-Heath Coalville, Leicestershire, now beautifully restored by the County Council. In his dream described in *The Mabinogion*, Rhonabwy probably gives a much fairer description of a hall at a lower social level:

> a black old hall with straight gable and smoke a plenty from
> it . . . inside a floor full of holes and uneven. Where there was a
> bump upon it it was with difficulty a man might stand thereon,
> so exceedingly slippery was the floor with cow's urine and their
> dung. Where there was hole it would go over the ankle . . .[9]

Rhonabwy slept on the dais under a 'flee-infested blanket' and as it was raining outside there were problems about relieving himself. Definitely a ground-floor hall!

This chapter deals with castles where defence had become the overriding consideration, where the preoccupation with the defensive *enceinte* overshadowed all else. There were no new arms to be taken into account; archery and engines of various kinds to hurl large missiles were still the main weapons. Rams, ladders, belfries and mining were still the main instruments of assault. What had changed was the attitude of the castle-builder: from a fairly *ad hoc* approach to a more rational and planned method of design by trying to foresee what an enemy was likely to do and take steps to counter it in his design. Domestic requirements still remained a very important consideration in this design. Inevitably the process of construction made much heavier demands in terms of administration on those engaged in it; the surviving documents, as well as the castles themselves, from Edward I's great enterprise in Wales, are a monument to this. It is forever a source of wonder that the very limited administrative apparatus of a medieval state could have achieved it.

To turn from the general to the particular, there are two or perhaps three especially significant features that we associate with castle defences of this period: a desire for a regular geometrical shape, a desire for a double line of mutually supportive defence ('concentricity'), and where possible to make use of water defences. Edward I's castles, which display these traits to a high degree, will be discussed in the final part of this chapter. The three features are to some extent interdependent, so can hardly be separated, but we may try to follow them consecutively in some examples.

A regular square or rectangular shape for castles had become normal in France from the time of Philippe Auguste at the turn of the century (p.43). The remarkable little regular rectangle at Barnwell, Northants probably belongs to the 1260s. At Somerton, Lincolnshire, a rectangular castle, with licence to crenellate in 1281, survives in a fragmentary state with one round corner tower preserved attached to a farmhouse, giving a distinctly French appearance to the ensemble.[10] Somerton is low-lying and so a wet moat was practicable; Goodrich castle, Hereford and Worcester, on the other hand is perched on the cliffs of a re-entrant valley of the river Wye (fig. 77). This has allowed the construction, in the later thirteenth century, of a fairly regular rectangular castle, some 45 by 40 m, incorporating an earlier Norman keep.[11] It has three round corner towers with its gatehouse at the north-east corner, protected by a bridge leading from a semi-circular barbican, similar to that of the same date at the Tower of London called the Lion tower. A rock-cut ditch protects the castle on the south and east, while the ground has been levelled off to form a kind of platform on the other two sides with a wall and parapet overlooking the cliff. On two sides, then, the defence was 'concentric'. The ground-floor great hall was on the west side with its kitchen in the south range, service rooms in the south-west tower (compare Carew) and chamber in the north range. The chapel is in the tower adjoining the gate passage.

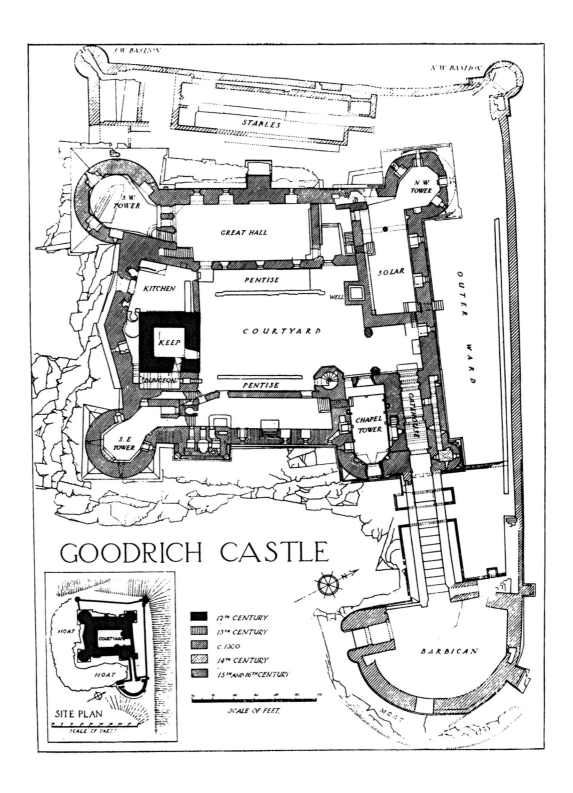

GOODRICH CASTLE

SITE PLAN

SCALE OF YARDS

■ 12ᵀᴴ CENTURY
▤ 13ᵀᴴ CENTURY
▨ c. 1300
▧ 14ᵀᴴ CENTURY
▤ 15ᵀᴴ AND 16ᵀᴴ CENTURY

SCALE OF FEET.

Goodrich castle, Hereford and
orcester. Plan showing the ear-
r twelfth-century keep. The
apel adjoining the gate, the
mi-circular barbican, the inter-
l domestic buildings, and the
rrace of 'concentric' defence on
e N. and W. sides are part of the
stle of *c.* 1300

The saving in cost by erecting a small rectangular enclosure rather than cutting off a whole spur, as at Beeston or Scarborough, needs no emphasis. Furthermore, a compact plan allowed the towers and gatehouse to play an ancillary part in the domestic arrangements. Lines of defence that were widely separated in a series of baileys were not only costly to build and maintain and demanded large garrisons, but rows of open-backed towers set at a long distance from the main domestic buildings could hardly supplement accommodation, as in the case of the outer curtain at Beeston, Cheshire (fig. 69). Far better was it to concentrate the defences in a small planned area, and omit outer wards, only creating, if possible, an encircling platform with its own parapet sufficiently narrow and low for archers to fire at the enemy from both levels of battlement, as at Goodrich. This is what is meant by the term 'concentric' applied to this form of defence in textbooks on castles.

Concentricity was not a new aspect of defence: it is a very distinctive feature of Iron Age hill-forts, especially of course in the famous example at Maiden Castle, Dorset.[12] The main missile weapon then was the sling, and apart from keeping the enemy at a distance the serried banks were calculated to break up a charge by Celtic tribesmen, but only the innermost bank carrying a palisade was manned by the defenders. In a medieval concentric work the intention was clearly to hold the outer defence as long as possible, so doubling the firepower. Even if the platform had to be abandoned to the enemy such a great step in front of the wall presented a formidable obstacle in trying to bring up a belfry to the face of the inner wall. Constrained by the outer wall of the platform, the enemy was far more vulnerable to missiles from the defenders. There was certainly no direct continuity from prehistoric times to the middle ages in such a form of defence, the advantages of which would be fairly easily recognised. Experience in the Mediterranean area no doubt provided stimulating examples, not least from the fourth Crusade when the western crusaders camped in front of the Theodosian land wall of Constantinople,[13] the great triple-tiered defence of the city (fig. 84). Edward I, whose name is especially associated with this type of defence, knew the Mediterranean and was indeed on a Crusade there when the death of his father Henry III brought him to the English throne in 1272.

The third element involved, water defences, now needs to be mentioned. We have seen how the menace of mining encouraged its use, notably at Kenilworth and Bolingbroke (p. 104). The heightening of the dam at Kenilworth and the enlargement of the mere, the large lake on its west side, created a new boundary for the construction of the curtain on that side, being sufficiently near to the inner one, indeed, to give a semblance of concentricity.[14] The whole of these waterwork defences were put to the test in the great siege of 1266 when the supporters of the late Simon de Montfort were besieged by the king, his sons, Edward and Edmund and others, including Gilbert de Clare of Gloucester.[15] The full range of royal resources was unable to take the castle by assault, the garrison after many months being persuaded to give up by the offer of favourable terms in the *Dictum* of Kenilworth. The success of the waterworks, which virtually rendered the castle impregnable, evidently made a deep impression on at least two of the attackers who shortly afterwards constructed castles in which water defences were the most significant feature.

The first of these was the great castle at Caerphilly, Glamorgan, just north of Cardiff, erected from 1268 onwards by Gilbert de Clare, Earl of Gloucester, to meet the menace of the Welsh Prince Llywelyn ap Gruffydd, whose expansion southward from his Gwynedd homeland was a matter of concern.[16] The partially constructed castle was indeed attacked and burnt by the Welsh at an early stage of the work. The domestic buildings have already been discussed (p. 113) but they are almost lost in the vast area of the defences (fig. 78). A huge dam running north–south, known as the north and south platforms, ponded back a

78 Caerphilly castle, Glamorgan. Aerial view showing the restored lakes, the fortified dam that created the waterworks, and the 'concentric' castle started in 1268

valley stream, the Nant-y-Gledyr, the waters of which formed two lakes to the north and south of the castle proper and an outwork on its west side, turning them both into islands. The dam itself was protected by a wet moat on the outside, so the person entering crossed first a bridge over this moat, then passed through a gatehouse, then over the dam, across another bridge and then through an outer and inner and larger gatehouse to reach the interior of the castle. The space between these gatehouses was an inner platform encircling the structure which was concentrically defended. A further pair of gatehouses on the other side led to the outwork (perhaps, like the Brays at Kenilworth, intended for tourneys) and so to the postern or back entry. This stupendous work fell into decay very rapidly, mainly because Edward I's conquest of Gwynedd in 1282 eliminated the threat that it was intended to counter. The clearance of later buildings and the restorations of the Marquess of Bute, followed by the re-creation of the lakes by the Ministry of Works, have allowed us to recapture something of its former majesty.

The second castle, which owes not a little to the siege at Kenilworth, is at Leeds, Kent, constructed soon after his accession to the throne by Edward I or perhaps by his queen, Eleanor.[17] In this case there had been an earlier motte and bailey (the Gloriette is thought to have been the motte) which the new works turned into two islands by ponding back a stream with dams to create a lake. This supplied a head of water for a mill, fortified like some medieval French mills. This was connected by a barbican and bridge to the main island which was enclosed with a new curtain wall outside the earlier one to form a sort of concentric defence. As well as defensive advantages, lakes have pleasure attractions which became increasingly important at Kenilworth in the fourteenth century and no doubt help to make Leeds so popular among tourists today.

Before turning to Wales, there remains one concentric castle to be mentioned, perhaps indeed the most important of all: the Tower of London. The earlier development in the thirteenth century has already been discussed (p. 102); work which now reached its full completion under Edward I. It is conveniently shown in green on the *King's Works* plan. The towered circuit around the White Tower was completed, and a platform created around it, giving the structure concentric defence. The outer circuit had a parapet but no towers and overlooked a broad moat (40 m wide) fed from the Thames. The castle was entered either from the south-west through a semi-circular barbican, across the moat controlled by two gate towers, the Byward and Middle towers. There was a moat on the south separated from the Thames by a solid embankment forming a wharf, reached directly from the river. As the normal method of travel for royalty was by water, a new river gate entered by a channel through the wharf was built on the riverside wall, St Thomas's tower. There was an entry behind this adjoining the Wakefield tower into the inner ward of the castle. Apart from certain additions by Henry VIII to allow the use of artillery, the Tower had now reached its final form.

Before his accession to the throne Prince Edward had had unhappy experiences with the Welsh who, in the first three-quarters of the thirteenth century under Llywelyn the Great and his grandson Llywelyn ap Gruffydd, were in a decidedly aggressive mood. As allies of Simon de Montfort the Welsh not only deprived the English prince of his lands in north Wales, but were a party to the capture of the king and himself after their defeat at the battle of Lewes. Clearly the day of reckoning was to come. On his rather leisurely return to England from the Mediterranean after his accession in 1272 the new king stayed in Savoy, to the royal house of which he was related, and it was there that he learnt of castle construction in progress and made the contacts that allowed him to introduce Savoyards at different levels in the execution of his great castle-building programme in Wales.[18] When he returned to England in 1274, friction with Llywelyn was not long delayed: Llywelyn refused to attend the coronation, wanted to marry the daughter of Simon de Montfort and so on. It is quite clear from these and other actions that the Welsh prince entirely misjudged the character of the man he was dealing with. In a book on castles further discussion of the political history would be out of place, and so we must turn to the campaigns.

The two campaigns, 1277 and 1282, were very different in their objectives and in the nature of the castles erected.[19] In the first campaign the intention was clearly to force Llywelyn back into his homeland of Gwynedd and establish firm English control of the east and south of Wales. In the second campaign, precipitated by the rash actions of Llewelyn's younger brother David, it is doubtful if Edward had intended to sweep away the independent Welsh princedom, but the almost accidental killing of Llywelyn in 1282 opened the way for the English king to regard himself as the feudal heir to Llywelyn's forfeited estate. The whole of Gwynedd had now to be subdued and securely riveted down with castles.

Although there was some overlapping between the two series, since the castles of the first campaign were not complete when the second campaign started and as, indeed, they had been attacked by the Welsh and severely damaged, there is a tendency to merge both series into one. This is a mistake, however, as A. J. Taylor has made clear in a recent article.[20] James of St George, the master mason from Savoy (St Georges d'Esperanches from where he took his name is in south-east France), who had over-all charge of the work, did not take over until 1278. The ground designs of the castles started in 1277 had presumably been already laid out before he took over, and so can hardly be attributed to him. There does seem to be a greater hesitancy and archaism about the earlier castles: the refurbishment of the motte and bailey at Builth Wells, Powys, the round keep at Flint, Clwyd, or the diamond shapes of Rhuddlan, Clwyd, or Aberystwyth, Dyfed, recalling Caerphilly where work was probably even then still in progress. As against this, the castles of the second campaign give a much more positive and individual impression.

There are several characteristics which the work of both campaigns share in common. The first is that most of the castles lie along the north coast (Flint, Rhuddlan, Conwy, Caernarfon, Beaumaris) or west coast (Harlech, Aberystwyth) of Wales. Rhuddlan is not by the sea, but is a few miles up the river Clwyd, the course of which was realigned in a canal skirting the foot of the castle, so that it could be reached by ship. The scale of the work involved in making such a canal brings home to us the crucial importance of supply by sea in the whole operation, not only because heavier materials were best carried by water, but also because they were not then at the mercy of Welsh guerrillas. Men usually travelled on foot overland. The exceptional inland castles like Builth, just mentioned, Ruthin and Hope in Clwyd, or the 'lordship' castles given by the king with large estates at Hawarden, Chirk, Denbigh and Holt, all in Clwyd, were fairly near the English border, and so could be supplied by land.

A second characteristic was that a number of the castles were associated with a fortified town, laid out as part of the original design, as at Flint, Aberystwyth, Conwy, Caernarfon and Denbigh, or a reformed town, as at Rhuddlan and Beaumaris. The intention clearly was that they would be settled by English craftsmen and tradesmen, on favourable terms, whose activities would radiate English culture all around them. It goes without saying that they were fortified (see chap. 9). By a strange irony of fate, these towns are now probably the most Welsh in Wales. In these *bastides*, as they are called, we see the castle in quite a new light, in a civilising or 'colonial' role as the dyed-in-the-wool nationalists might call it. It was a secular influence that was to be experienced, for unlike the twelfth-century foundations, no monasteries were associated with these castles.

The third characteristic, a fairly obvious one, is that with the exception of the lordship castles they were all official, royal or state enterprises, erected more or less simultaneously with resources provided by the English Exchequeur; in contrast, the castles of the March had been erected piecemeal by the barons in their different conquests in the eleventh and twelfth centuries. Some of the marked differences between north and south Wales, particularly in their attitude towards the English, can be traced back to this varied experience. South Wales was, after all, the springboard for the conquest of Ireland in 1169, while countless archers, particularly from Gwent, served in English armies of the thirteenth to fifteenth centuries.

In the comparable constructional campaigns of Henry II in England a century earlier the work was largely carried out at existing castles, at places where the king was certainly intending to reside, from time to time, but it is difficult to believe that Edward I saw his Welsh castles in these terms. At Caernarfon, the intended capital, and Conwy, the secondary capital, of the new province the castles were divided into two, with one part reached by boat (as in the Tower) and furnished with accommodation clearly intended for the king and queen. It is known that they stayed in them, and the later Edward II, Edward of Caernarfon, took his name from his birthplace. However, these two castles were exceptional; the others have no such clear indication of royal intentions. They were no doubt designed principally as garrisons in hostile territory, but they were not forts, since their builders only knew feudal castles and it was in that form that they were cast. They were built on a grand scale to reflect the royal authority (or imperial status at Caernarfon, to judge by the allusions to Constantinople), of the builder, as well as to overawe and subdue a recalcitrant native population. In 1294 the Welsh insurgents in Madoc's rebellion badly damaged the incomplete castle at Caernarfon; the English response was not only to repair Caernarfon but to plant one of even more ingenious design at the other end of the Menai Strait at Beaumaris in Anglesey.

The Savoyard presence, so skilfully demonstrated by A. J. Taylor,[21] not only in the directing architect represented by Master James but also at craftsman level below and administrative level above, as in the case of Otto de Grandison, must raise questions as to how far this directly influenced the architecture. Five Continental traits were identified by Taylor: the spiralling scaffold used on the towers, leaving its traces in the form of putlog holes where horizontal supports were inserted into the masonry; the semi-circular arch (found elsewhere); the peculiar inverted semi-conical latrines corbelled out from the wall face as at Harlech; the triple points or finials on the merlons at Conwy; the distinctive form of windows in the back of the Harlech gatehouse. At first these seem rather small beer, but we must assume that just as at Canterbury cathedral or Westminster abbey Continental intrusions became anglicised during construction, so something analogous happened in Wales. The great gatehouses at Harlech and Beaumaris, with their splendid first-floor accommodation at the rear, could have served as first-floor halls; it has been suggested that Master James, who was appointed constable at Harlech in 1290, lived in the gatehouse. Putting aside minor variations, there is an indefinable sense of completeness of design and boldness of conception in these castles, which recalls the difference between a French and an English cathedral, and betrays an alien hand at work.

Before turning to domestic accommodation in the castles, something must be said of the logistics of construction, not our main concern in this book and treated at length elsewhere, which the wealth of documentary sources provides.[23] The main supply base and assembly point was Chester in the north (Bristol in the south). Craftsmen and labourers were recruited from all over England, in effect pressganged, and marched under escort to the construction sites. There were up to *c.* 4,000 men occasionally working on a site, but as so much work was going on simultaneously large bodies of men moved about from one site to another. The first step was to set up temporary wooden buildings and defences, and then set about digging the great ditches that would surround the masonry structures; hundreds of *fossatores* were set to work. This was followed by construction starting in earnest with stonecutters and masons, who were supplied by quarrymen and limeburners, the latter burning the local limestone to quicklime for making the mortar. Numerous also were carpenters or joiners working on scaffolding, doors, bridges, floors, roofs and so on. For covering the roofs, plumbers and tilers were necessary, while windows and doors required smiths. This great army of people had to be paid, adding considerably to the costs of materials, transport etc. For the whole Welsh undertaking the recorded minimum cost was £93,000.[24] By comparing the wages of workers of a corresponding grade today one can arrive at a very rough multiple of 700, yielding a modern equivalent of, say, £65,000,000. Taking into account the lower standard of living and the minute GNP this comparison is quite unrealistic, and in any case because of incessant modern inflation is subject to constant upward revision. Perhaps if we see the enterprise as something equivalent to the construction of the modern motorway system over the last thirty years a more telling analogy may be envisaged.

Of the Edwardian castles, six remain as very substantial ruins (Flint, Rhuddlan, Conwy, Beaumaris, Caernarfon, Harlech) and discussion may be confined to these.[25] Of the lordship castles, there are very substantial remains at Chirk, which is still inhabited, and Denbigh, while we know a good deal about Holt from a surviving Tudor view.[26] No two are alike and we may suspect that had it not been for the written sources architectural historians would happily have given them different dates. Flint and Rhuddlan were started in 1277, Conwy, Caernarfon and Harlech in 1283, and Beaumaris in 1295. The climax of the whole operation was in 1283 to 1289 when Harlech and Conwy were being erected at breakneck speed and were virtually complete by the last date, while Caernarfon, an altogether bigger operation, was under way but not completed until much later. Beaumaris in Anglesey was started in 1295 after Madoc's rebellion, but after two or three years of intensive effort Edward I's attention was distracted from Wales to Scotland; it was never completed. The lordship castles were probably started a little later, but are of course less well documented.

  No internal buildings survive at Flint, Rhuddlan or Beaumaris and at Chirk none of the existing ranges are contemporary with the original castle, which may have been larger before the Civil War.[27] At Denbigh there are the remains of a ground-floor hall and a two-storeyed range further south (Green Chambers). At Harlech, the domestic lay-out is clear although the buildings are ruinous (fig. 79). Opposite the gatehouse, almost exactly so, is the screens passage of the hall, the standard late medieval domestic fashion; it extends to the right with the chapel at right angles to the upper end, while normal service buildings extend round the left (south) side of the castle. The outside wall of the buildings was formed by the curtain. The missing feature from the lay-out is the standard two-storeyed chamber block; the first floor of the colossal gatehouse may have contained this as well as a Continental-style first-floor hall, as mentioned above; in point of fact the kitchen is hardly further away from it than it is from the main hall.

  At Caernarfon and Conwy castles we are dealing with something quite different; in each case the castle is divided into two sectors or wards which were evidently intended to have two different types of accommodation. In both cases, the foundations of the large ground-floor hall survive in what we may presume was the ward intended for

79 Harlech castle, Gwynedd. Built between 1283–7, the great gatehouse, the hall (foundations) opposite, the 'concentric' design and the fortified track down to the sea, which then reached the cliff bottom, deserve attention

use by the garrison, the western one in both cases. At Caernarfon, the original buildings in the eastern or royal ward do not survive which embraced, perhaps significantly, the eleventh-century motte of the earl of Chester's castle (where the Investiture platform now stands), but at Conwy the author of the official guidebook has been able to identify the first-floor hall, served by a chapel in the adjoining tower, and the other royal apartments (fig. 80). The contrast with the long (25–30 m) ground-floor halls in the lower wards of the two castles is impressive; one could hardly need a better demonstration of the social superiority

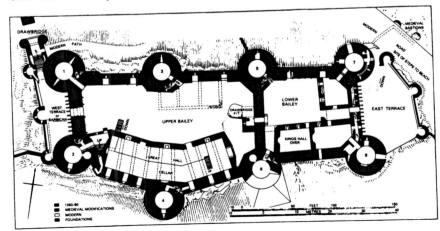

80 Conwy, Gwynedd. Plan of the castle erected 1283–9, showing the sharp division into two wards, the hall which takes the shape of the curtain wall, the cylindrical mural towers and the form of the entry at the W. end up a ramp from the town

of the first-floor hall. It is unfortunate that the domestic buildings at Beaumaris castle either were not erected or have been demolished, since it may be reasonably supposed that a large hall was intended in the courtyard, although the vast gatehouses suggest that they were to be used after the style of Harlech.

Turning now to aspects of the defence, the shape may be considered first. Clearly a desire for a square or, at all events, quadrilateral form was almost universal. At Caernarfon the line of the curtain may have followed the sinuous circuit of the earlier motte and bailey, while at Conwy a square shape was clearly intended for the inner ward, although the outer one tends to take the shape of the rock. At Flint, Rhuddlan, Harlech, Beaumaris, and Chirk the intention is plain; it may be that there is a Continental influence at work here. As shown in a plan of 1562 the lordship castle at Holt, which was pentagonal with a round tower at each corner, an unflanked entry in the middle of one side and continuous two-storeyed ranges all the way round[28] was quite out of step and seems to hark back to Bolingbroke, Boulogne or Castel del Monte (p. 105). Unfortunately its date of construction is less firmly fixed, although the 1280s seem the most likely. At Denbigh, the town wall was built first and the castle tucked into one corner, formed by cutting off a segment of the town enclosure with a wall defended by octagonal towers (fig. 81).[29] In other cases the town enclosure was

81 Denbigh castle, Clwyd. This aerial view shows the castle created by cutting off an angle of the pre-existing town enclosure, and the octagonal towers of its gatehouse and walls

usually erected at the same time as the castle, but Denbigh illustrates the crucial importance attached to the creation of towns in the whole undertaking.

The intervals of curtain wall between mural towers varied from 15 to 35 m, and so always allowed the wall face to be within archer's range from one or both sides. The walls were surprisingly thick, 3–6 m, usually solid but sometimes pierced by arrow slits, as at Rhuddlan. Caernarfon, special in so many ways, has wall galleries at two levels on the riverside, and on the town side where the wall was built later after Madoc's rebellion, embrasures with triple arrow slits that are either convergent or radiating. The main defence of the walls was from the top, where the merlons have a central arrow slit, emphasising the vulnerability of the defender even at this height (p. 108). At Conwy the merlons have triple finials on them, while at Caernarfon the Eagle tower has the famous eagles on it. The walls were faced with partially dressed stone, not ashlar, and the patches of rendering on the face of Conwy indicate that it was originally like that all over, and possibly painted or whitewashed. The present dark, almost black, walls of Conwy are quite misleading as to its original light appearance.

The other defensive element were the mural towers, set at each change of direction in the circuit and rising a stage above the wall walk of the curtain. The wall could be carried round, through, or stopped at, the tower. The towers were normally round and closed, unlike the open-backed ones on the town walls at Conwy and Caernarfon. Flint is exceptional in that it has a veritable keep or donjon with its own moat separating it from the castle. It is an unusual structure consisting of concentric cylinders, the inner one evidently rising higher than the outer; it would seem to have a continental pedigree. The mural towers normally contain habitable rooms which at Caernarfon are very large. Caernarfon and Denbigh have very distinct towers which are octagonal rather than round (figs. 81, 82–3). At Caernarfon, the octagonal shape was undoubtedly meant to simulate the Theodosian walls at Constantinople which have towers of variable shape, sometimes polygonal, just as the banding at Caernarfon is intended to simulate their tile courses (fig. 84). The banding, created by using a darker-coloured stone for two or three courses at intervals, only occurs on the outer face, the earlier part of the castle overlooking the river. Special emphasis could be given to the towers by allowing a stair to rise as a turret above the main tower, as in the inner ward at Conwy, the seaward side at Harlech, or more generally at Caernarfon.

One of the puzzling features of the Edwardian castles is the inconsis-

82 Caernarfon castle, Gwynedd. Erected from 1283 onwards, the curtain is shown, across the river Seiont, with octagonal towers, turrets and banded masonry

83 Caernarfon, Gwynedd. The castle showing Eagle tower, with its three turrets and eagles on top

84 Constantinople (Istanbul), Turkey. The Theodosian land wall (fifth century) to compare the polygonal towers and tile banding with Caernarfon curtain

tency on gatehouses: impressive ones at Beaumaris, Caernarfon, Harlech and Rhuddlan, but no real gatehouse at Conwy, Flint, Holt and Chirk. At Conwy the causeway, outer gate and barbican might be regarded as adequate defence for the entry, but this hardly applies in the other cases. At Chirk, a gatehouse might have been demolished in the Commonwealth period, for the surviving gate set between a corner tower and another set slightly off-centre seems a rather feeble defence (fig. 85). At Rhuddlan, the opposed gatehouses at the angles of the

85 Chirk castle, Clwyd. Aerial view showing Mortimer castle of c. 1300 with nearly half of the design missing, due probably to demolition during the Commonwealth

rhomboidal shape remind one of Caerphilly castle (p. 118). They do not project backwards into the court in the way that those at Harlech and Beaumaris were planned to do, clearly for the purpose of creating rooms in the upper storeys, and not with a defensive intention. The lengthened gate passage allowed more portcullises, but that clearly was not the motive. The *tour de force* of the whole series was the great triangular gate at Denbigh, now sadly very ruinous, a composite structure made up of three octagonal towers with a covered court in the middle. It must have been intended as much for display as defence, and the seated figure over the gate, interpreted as Edward I, was presumably a grateful acknowledgement of favours bestowed on Henry de Lacy, earl of Lincoln, a confidant of the king and grantee of the site.

The low-lying flat site at Beaumaris, its French name referring to its situation, allowed a very regular geometric plan to be adopted, which is intellectually satisfying and is usually hailed as the greatest triumph of the concentric plan. This is best studied on a drawn plan or aerial photograph (fig. 86), because it cannot be appreciated at ground level when the remains are somewhat disappointing. The castle had its own dock, and the adjoining outer gate is not set opposite the inner one, but staggered. The walls and southern gatehouse have not been carried to full height, but the great northern gatehouse opposite gives an idea of

86 Beaumaris castle, Anglesey. Started in 1295 but never completed, this is the classic concentric castle, where level ground allowed the full scheme to be worked out. Note the huge gatehouses, the partly reflooded moat lapping the outer curtain and the dock allowing ships to come right into the entry

what its twin should have been like if completed. The walls of the inner ward are straight, but those of the enclosing platform, which are strikingly bowed in the middle have their own set of smaller towers. The moat outside has been partly reflooded. The scale of building is very much greater than that in the other castles, except perhaps for Caernarfon, so one can appreciate why this vast work was never completed. Both Harlech and Rhuddlan are concentric, with a fortified platform outside the main curtain wall, but it is to Beaumaris that one must go to understand fully what is meant by the term.

Set on their rocks, Harlech and Conwy have powerful aesthetic support from their surroundings; they made a deep impression on the seekers of the picturesque in the late eighteenth and nineteenth centuries.[30] Conwy has usually been awarded the palm, for, with the broad estuary on one side, the walled town on the other and green hills to the north and south, the setting cannot be rivalled. Being low-lying, Caernarfon does not make the same impact as Conwy, although there is little doubt that Edward wanted it to make more. The conscious imitation of the Theodosian land wall of Constantinople in the polygonal towers and the banding in the stone work, not to mention the eagles, is surely one of the most remarkable achievements in castle history (figs. 82, 83). In Welsh legend, the messengers of Macsen Wledig, the Roman emperor, came to 'a great city at the mouth of the river and in the city a great castle, and great towers of various colours on the castle'.[31] Although the Roman station of Segontium on the outskirts of Caernarfon was intended in the legend, there is still a dreamlike quality about Edward's castle when seen from across the river Seiont that almost outdoes the legend.

Chapter 8

The castle as midwife: monasteries

C. V. Langlois[1] has compared the life of the feudal aristocracy in thirteenth-century France with that of the landed aristocracy in nineteenth-century England in its complete divorce from the practical side of life and its sole preoccupation with sport and pleasure. The fifteenth-century pursuits listed as suitable for a French nobleman, culled by another Frenchman from the contemporary vernacular literature, illustrate the point: hunting, fishing, fencing, jousting, watching bear-baiting, playing chess, eating and drinking, listening to the minstrels, receiving guests, chatting with the ladies, walking in the meadows, holding a court, warming himself, being cupped and bled, and watching the snow fall.[2] If one adds billiards and smoking, comparison with the nineteenth-century English aristocrat can be understood. There was one major difference – religion.

In the twelfth- or thirteenth-century castle, for the nobleman as much as for his humblest servant, the hand of God or of the Evil One was present everywhere. Both were constantly intervening in everyday events; life was a permanent siege by the forces of evil in which unending recourse to prayer either to God or to the saints for intercession was essential if one was not to succumb. Even more important than the present life was the hereafter, for the soul would then be judged by the present conduct of the person to whom it belonged.[3] We will never understand life in medieval castles unless we take into account the background, so alien to present modern life.

Some idea of piety in normal castle life can be gleaned from the way the mythical characters behave in the *chansons* sung or recited by the minstrels in the castle halls,[4] the true culture of the castle. Crossing oneself and praying on waking, the first mass would follow after dressing and there would probably be two more during the day, while an unusual event like a journey would require another. The main meal of the day was between nine and noon (between terce and sext, since the canonical hours were normally used) and there would be a second later in the afternoon; the day concluded with a further prayer.

This piety has left a permanent record in the castle chapels that survive in large numbers, for some kind of chapel certainly existed in every castle. The subject is still largely neglected, waiting for classification, study of dedications, and written sources. We can make, however, a broad distinction between those chapels within another building and those that are free-standing.

The first type occurs in eleventh- and twelfth-century keeps: the most famous is the chapel of St John, with its aisles and gallery, in the White Tower in London (fig. 87). There and at Colchester a special

87 London: the eleventh-centur St John's chapel in the White Tower. Note the arcades, the vaulting and the gallery, terminating in an eastern apse (cf. fig. 5

projection had to be made on the rectangle for the apse. At Conisbrough a small chapel or oratory is tucked into one of the six great buttresses at second-floor level (fig. 88). Most large keeps (hall keeps, p. 64) contained a chapel or oratory at an upper level, like the one over the forebuilding at Rochester. In the thirteenth century, when the residential buildings were free-standing, a chapel could be accommodated in an adjoining tower, like the one juxtaposed to the royal apartments at Conwy, or on the first floor of an eastern mural tower at Beaumaris, perhaps designed to adjoin an intended chamber block. The small chapel in Marten's tower at Chepstow, Gwent, evidently served a similar purpose, as a private oratory where the lord and his family could pray or take mass first thing in the morning after rising at an earlier hour than we are accustomed to, or as occasion might require during the day.

A distinct kind of chapel contained within another building is the chapel in or adjoining the gate. There is a good example at Goodrich (p. 115) and there was probably one in the collapsed gate at Conisbrough (p. 103). At Harlech, Gwynedd, the chapel in the great gatehouse was only usable when the portcullis was down.[5] This perhaps served as a private chapel for the adjoining chamber, but the chapel at the gate, like the chapel on a medieval bridge, was evidently intended for a traveller to say a mass before or after making a journey.

Two-storeyed chapels occur in German castles and in France; the surviving example of Sainte-Chapelle in the Palais Royal in Paris is the most famous.[6] They are not unknown in this country: in Durham castle the vaulted under-chapel with fine capitals on its columns is earlier than the adjoining hall of Bishop Pudsey. We know there was one in the palace at Bishop Auckland before its destruction in the seventeenth century. St Stephen's chapel in Westminster palace owed not a little to Sainte-Chapelle in Paris. Two-storeyed chapels or chapels on the first floor are evidently connected with first-floor halls, as is vividly demonstrated at Manorbier, Dyfed, where the two, with their external steps, stand side by side (p. 89). This is not, however, the normal type of free-standing chapel in the English castle.

There was patently a need for a chapel to satisfy the requirements of the whole household or garrison which might run to dozens or scores of people. The answer was a free-standing structure in the bailey. There could still be an element of privacy about this if it stood immediately adjoining the upper end of the hall, as in the earlier phase at Framlingham, Suffolk. Throughout the middle ages the preferred position was one that was easily accessible from the upper end of the hall. A final category of chapel was situated free of the domestic buildings, even in a separate ward or bailey, with a building of some size, as at Kenilworth or the Tower of London (St Peter ad Vincula). This could reach churchlike proportions. The climax of castle chapels is presumably St George's chapel at Windsor, but that lies outside our period. It was collegiate and in other cases, like Warkworth where there was a collegiate establishment, the structure was a large one.

The form of chapel reflected the ecclesiastical architecture of the time, so that Romanesque apsidal chancels are found not only in the White Tower but in free-standing buildings. The most remarkable case is at Castle Rising, Norfolk, where a small churchlike structure with nave and chancel with apsidal end is partly buried by the huge earthen bank that encircles the keep.[7] It was apparently free-standing at first within the bailey but became engulfed by an enlargement of the bank.

88 Conisbrough castle, S. Yorkshire. The vaulted chapel in the keep buttress adjoining the second-floor room

At Pontefract, Yorkshire, excavations have revealed the lower parts of two chapels:[8] an apsidal structure probably to be associated with an eleventh-century college and a later Elizabethan work. At Hastings and Pevensey on the south coast A.J. Taylor has suggested that the castles were constructed around a pre-Conquest chapel.[9]

The most striking example of this type of building is undoubtedly the round chapel at Ludlow castle, Shropshire.[10] Like the Round church at Cambridge it had a round nave, the rectangular chancel being known only from excavation (fig. 89). It is not aisled as at Cambridge but has a highly decorated west door and blank arcading running round the inside that recalls a monastic chapter house (fig. 90). In

both cases there appears to be no connection with the knightly order of Templars who built round churches in allusion to the round structure surrounding the Holy Sepulchre at Jerusalem. In this instance it is perhaps more likely to be an allusion to the capture of Jerusalem by the Crusaders in 1099 rather than to be modelled on Charlemagne's church at Aachen, as has recently been suggested.[11]

However the normal castle chapel was usually a plain rectangular building often with no distinguishable chancel. A good example is at Pickering castle, Yorkshire (fig. 91) which is still largely intact.

In major castles then we should envisage a large communal chapel, but not parochial, and several smaller chapels or oratories for private use, served by chaplains who might be secular or regular canons. This

89 Ludlow castle, Shropshire. W. doorway of the round nave of the chapel in the inner ward

90 Ludlow castle, Shropshire. The foundations of the rectangular chancel, and the blank arcading within the round nave of the chapel

Pickering castle, N. Yorkshire.
. side of the chapel with the
otte and shell keep in the back-
round. The chancel is only distin-
uished by a step inside

made adequate provision for everyday requirements for worship, for the frequent masses that formed such an essential ingredient of medieval life. The soul needed more than this, however, in the perilous journey that lay ahead of it after death. This need was met by the foundation of monasteries, a medieval solution to which we must now turn in so far as it concerned castles.

According to William of Poitiers, a contemporary chronicler, Normandy under Duke William rivalled Egypt in the number of its monasteries.[12] Before the Conquest of England he had already adopted a vigorous 'monastic' policy in Normandy, not only founding monasteries but controlling the appointment of abbots, as well as encouraging his barons to establish and endow numerous foundations.[13] After 1066 this policy was extended across the Channel, so that some thirty-five existing pre-Conquest monasteries had multiplied tenfold by the end of the twelfth century. Lanfranc and Anselm, Benedictine monks from Bec in Normandy, became archbishops of Canterbury, acting as the king's chief ministers. The unique Old English institution of monastery–bishopric was not only sanctioned but its numbers were augmented by new additions.[14]

Old English pre-Conquest houses, like Glastonbury, were already richly endowed; monasteries were institutions that were familiar, in the southern part of country at all events – not like castles that were virtually unknown before their introduction from Normandy. After the Conquest there is a surprising parallelism in the vicissitudes experienced by both types of institution. The great outburst of foundations reached a climax in both cases in Stephen's reign and then there is a falling off; for monasteries of the main orders (not friaries) there was almost a cessation in the thirteenth century. For castles, there is less available information, but it is reasonable to assume a sharp decline in the number of foundations in the thirteenth century. Great castle-builders like Fulk Nerra (p. 36) were often great founders of monasteries; what if anything did these two institutions, which so epitomise the middle ages, have in common?

The foundation of a monastery was a protracted business, but the real act of creation was the gift of a site for the conventual buildings and land as an endowment for their maintenance by a founder. There had to be monks to occupy the site, but in the eleventh and twelfth centuries this presented no problem; in the case of Cistercians, Cîteaux had to call a halt because the number of foundations was getting out of hand. No doubt the initiative often came from the monks' side, but the founder disposed of the means and had a strong motive for employing them in this way, as the charters reveal.[15] Almost invariably the reason given in the foundation charter is for the health or salvation (salus) of the souls of the founder and his wife, and sometimes of his successors and predecessors. The everlasting performance of divine offices day in and day out must influence the Deity in favour of the soul of the person who had brought it about, especially as masses for their souls' salvation would also be said. For the feudal lord, his castle provided security for his body in this world and his monastery security for his soul in the next. There was no need for the castle and monastery to be close together since the merit lay in the foundation, not in its location, but it was much more satisfying for the founder if it was close at hand. In the majority of cases they were not in proximity, but it is the significant number where there evidently was an association that is our concern.

The table shown here[16] represents century by century the cases where there seems to be a clear association between castle and religious house, with a distinction made between the main orders. In the eleventh and twelfth centuries the foundations were mainly of regulars, living a common life, and after something of a hiatus in the thirteenth century the foundations of the later middle ages were primarily chantry colleges of secular canons, not living a common life according to a fixed rule. The latter provided a specific service, saying masses for the soul of the founder, whereas the earlier monasteries had a quite independent existence which might incidentally include masses for the

Monasteries associated with castles in the middle ages

Religious order	11th C.	12th C.	13th C.	14th C.	15th C.	16th C.
Benedictine	14	13	—	1	—	—
Cluniac	7	6	—	—	—	—
Alien (Benedictine)	15	7	—	—	—	—
Augustinian	2	27 (1 alien)	2	3	—	—
Premonstratensian	—	6	—	—	—	—
Cistercian	—	13	1	1	—	—
Others	1	2	3	2	3	1
Secular canons	6	6	3	16	8	2
Totals	45	80	9	23	11	3

soul of the founder. It is a revealing change which throws some light on the nature of religion in the earlier and later middle ages. One can understand why the more self-centred attitudes of the later period have repelled many modern students.

To return, however, to the reasons for association, Charlemagne's great palace at Aachen had the secular domestic block connected by a long corridor to the chapel, the present cathedral. The *Klosterpfalz*, to use the expressive German word, envisaged the church and palace as of equal status, or even the latter as subservient to the former. In the Continental palaces of the tenth and eleventh centuries a collegiate church served by secular canons was an essential element of the establishment.[17] The most vivid account of such a palace is in the contemporary record of the murder of Charles the Good at Ghent, in 1127, where the polygonal church (known from excavation) was evidently modelled on the *Dom* at Aachen.[18] In England the collegiate church was transformed into a Benedictine abbey or priory, as at the Confessor's palace at Westminster. The Confessor had been brought up in Normandy and after the Conquest the preference for Benedictines became even more marked.

Royal example suggested, then, that a palace or castle that laid any claim to importance was incomplete without an attached priory or abbey in its proximity. There was in fact a problem, in that before the Conquest the native clergy, including the secular canons, were decidedly lax and often married; the introduction of Benedictines from the Continent could set an example and raise standards. The papal, Gregorian reforms gave impetus to such ideas. At Rochester and Durham the seculars were driven out and replaced by Benedictines.

The exercise of power over a house, choosing its head and so on, must also have had attractions for the lord of the castle, human nature being what it is. Furthermore, there was the very important consideration that a religious house close by could service the castle chapels. No doubt one of the reasons for the special popularity of Augustinian houses was that the black canons were nearly all ordained priests who could take mass. While the more enclosed orders could not provide services of this kind some kudos accrued to the lord for having such a house near by, since the medieval mind tended to equate the severity of the order with its degree of merit and dedication.

With the Knights Templar in the Holy Land the boundary between castle and monastery might be blurred, but in Europe the distinction was clear one. Secular canons might live in the castle at Windsor, but with regulars the monastic regimen and timetable was not compatible with the lay, probably unsympathetic, possibly hostile, environment of the castle. The situation at Tynemouth, where castle and priory were on the same site, was most unusual. When the Augustinian priory was founded within the Roman enclosure at Portchester, Hampshire (fig. 92), diagonally opposite the castle, it was intolerably close and had to

92 Portchester, Hants. Aerial view of the Roman coastal fort (fourth century AD) and the castle with keep set in one corner. The former Augustinian priory, now the parish church, is diagonally opposite

be moved to Southwick. Probably the ideal was an interval of a few minutes' walk, as at Kenilworth or Castle Acre, but much greater distances were common, especially with severer orders, as at Helmsley castle and Rievaulx abbey in Yorkshire, or Chepstow castle and Tintern abbey in Gwent.

The rest of the chapter will be devoted to actual examples to see how the association of castle and monastery worked out in practice. We can start with Gwent in Wales where the late Rose Graham has described the foundation of four alien priories,[19] three of which were closely associated with castles.

William FitzOsbern, lord of Breteuil and Seneschal of Normandy, friend of William the Conqueror with whom he came to England, had been created earl of Hereford. From this base he launched out into Gwent where he built the castle of Chepstow on the bank of the river Wye (p. 73). He had founded the abbey of Cormeilles in Normandy and he now gave the tithes between the rivers Usk and Wye to support it in forming a priory at Chepstow. Monks came from Cormeilles and probably lodged in the castle at Chepstow while the church was under construction (fig. 93). One of the conditions of the grant was that the monks held three services a week in the castle chapel. This all happened before 1071, very soon after the Conquest.

Chepstow is an example of an 'alien' priory, of which some two hundred were created in the country after the Conquest, but only a minority of which were connected with castles. They were 'cells', 'branches' in modern parlance, of an overseas abbey and did not have independent status. From the founders' point of view they had the con-

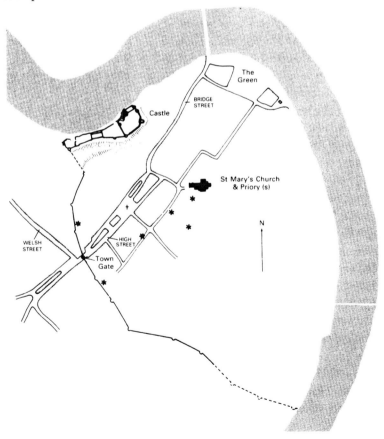

93 Chepstow, Gwent. Plan of the town in a loop of the river Wye showing the castle, town wall and gate, priory and bridge. Scale c. 1:10,000

siderable advantage that the administrative problems associated with their creation and maintenance fell upon the parent abbey. Often the nave of the church of the new foundation was still parochial, the monks making use of the chancel and crossing for their choir. At Chepstow, the much-restored early Norman nave survives in the present parish church while the plan of the claustral buildings has been recovered by excavation.[20]

At Monmouth the castle belonged to Guiheroz, a man from Dol, who made a rather similar arrangement with the abbey St-Florent near Saumur in Anjou. Again, the castle chapel was to be serviced by the monks. The church was dedicated in 1101 or 1102, and its nave survived until it was rebuilt in the nineteenth century.

At Abergavenny, in a joint venture, the brothers Hamelin, who held the castle, and Wynebald of Caerleon castle, both of whom came from near Le Mans, gave the castle chapel, with other endowments, to the abbey of St-Vincent at Le Mans to create a priory outside the wall at Abergavenny. This foundation outside the wall, presumably to exclude it from town jurisdiction, can be compared with Benedictine abbeys of the same date at Shrewsbury, Colchester, or York. The priory of Abergavenny had a complement of a prior and twelve monks, the desirable minimum for a viable house. The church survives today as the parish church of Abergavenny.

In the west of Wales in Dyfed the juxtaposition of castle and priory church at Pembroke well illustrates the subject under discussion (fig. 97). The priory of St Nicholas, Monkton, facing the castle on the other side of the river, was formed in 1098 by Arnulph de Montgomery soon after he had granted the chapel in the castle to the abbey of Seez.[21] The house received further endowments from the earls of Pembroke.

To return to England: substantial remains survive of the motte, walls and gatehouse of the eleventh-century castle at Tickhill, Yorkshire, and some five miles to the south over the border into Nottinghamshire the well-known early Norman church at Blyth represents the remains of the priory church of St Mary the Virgin, founded by Robert de Builli of Tickhill castle in 1088. It was a cell of Holy Trinity, Rouen. As there was a college of secular canons within the castle at Tickhill it evidently had no responsibility for the castle chapel.[22]

Not all the foundations were alien priories. At Colchester, Essex, the dapifer or sewer of William II, called Eudo, who was presumably involved with the construction of the great keep (p. 75) had decided when it was complete to found a Benedictine abbey.[23] This was marked out in 1096 on a site 500 m to the south of the castle outside the Roman wall. It was some time before it had its full complement of monks. Nothing now survives above ground except the gatehouse. Although not so obviously related to the castle, the Benedictine abbeys at Shrewsbury and Chester illustrate the same partnership.

Two Cluniac priories founded by William de Warenne who came over with the Conqueror were intimately associated with the castles that he had founded at Lewes, Sussex, and Castle Acre, Norfolk, on land that he had been granted.[24] Warenne, while on the Continent, had visited Cluny and was so impressed with what he saw that he determined to found a priory of this type at Lewes, which he did on a site some 500 m south of the castle. Monks came from Cluny to the abbey of St Pancras, a very well-endowed establishment. Unfortunately nothing now remains visible. It had been founded before 1076; its offshoot at Castle Acre was created about twelve years later. The monks were probably settled first in the castle (perhaps in the curious unfortified 'keep' revealed in the excavations) before moving to the site of the present ruin a short distance away. The other main Cluniac priory of East Anglia may have followed the example, being set up a few years later by Roger Bigod near his castle in Thetford, Norfolk.[25]

From the 1090s a new order, Augustinian canons, that is canons living by the rule of St Augustine and mainly ordained priests, appeared on the scene.[26] One of the earliest houses was the priory at Huntingdon founded by Eustace de Lovetot, the sheriff, who had charge of the royal castle.[27] Among its benefactors was Maud, queen to Henry I, who showed special favour to this order. In the Border area William II had founded the castle at Carlisle, but it was under his successor that a priory, served at first by secular canons, became the cathedral of a new diocese with its bishop as head of the new Augustinian priory.

Of the major Augustinian priories Kenilworth (promoted to abbey in the fifteenth century) had one of the closest connections with its castle.[28] The latter is mentioned in such a way in the original and confirmation charters, with increasing perquisites from it (fishing one day a week in the castle pool, tithes of everything brought into the castle pantry, larder, hall, granary etc.) that clearly construction was going on simultaneously on both sites. It is worth quoting the foundation charter:

Geoffrey de Clinton, chamberlain of King Henry . . . take notice all of you, French and English, strangers and relatives, that I Geoffrey for the redemption of my sins, and for the salvation of my lord the king Henry and of my wife and children and all relatives, with royal permission, have founded the church of Kenilworth in honour of St Mary; and I have conceded to the canons there regularly serving God, the whole of the low ground of Kenilworth, with woods, and all the remaining part of the vill, excepting that particular part that I have retained on which to make my castle and park[29]

The subsequent confirmation charter allowing the canons to fish one day a week in the castle pool (*in vivario de castello*) shows the streams had been ponded back to create the early form of the mere before its enlargement in John's reign. Subsequently, by the construction of dams and locks a series of pools were formed down the valley and the priory a little way down had its own fishpond (fig. 94). The two foundations were intimately bound together and so it is not surprising that the priory suffered severely when the castle was under siege in 1266 (p. 118). At the time of the Dissolution there were fifteen canons in the abbey, and it is fair to presume that this number had been exceeded in earlier times.

A new order that appeared in England from 1128 onward, the Cistercians, grew in an astonishing way. The Savignacs were combined with them in 1148. The White Monks, so called from the colour of their habit, were excluded by their rules from settlement in castles and towns, and chose for preference remote waste ground which could be won back by their labours. Not many can be deemed to be associated with castles. Calder abbey in Cumberland is only a mile or two from its founder's seat at Egremont and can fall into this category. After the first monks decamped to Byland the site had to be recolonised from Furness.[30]

Rievaulx Abbey in North Yorkshire was founded by Walter Espec of Helmsley castle, which is within walking distance of it.[31] It was colonised by White Monks from a mother house in France, Clairvaux itself, and subsequently sent out colonies to Warden in Bedfordshire, Melrose in Scotland and Revesby in Lincolnshire. Walter Espec, the founder, entered the monastery as a monk towards the end of his life.

An interesting case of a very late transfer of a monastery at the behest of a castle owner was the Cistercian abbey of Dieulacres in Staffordshire,[32] which Ralph de Blundeville, earl of Chester, in 1214, caused to be transferred from Poulton, Cheshire (the original foundation had been in 1158). The new site was near Chartley castle, a motte and bailey that had been reconstructed in stone by Blundeville (p. 104). He had arranged for his heart to be buried at the abbey so there can be no doubt about his feelings in the matter.

Kenilworth, Warwicks. Aerial
 showing the site of the mere
 e foreground, the castle to the
 (note the keep and John of
 nt's hall). Downstream
 nd, is the Abbey pool with
 site of the Augustinian abbey
 e left near the parish church

The more extreme enclosed orders were rarely associated with
castles. An exception is the Grandmontine house founded in the 1220s
by Fulk fitzWarin of Whittington, Shropshire, at Alberbury[33]. Significantly, the original intention was to colonise it with Augustinians from
Lilleshall in the same county, but this did not work out. The house
came under the direct control of the Grandmontine centre at Limousin
in France. The site of the priory is near the village of Alberbury where
Fulk had a seat, probably in the motte and bailey; the tower at Wattlesborough belongs to the next century[34].

The fourteenth century saw a great growth in the foundation of colleges of secular canons, sometimes attached to castles. A particularly instructive example is at Maxstoke, Warwickshire[35]. In 1331 Sir William de Clinton purchased the advowson of the church and obtained licence to found a college of secular canons, warden and chaplains, who would pray for the souls of the king, the bishop of Coventry and Sir William and his wife. In 1336 he changed his mind and founded an Augustinian house instead. The licence to crenellate of 1345 suggests that the very fine square moated castle (fig. 108), still inhabited, was built after the priory of which the gateway, with its fine wooden gates, still exists by the roadside.

An interesting point is raised by the sequence of events at Maxstoke, since it is clear that in most cases the castle was built first and the monastery, perhaps intended from the beginning, added afterwards, partly because it was a protracted business to found a monastery. Simultaneous construction, as at Kenilworth, was probably not usual. The mottes adjacent to the cathedrals at Peterborough, Ely and Worcester, pre-Conquest monasteries, fall into a different category. More analogous is Wingfield, Suffolk, where college and castle were built in the same inverted sequence.[36]

Late medieval colleges do not stir one's feelings in the same way that a great twelfth-century monastery does, so we will conclude with only one example from Cumbria: Greystoke castle and college[37]. The great pele-tower hidden behind Salvin's buildings was probably constructed after the licence to crenellate of 1353 was obtained by Lord William Greystoke. Steps to found a college had started in 1342 but it was not formally set up until 1382. Although much altered in later times, the present parish church presumably is substantially the college church.

Chapter 9

The castle as midwife: towns

> The deeper that research is pursued into the origins of German towns, the clearer it becomes that in normal circumstances earlier settlement had preceded the foundation of the town; throughout the thirteenth century beside the market the castle (*Burg*) was the persistent predecessor.
>
> H. Planitz, *Die deutsche Stadt im Mittelalter* (Cologne, 1965), p. 165

Planitz was speaking of the huge expansion of town foundations in Germany in the thirteenth century. In England castle, although not town, foundation was probably falling off (p. 136) so it does not represent conditions here. It applies far better to Wales, where some 80 per cent of the towns of medieval times owe their origin to a castle[1]. The other element mentioned by Planitz, the market, was the reason for the creation of a town: trade, local trade in a weekly market and shops, and more far-flung trade in an annual fair, like the famous Stourbridge fair outside Cambridge. Trade, of course, promoted craft industries which thrive best in an urban setting.

The erection of a castle was bound to have an impact over a considerable area, however rural or isolated it might be. The waterworks, the transformation of the valley, the park, the priory, could not be created at Kenilworth without setting off all sorts of associated changes in the neighbourhood. The labourers and craftsmen engaged in building the castle and maintaining it, the staff (constable, chaplain, porters, garrison and so on) generated new needs; in fact created a market. Stone, lead, iron, tools, clothes, food had to be bought. This activity by itself would prompt thoughts about forming a borough; the revenue from burgage plots, tolls, fines and the dispensation of justice could be a useful addition to income. It might be worthwhile actively to promote this by enclosing an area with defences, seeking a charter, and so on. It is surprising that in fact only a small proportion of castles did stimulate the formation of a town.

We have had to make frequent reference to Ludlow castle in Shropshire as it was so well described for us by W. St John Hope in an article

95 Ludlow, Shropshire. Aerial view showing the street design with the castle top left, parish church top right and the streets set at right angles to the market in front of the castle

in the early years of this century, but Hope was also impressed by the design of the town[2]. This has a broad street, a market place, extending eastwards from the castle with four streets at right angles on the south side running down towards the river. The design of the town can leave no doubt but that it was intended, not haphazard, and that it was intended as an adjunct of the castle, the outer bailey of which appears indeed to be an afterthought, unforseen in the original lay-out (fig. 95). The castle was evidently the primary foundation, set on the precipitous bank of the river Teme, perhaps at first without the intention of forming a town. The surviving town wall and gate are much later, although there were no doubt timber and earth defences preceding it.

The example of Ludlow illustrates what is meant by the term 'midwife' in the chapter title, the formation of a town as an appendage to a castle, a not unusual method of town creation in England during the eleventh and twelfth centuries, and the standard method in Wales from the eleventh to the thirteenth centuries. In the east of England, at Bury St Edmunds, Suffolk, the grid-shaped plan of the town aligned on the abbey gate on the west side of its outer court demonstrates that not only castles but also abbeys (St Albans, Hertfordshire, is another example) could act as midwives in town creation. It is equally clear that in England at any rate towns could be formed spontaneously or as a deliberrate act on a virgin site. Coastal towns, in particular, where maritime trade was the generating factor, did not usually arise as offshoots from another establishment.

The difference between England and Wales is a fundamental one. In the former there were a substantial number of towns born or reborn in late Anglo-Saxon times, as Martin Biddle's work in Winchester has so vividly revealed, which constituted the main centres throughout medieval and into modern times. In Wales, where there had been no real urban centres before the Norman Conquest, towns had to be freshly created, and not surprisingly in the midst of a hostile population the protection of a castle was of paramount importance. In England, only in the early years after the Conquest were there comparable conditions leading to an analogous importance for the castle in town foundations[3].

One of the first actions of William the Conqueror after the Battle of Hastings and his coronation was to erect castles in the existing English towns[4]; the destruction of houses to make way for them is several times recorded in the Domesday Book. The majority of eleventh-century castles recorded by E. S. Armitage in her well-known account were urban, although one may suppose that the construction of a castle in a town was much more likely to be recorded than a similar event in the countryside[5]. These and later insertions of a castle into an existing town must have had a profound influence on the town's development, not merely on its defences but on its shape and later expansion. Of some 147 cases of town defences, about 100 had a castle[6]. The anonymous author of the *Gesta Stephani* tells us of the importance of the castle in the defences of Gloucester[7], and no one looking at a plan of Oxford can fail to be struck by the castle's key role in the urban defences. A glance at the series of town plans in the two volumes of M. Lobel's *Historic Towns* will reveal the important influence an inserted castle had on a town's development, as for example at Banbury. No two cases are alike, but this interesting aspect of castle history must be set aside as we return to towns that owe their existence to a castle.

The charters for Kenilworth priory have been mentioned already (p. 142). The *Monasticon* recites the original foundation charter and six subsequent confirmation charters all issued within a period of 40 to 50 years by Geoffrey de Clinton, his son Henry and the Crown.[8] The charters provide a sort of running commentary on the construction of the castle and its ancillaries. Initially Clinton had reserved land for his castle and park, then there was the pool on which the canons of the priory could fish once a week, and buildings (hall, kitchen etc.) from which a tithe of what was brought in would be given to the canons. Later we learn that land had been reserved, not only for castle and park, but also for a *burgus*, a borough. Evidently this was an afterthought dependent on a pragmatic decision as to whether sufficient trade had been generated to make it a viable proposition. In fact, no subsequent record of the borough survives,[9] so the settlement at Kenilworth may never have achieved that status. No doubt this was not an uncommon occurrence, an important point to bear in mind when considering towns or other settlements that castle foundation may have generated.

At Richards Castle (two villages with the same name straddle the Hereford–Shropshire border) the excavations on the castle in 1962–4 revealed a splendid late twelfth-century octagonal keep on top of the motte, assumed to have been thrown up in *c*. 1050 and certainly of eleventh century origin.[10] The outer enclosure of the castle, delimited by the 'village bank', was thought to be of the same date or even of Iron Age origin (fig. 35). In the event both theories proved to be wrong, since pottery from within and under the bank (i.e. earlier in date) was medieval, probably of *c*. 1200. A charter from the end of John's reign, 1216, granted a market to Richards Castle. It may be, therefore, that market and earthwork were part and parcel of the same thing, the formation of a town. The base of a fine circular dovecot with two or three tiers of nesting holes evidently belongs to a later construction on the line of the earthwork, mistaken indeed by more than one unwary historian for a mural tower. So far as we can tell, the defence was always of earth and timber except immediately adjoining the castle, in its ditch. M. W. Beresford spotted a reference of 1304 in the Patent Rolls to burgage plots at Richards Castle,[11] so we must assume borough status was achieved even if no charter has survived. The 'borough' went into steep decline in the later middle ages; only two or three houses and the church exist there now. There was evidently a gap, this time of perhaps 150 years, between the foundation of the castle and the creation of the town, the proximity of Ludlow perhaps being a deterrent. Only the fortuitous record in the Patent Rolls allows us to know that the site ever achieved borough status.

In Wales, where we start with a pre-Conquest *tabula rasa* for both monasteries and towns, the picture is very much clearer. The anonymous author of the *Gesta Stephani* tells us of the great benefits brought to Wales by the castles planted there particularly by Henry I, later nullified by the ungrateful Welsh who destroyed them after the king's death.[12] He makes no reference to towns, which would be no matter for surprise if most of them had not yet been created. Writing some 50 years later Giraldus Cambrensis, speaking of Ireland, makes repeated reference to castles being erected, but the lack of success of the English conquest he attributes to their not founding 'towns and castles' across the land from sea to sea.[13] He evidently saw the two as obverse and reverse of the same coin. In Wales, what impresses one is the delay, often protracted, between the first reference to a castle and the first reference to a town, strongly suggesting the pragmatic nature of the foundation of the latter.[14] As Lewis put it, contrasting this delay with the Edwardian foundations: 'We miss that period of vagueness between the formation of the castle and the appearance of the town charter, so characteristic of the baronial boroughs'.[15]

Hundreds of castles, the majority in fact, never acquired a borough, so the 'period of vagueness' was presumably the time of weighing up by the lord whether a borough was a viable project. One might apply the word 'plantation' to the castles planted in England, Wales and Ireland, but to use the word for the towns as M. W. Beresford does in his fascinating book *New Towns of the Middle Ages* is probably to over-dramatise a fairly haphazard business. Even a charter where it exists is probably misleading for a foundation date for a town before 1200.

The situation regarding new foundations after 1200 when the documentation is much better is very different, and the contrast between England and Wales is even more marked. The classic case is the transfer of the cathedral and city from Old Sarum in Wiltshire to a site a mile to the south in the meadows of the river Avon.[16] Apart from mundane matters like shortage of water, wind and weather, part of the motive for the move was to end friction between the cathedral canons and the castle garrison, so at all events it is alleged. Whatever the truth of this, there was no castle in new Salisbury, which was laid out on a grid plan. There was no castle at the two coastal foundations of Edward I later in the century at New Winchelsea, Kent, and Kingston upon Hull, Humberside. On the other hand, a significant contrast, the king's reconstruction of the defences of Berwick on Tweed after its capture from the Scots included a castle.

The contrast with Wales is dramatic, well illustrating the military necessity for a castle in hostile territory. In south Wales, among a number of formidable castles, the outstanding example is of course at Caerphilly, Glamorgan (p. 118), the huge structure with its extensive waterworks erected from 1268 onwards to counter the menace of Llywelyn ap Gruffydd. It was the harbinger of the series of great castles erected in north Wales from 1277 onwards by Edward I (p. 120). Although often compared with the Gascon *bastides* of south-west

France, the foundation of some of which were due to Edward I, the towns really are very different. The Gascon *bastide* did not as a rule have a castle and commonly took a geometrical shape. The prosperity of the area was in some measure due to the production of wine for export, and there was presumably some element of spontaneity, whatever the formality of the foundation. The Edwardian borough in Wales was an excrescence or emanation from a dominating, vastly more expensive castle, imposed on an alien land and intended to be inhabited by an alien population. Where the town had no town wall, as at Harlech, the borough is scarcely detectable beside the bulk of the castle. No doubt the king was influenced by his experience in France, but the circumstances of foundation in the two countries were entirely different.

Tailing off in the fourteenth century, town foundation ceased with the creation by Edward III of the castle and town at Queenborough, Kent, in 1368, a coastal defence against France.[17] The self-conscious builders of the ostentatious 'castles' of the later middle ages were not interested in urban growth and were in any case ill at ease with the powerful guilds who dominated the towns of the period.

The lists on the right of towns that owe their foundation to a castle, first in England and then in Wales, have been abstracted from M. W. Beresford's *New Towns of the Middle Ages*. They are certainly incomplete, omitting large settlements that either did not achieve borough status or are not recorded as so doing. Some sites survive today merely as hamlets or even quite abandoned earthworks.

Most of our examples will be drawn from Wales, but two English cases of very different kinds may be mentioned. Newcastle upon Tyne takes its name from the castle founded there in 1080,[18] at the point where the Romans had had a bridge over the river. The castle built by Robert, son of the Conqueror, acted as a bridgehead on the north side of the river, as likely a place to attract a market from waterborne and land trade as one can imagine. No doubt at first a castle of motte and bailey form, the present stone keep was added by Henry II in 1168 to 1178.[19] The same monk who recorded the construction of the castle here in 1080, Simeon of Durham, noted that three monks had been sent to this place (*locus*) in 1074[20] when it was called Monkchester (*Monecacaestre*), which, it is tempting to think, was the site of a Northumbrian monastery on the Roman settlement, and destroyed by the Vikings. However, the existence of a mid-twelfth-century document reciting the 'laws and customs' of Newcastle upon Tyne has led to the

Towns in England and Wales owing their foundation to a castle (after Beresford)

ENGLAND
Appleby, Cumbria
Arundel, Sussex
Barnard Castle, County Durham
Bishop's Castle, Shropshire
Boscastle, Cornwall
Bridgnorth, Shropshire
Castleton, Derbyshire
Caus, Shropshire
Clitheroe, Lancashire
Corfe, Dorset
Devizes, Wiltshire
Downton, Wiltshire
Durham
Egremont, Cumbria
Hastings, Sussex
Henley in Arden, Warwickshire
Kington, Hereford and Worcester
Launceston, Cornwall
Liverpool, Merseyside
Ludlow, Shropshire
Malton, N. Yorkshire
Midhurst, Sussex
Mitford, Northumberland
Morpeth, Northumberland
Mountsorrel, Leicestershire
New Buckenham, Norfolk
Newcastle under Lyme, Staffordshire
Newcastle upon Tyne, Tyne and Wear
Okehampton, Devon
Oswestry, Shropshire
Pleshey, Essex
Plympton, Devon
Pontefract, W. Yorkshire
Queenborough, Kent
Reigate, Surrey
Richards Castle, Hereford and Worcester
Richmond, N. Yorkshire
Ruyton, Shropshire
Skipsea, Humberside
Sleaford, Lincolnshire
Thirsk, N. Yorkshire
Tickhill, N. Yorkshire
Tregoney, Cornwall
Trematon, Cornwall
Truro, Cornwall
Windsor, Berkshire

view that there must have been a pre-1080 English town there already. Customary laws and practices in a locality surely are usually tied as much to the name as to the place, so this is hardly a conclusive argument when only the new name is used in the document. Whether the castle was erected on a deserted site or not, the town's name has referred to it ever since.

The second example is at Pleshey, Essex, where a splendid motte mound approached by a fifteenth-century brick bridge is flanked by what is clearly a bailey on one side and a larger borough enclosure on the other; although no charter exists there were a church, active markets and shops there in the fifteenth and sixteenth centuries.[21] Excavations in the bailey have thrown some light on the buildings there. The disposition of the earthwork bank of the abandoned town vividly demonstrates the dependent relationship of town to castle of which the former makes a sort of emanation.

The survival of the town defences in Wales has made the shape of early towns and their relationship to the present castle much easier to understand, especially as a series of plans at uniform scale have been made for the Urban Research Unit at University College, Cardiff, by Ian Soulsby.[22] I have made extensive use of these.

At Chepstow the castle (see fig. 93) lies on the edge of a cliff on the right bank of the river Wye where it forms a loop on its passage to the river Severn. The town was enclosed by linking the castle with a wall, the port wall, to the river on the other side of the loop. A good deal of this wall, including the town gate, survives, although the present masonry structures must be much later than the original town which, like the castle, traces its origin back to soon after the Norman conquest.[23] The wall extended over nearly a kilometre and it is quite clear that the wide area it cut off can never have been built up with houses. The special interest of the site is the very early recorded date of castle, priory (p. 139) and town. The naturally strong defensive position of the castle on the cliff suggests that this was uppermost in the founder's mind, the town being a lesser consideration if not indeed an afterthought.

At Kidwelly in Dyfed, south of Carmarthen, early in the twelfth century Bishop Roger of Salisbury set up his castle adjoining a small river.[24] As at Chepstow, there is a steep bank or cliff on one side down to the river (fig. 96). A diverted stream from the river provided a head of water for a mill. The town was formed on the south-west side of the castle, rectangular in shape, enclosing a very small area some 60 m by 40 m. The earthworks of a proposed extension on the north side are visible. The present stone structures of town wall, gates and castle are a

96 Kidwelly, Dyfed. The castle the river with the ancillary town and its gate at the top of aerial view. The proposed extension to town is in the foreground

good deal later than the original foundation. The alien priory founded by the bishop lay on the other side of the river, where a new town was created in the later middle ages.

At Tenby, Dyfed, the castle is not recorded until 1153 although there are good reasons for thinking that it belongs to the late eleventh century.[25] The castle was almost surrounded by the sea on a promontory linked to the mainland by a narrow neck of land, the town forming a narrow strip at right angles to this. It was protected by a fine, largely preserved town wall, and had a regular street plan, probably laid out by William de Valence in the 1280s. The bay on the north side of the promontory formed a good harbour, so the town achieved considerable prosperity in the later middle ages. The plan, and especially the narrow neck of land between castle and town, makes the latter look like a sort of balloon inflated by the former.

Pembroke in Dyfed, one of the most dramatically situated of Welsh towns and our last example from south Wales, lies on a ridge or spit of land turned into a peninsula by the waters of the Pembroke river on one side and a small stream on the other (fig. 97). The tip of the peninsula at the west end is occupied by the castle, founded by Arnulf de Montgomery in 1093, with the west gate of the town adjoining it and giving access to a long spinal high street which emerged at an east gate nearly 800 m away.[26] As there are two churches at either end it is possible that at some time in its history the town was extended eastward. The castle

97 Pembroke, Dyfed. The castle in the background with the alien priory (Monkton) to the left, and the formerly walled, ancillary town extending along one street into the foreground

with its splendid keep is subdivided into two wards and was undoubtedly the primary foundation, although it may well have been sited so as to allow the creation of a town if circumstances required it.

The four instances in south Wales that have been chosen clearly demonstrate the primacy of the castle, which occupies the strong position with one side at least rendered inaccessible by cliff, river or sea. At Pembroke, the siting of the castle suggests the addition of a town may have been envisaged from the beginning but this is by no means demonstrable in the other three cases. The attitude may have been pragmatic, as suggested, and if a town was viable commercially then it could be added. To have an adjoining town inhabited by compatriots in a hostile terrain clearly had a great deal to be said for it.

To leave the Marcher castles and turn to those of Edward I in the north: mention has already been made of these structures erected in the latter part of the thirteenth century (p. 120). The abundance of documentary sources allows a much fuller understanding of the relationship between castle and town; both were erected as part of the same operation. The lion's share of the expenditure was always incurred by the work on the castle; the town emerges as a necessary but subordinate adjunct. It was an entirely unequal relationship in which sometimes, as at Harlech, the borough was lost beside the bulk of the castle. Only at the lordship castle of Denbigh (fig. 81) is the archaeological evidence clear that the town wall was built first and the castle created by walling off a corner of it, although even here the castle wall and gatehouse were constructed on such a massive scale that they overshadowed the town.

By November 1284, after two seasons of work at Conwy, a sum of £5,819 14s. had been issued by the Keeper of the Wardrobe to John of Condover and Master James of St George specifically for the works in the castle and town of Conwy.[27] A further £3,313 15.2d. was paid for the third season, which included £472 10s.4d. for the town wall and ditch.[28] The figures show not only the work on castle and town in progress simultaneously but also the relatively small scale in cost terms of the town wall in relation to the castle. There is no need to pursue the published figures further to understand this point. Expenditure fell sharply from 1287 when castle and town wall were undoubtedly nearing completion, although there was a murage grant for work on the walls in 1305.

Although there is a contrast between the towns of the Marcher lords following at some interval of time after the foundation of the castle, yet the physical lay-out at Conwy recalls the situation of the southern sites

98 Conwy, Gwynedd. The castle and the whole circuit of the town walls (built between 1283 and 1287) seen from the air; note the mural towers, gates, and protected quayside along the estuary (see plan of castle in fig. 80) The Welsh Cistercian abbey was on the site of the parish church

(fig. 98). The plan shows the primacy of the castle at Conwy in terms of the defensive siting, for it has been placed in an angle between the Conwy estuary and a small stream entering from the west, the Gyffin. Part of the shore was isolated to be used as a quayside by projecting the town wall into the sea at the north end and the castle at the south end. The circuit of the walls was 1,100 m forming a roughly triangular shape extending outwards from the castle. Twenty-one open-backed circular towers were built along its outer face; the wall, towers and three gate-houses are in a remarkable state of preservation, constituting indeed the finest monument of this kind in the country. The Welsh Cistercian monastery that formerly stood on the site was transposed to Maenan[29] a few miles up the river, but part of the walls were incorporated into the new parish church of St Mary's, the retention of which caused a central disturbance in the street plan that might otherwise have been a regular grid.

It was a very different case at Caernarfon. Although started also in 1283, probably only a few weeks after Conwy, the king had decided to make this a provincial capital with special architectural treatment that a legendary imperial seat and former Welsh royal centre demanded.[30] The result was the construction of a castle with large polygonal towers on an altogether grander scale than Conwy (p. 127). The town is much smaller than at Conwy and surely there is no more telling evidence of the relative importance, in the medieval view, of town and castle than that the distinctive Byzantine features, polygonal towers and banding are confined to the castle, the town wall having to make do with plain round towers (fig. 99). The circuit of the Caernarfon town wall which is only about 700 m had eight mural towers more widely spaced than at Conwy. Only the sea gate, the Golden Gate (*Porth yr Aur*), if the name is original, recalls imperial grandeur, although the High Street which runs from gate to gate perhaps recalls a Roman *via decumana*. The situation of the castle was predetermined to some extent by the eleventh-century motte and bailey of the earl of Chester (p. 125), but the skilful use of the rivers Seiont and Cadnant to south and north respectively to create the defences is impressive. There could be no better example, however, of the complete dominance of the castle over the town in a very unequal partnership.

99 Caernarfon, Gwynedd. Aerial view of the castle and town in the angle of the Menai Strait and river Seiont; note the huge octagonal towers of the castle, round towers on the town wall, and the straight street transecting the town between the east gate on the land side and the 'Golden Gate' on the quayside

Chapter 10

Indian summer: the fourteenth century

the fourteenth century . . . to summarise its military architecture in a concrete formula one is tempted to say that, its engineers being unable to achieve a new doctrine, it marked time
with empiricism . . . On the contrary in what concerns the
seigneurial residence a transformation manifests itself that is a
veritable revolution.

P. Ritter, *Chateaux, donjons et places fortes* (Paris, 1953), pp. 98–9

The observation above on French castles can also in large measure be
applied to this country. The two large castles that demonstrate this
most clearly are the royal castle of Windsor where huge works were
carried out by Edward III, well documented in the sources but unfortunately much altered later,[1] and Kenilworth where the extensive but un-
documented works of the dukes of Lancaster survive in the present
ruin.[2] Looking at plans of the two castles one is immediately struck by
the fact that the largely unaltered defences enclose buildings that un-
derwent massive alteration in the middle or late fourteenth century. I
have described the cellular lodgings on the east and south sides of the
inner ward at Windsor elsewhere[3] and the surviving domestic buildings are described in the *King's Works* volume II,[4] Hollar's view of the
interior of the new hall being reproduced there. This shows its division
into at least ten bays, with traceried windows and a roof supported
on huge arched braces. The floor presumably rested on a vaulted
undercroft.

Whether the earlier hall at Windsor was aisled, as we might reasonably suppose, is uncertain; at Kenilworth there is a strong presumption
from the dimensions that it was so. The lay-out of the twelfth-century
buildings had fixed their position for the future, so alterations had to be
made to an existing hall. A surviving contract of 1347 shows that a
carpenter came from London to put a new roof over a hall with the
dimensions of the existing one, probably arising from the removal of
the aisle posts of the original hall.[5] He had the skill, using either ham-
mer beams or arched braces such as those at Windsor or Penshurst

100 Penshurst Place, Kent. A nineteenth-century view of the interior of the hall of *c.* 1345. Note the central hearth, and arch-braced roof with crown posts. In medieval times the tables would have been demountable, resting on trestles

Place, Kent, (fig. 100) to span this great width. The architectural detail of the hall indicates that it must have been further transformed into its present two-storeyed state later in the century by John of Gaunt, when the vaulted ground floor and the great fireplaces and windows were put in on the first floor. If these three stages of the hall at Kenilworth have been correctly interpreted there are interesting implications for the architectural historian. The preference for a Continental-style first-floor hall in a man of John of Gaunt's cosmopolitan background is understandable; the alteration perhaps implies a more personal use for the hall, and is clearly extremely revealing about the whole question of first-floor and ground-floor halls. The highly ornate undercroft surely can hardly have been intended for storage, but rather as a *salle basse* or servants' hall. This perhaps gives the clue to the attraction of the first-floor hall for a nobleman. If aisle arcades were removed from an earlier hall as suggested, then we have another example of the greater skills in carpentry which allowed greater unsupported spans, so vividly demonstrated in the contemporary Octagon in Ely cathedral. The abandonment of aisles in halls at this date no doubt was made possible by these new skills, but if the bays were used for bedrooms at night, a desire for greater privacy and independence in a separate room may have been as powerful a factor. The simultaneous increase in the number of rooms required and the creation of cellular lodging ranges might be a related process.

Turning from the refurbishment of older castles to the planning of entirely new ones, the fourteenth century furnishes us with a number of examples. A general point first needs to be made: the fourteenth century saw something of a retrogression to a fortified dwelling, to a keep-like tower recalling twelfth-century structures. The motivation in the case of the scores of pele-towers of the Border or Ireland was clearly defensive, with the domestic rooms arranged vertically as in a keep. Further south a very different motive produced a different response: the desire to create an idealised castle, so that appearance became an overriding consideration. Although widespread in Europe, in England we are evidently dealing with notions that had come across the Channel.

   A cult of the castle is most strikingly revealed in the form of the greetings met by Queen Isabel when she came to Paris in 1389 for her marriage to the king, and which are so vividly described by Froissart.[6] She was greeted by castles all along the way culminating in the massive rectangular wooden structure complete with central tower (recalling Vincennes (fig. 101) or the Louvre to judge by Froissart's eye-witness account), set on wheels but immobilised because of the crowd at the Palais Royal. It was meant to represent Troy. The real castles of cult-type are depicted for us in the famous calendar of the *Très Riches*

101 Vincennes, Seine. A sixteenth-century view of the fourteenth-century castle. Note the shape of the towers and the huge keep with its independent moat

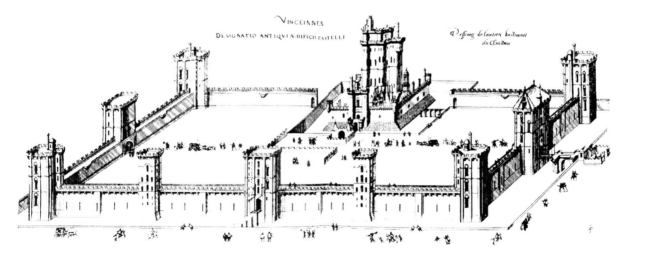

Heures of the Duc de Berry,[7] as at Saumur, Vincennes, Mehun-sur-Yèvres. In England examples of this style, where appearance was the primary consideration, are not far to seek: Guy's and Caesar's towers (fig. 105) at Warwick are the most dramatic, but Nunney, Somerset (fig. 111), Old Wardour, Wiltshire, Bodiam, Sussex (fig. 106) fall into the same category, while the Yorkshire castles like Bolton, Danby, Sheriff Hutton, and Wressle owe not a little to the same motive. It is like a preface to the Renaissance when the façade dominates; the subordinate position of internal planning to this is not always appreciated.[8]

Throughout the middle ages, the twice-daily assembly for meals in hall provided the social cement for binding together the household, the essential medieval secular aristocratic unit. In royal or episcopal palaces two halls with different functions are understandable, but in a normal household two halls would be a contradiction in terms; the documentary evidence leaves no doubt on this point. Even in a bishop's palace the portmanteau term *camera* probably would be applied to, say, the east hall at Lincoln. At Goodrich castle, Hereford and Worcester,[9] the 'north hall' may be the enlarged chamber or 'parlour' of the late fourteenth century, perhaps a mess room for senior staff, and the 'west hall' the *salle basse* equivalent (the alleys suggest it was isolated like the lay brothers' quarters in a Cistercian abbey: fig. 77). In both cases 'hall' is a modern appellation that would have bewildered the medieval inhabitant who knew only one hall.

The main social change in the fourteenth century, reflected in the architecture, was the creation of a large number of rooms, *camerae* in medieval Latin, lodgings in English or bed-sitting rooms in modern parlance. In the fifteenth century they formed the ranges of the courtyard house;[10] in the fourteenth century they had to be fitted in as best as may be, often stacked vertically in mural towers as at Warwick or Bodiam. The lord's suite certainly saw a multiplication of rooms also, sometimes at both ends of the hall. The virtual absence in medieval rooms of furniture, which fixes the function in modern houses, meant the uses of the *camerae* could change with bewildering rapidity. Only the bipolarity of the hall with service rooms at the lower end and lord's rooms at the upper end linked to the chapel remained constant.

The distribution of rooms in the block plan of a late fourteenth-century castle can be of baffling complexity: fortunately Patrick Faulkner has devised an ingenious method of showing intercommunicating rooms in a diagram that at first sight looks like an electric circuit (figs. 102, 103). The relative sizes of the rooms are shown and a known or suggested function is indicated.[11] It certainly makes it easier

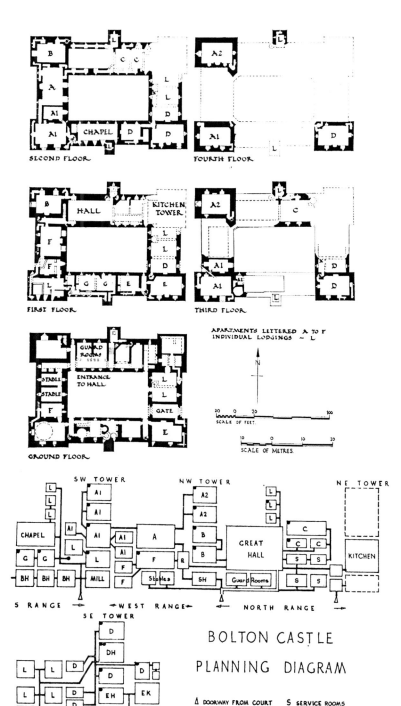

102 Bolton castle, N. Yorkshire. Plans at five levels to show the complexity of the lay-out

103 Bolton castle, N. Yorkshire. Patrick Faulkner's diagrammatic elevation to illustrate intercommunication between rooms and throw light on use. Principal apartments are lettered A–F, and individual lodgings L, as in fig. 102

to take in, almost at a glance, the complexities of a building which on a visit are quite incomprehensible. The particular functions of many of the rooms may be open to doubt, if indeed they were designed with specific functions in mind, but comparison of the floor plans with the circuit diagram at once shows how much the latter has deepened our understanding of the building.

We may pause briefly to consider Bolton castle, Yorkshire, the circuit plan of which has just been discussed; it is one of the most impressive of fourteenth-century castles erected by Richard Lord Scrope in the last years of the century. A glance at the plan (fig. 102) shows a rectangle with slightly projecting rectangular towers at the corners, recalling Avignon or papal palaces of the period. Symmetry and appearance were paramount; gatehouse and barbican would have spoilt this and so were omitted; a corner tower adjoins and protects the gate. The four internal ranges were three-storeyed, service rooms on the ground floor and the main accommodation on the first and second floors. The towers formed part of the accommodation. Lodgings could be stacked. I would regard F as the parlour and A as the great chamber, but this, as well as the possibility of separate accommodation for women and guests, must be a matter for discussion. Some of these points will be referred to later in the chapter.

Our views of the fourteenth century are very much coloured by the long chronicle of John Froissart (a contemporary of Chaucer), available in the splendid early Tudor translation of Lord Berners.[12] Froissart's main experience was in France and the Low Countries, although he visited England more than once, journeys which he describes in some detail. He also had a good deal to say about happenings in Spain and Portugal, although this was not based on first-hand experience of them. Froissart's main interests were in war and politics, so he has left us a detailed account of the first half of the Hundred Years War in France. In many ways it is the most instructive account of castle warfare that we have, since defending and attacking castles – Froissart is particularly strong on methods of assault – were the chief features of warfare. Methods of scaling walls, forcing holes through them or undermining them[13] interested him especially. Open battles were less common, but his vivid accounts of Crecy and Poitiers reveal the extent to which the English owed their success to the longbow. The volleying (shooting together was regarded by Froissart[14] as the key to its successful use) of several thousand archers was a terrible weapon, as readers who have seen Olivier's film of *Henry V* will readily appreciate. Froissart surprisingly says the same device was successful in sieges by preventing the defenders from exposing themselves. He refers also to cannon in use from the middle of the century, although their value seems to have been somewhat limited.[15]

Two other features which are of especial interest to the student of the castle are identified by Froissart: the persistent Scottish invasions of the north of England[16] and the French raids on the south coast, as well as their intended invasion.[17] On castle warfare in England Froissart has hardly anything to say, a perhaps significant omission. It is noteworthy that both Edward III and Richard II seemed to use only two castles consistently, Windsor and Leeds, Kent, otherwise moving along the Thames from one courtyard palace to another: Sheen, Kingston, Westminster, Chertsey, Eltham, Greenwich.[18] In France the king used the Palais Royal and St-Pol, but the castle had a social cachet unrivalled in England; not only the reconstructed Louvre, for instance, but also a rural retreat like Mehun-sur-Yévres for the Duc de Berry.[19]

The fourteenth century has the distinction of having 380 licences to crenellate recorded, an authority by the Crown to erect some kind of fortification, copied on to the back of the Patent Roll.[20] The practice started early in the thirteenth century and continued until the sixteenth. The grantees might be private individuals, towns, monasteries or other institutions, and the range of works licensed varied from relatively minor construction to the erection of complete castles. It is clear that a great deal of fortification never was licensed, unfortunately, even excluding the Crown's own works, so the licences cannot serve as a reliable guide to the volume of fortification in the thirteenth and fourteenth centuries. Furthermore, there was something of a change of motive in the fourteenth century: the conversion of a manor house to a castle gave an important rise in status for which the licence was a certificate, a diploma one might say. Nevertheless, the increase in the number of licences over the previous century, whatever its cause, is worth bearing in mind.

There is a very marked regional variation in the amount of castle construction during this period. In the table I have tried tentatively to list castles (excluding simple pele-towers) where there was substantial construction work during the century, dividing the list into three parts by regions: North, Midlands (including East Anglia) and South. References to the literature will be found in Cathcart King's *Castellarium Anglicanum*. Much work of the period has disappeared, but where there is reasonable documentary evidence I have included it, and the difficulties of architectural dating to just before or just after

1300 or 1400 must be born in mind. The table is necessarily rough and ready, but should serve as a basis for discussion.

The first point to strike one in looking at the list overall is the comparative rarity of major work by the Crown, in contrast to lists of the eleventh, twelfth or thirteenth centuries where it would have had a predominant role. The last new castle erected by the Crown in the middle ages was at Queenborough in the Isle of Sheppey in the 1360s.[21] The failure of the Crown to take part in the construction of what I have termed 'cult-castles' perhaps indeed throws some light on the aspirations of those who did construct them.

The North clearly differs markedly from the other two regions: although smaller in area the volume of new work was much greater

Major construction work on English castles in the fourteenth century

North

Alnwick (Northumb.)	Dunstanburgh (Northumb.)	Kendal (Cumbria)	Raby (Dur.)
Aydon (Northumb.)	Durham	Kilton (Yorks.)	Ravensworth (Dur.)
Bewley (Cumbria)	Egremont (Cumbria)	Knaresborough (Yorks.)	Ravensworth (Yorks.)
Bolton (Yorks.)	Ford (Northumb.)	Lumley (Dur.)	Rose (Cumbria)
Brancepeth (Dur.)	Gilling (Yorks.)	Middlehall (Yorks.)	Sheriff Hutton (Yorks.)
Bronsholm (Yorks.)	Halton (Ches.)	Millon (Cumbria)	Skipton (Yorks.)
*Carlisle (Cumbria)	Harbottle (Northumb.)	Morpeth (Northumb.)	Slingsby (Yorks.)
Cartington (Northumb.)	Harewood (Yorks.)	Mulgrave (Yorks.)	Tynemouth (Tyne and Wear)
Cawood (Yorks.)	Hartley (Cumbria)	Naworth (Cumbria)	Upsall (Yorks.)
Chillingham (Northumb.)	Haughton (Northumb.)	Ogle (Northumb.)	Warkworth (Northumb.)
Cockermouth (Cumbria)	Hay (Cumbria)	Penrith (Cumbria)	Wolsty (Cumbria)
Dacre (Cumbria)	Howgill (Cumbria)	*Pickering (Yorks.)	Wressle (Yorks.)
Danby (Yorks.)	Hylton (Tyne and Wear)	*Pontefract (Yorks.)	
Doddington (Ches.)			

Midlands

Bampton (Oxon.)	Cheney Longville (Shropshire)	Maxstoke (War.)	Shirburn (Oxon.)
Banbury (Oxon.)	Cheveley (Cambs.)	Melbourne (Derby.)	Stafford
Beaudesert (War.)	Codnor (Derby.)	Mettingham (Suffolk)	Tong (Shropshire)
Brampton Bryan (Hereford)	Fotheringhay (Northants.)	Moor End (Notts.)	Tutbury (Staffs.)
Broncroft (Shropshire)	Greasley (Notts.)	Myddle (Shropshire)	Warwick
Castle Ashby (Northants.)	Kenilworth (War.)	*Nottingham	Wigmore (Hereford)
Caverswall (Staffs.)	Kingsbury (War.)	Rotherfield Greys (Oxon.)	Wingfield (Suffolk)

South

Amberley (Sussex)	Farleigh Hungerford (Som.)	Powderham (Devon)	Sterborough (Surrey)
Beverstone (Glos.)	Hadleigh (Essex)	*Queenborough (Kent)	Tiverton (Devon)
Bishop's Stortford (Herts.)	Hemyock (Devon)	*Rochester (Kent)	Wardour (Wilts.)
Bodiam (Sussex)	Lanihorne (Corn.)	Ruardean (Corn.)	Wells palace (Som.)
*Carisbrooke (Isle of Wight)	Nunney (Som.)	Saltwood (Kent)	Westenhanger (Kent)
Cooling (Kent)	Okehampton (Devon)	Scotney (Kent)	*Windsor (Berks.)
Dartmouth (Clifton) (Devon)	Pleshey (Essex)	Southampton (Hants.)	Woodsford (Dorset)
Donnington (Berks.)			

Note: castles marked with an asterisk were in Crown hands

and, had pele-towers been included, would have completely over-shadowed them. A striking feature of the North is the creation of new foundations: Bolton has been described (p. 161), but there are others like Dunstanburgh, Lumley, Cawood, Sheriff Hutton, Wressle and so on. Furthermore, the new castles largely belong to the last decades of the century, followed by a fairly abrupt end in around 1400. The castles differ from those in other parts of the country in several respects, but most notably by their square or rectangular corner and mural towers, a preference for rectilinear shapes both overall and in the towers being a marked northern feature. This may have some connection with the pele-towers of the same area, especially as at Bolton they were used in the domestic accommodation, and certainly ties in with the presumed late use of firearms indicated by the absence of gunports, in contrast to the south.

The incursions of the Scots recorded by Froissart (who visited Scotland) are clearly sufficient explanation for the differences between the north and the rest of the country. These were not occasional rebellious outbursts as in Wales, but attacks by an organised army of an independent kingdom. Sometimes the construction can be directly related to a Scottish invasion. After the disastrous expedition of Edward II into Scotland the Scots retaliated by invading England, almost capturing the king. Pickering castle, Yorkshire, although not taken by the Scots, was felt to be vulnerable, so on the king's personal orders, given when he spent three weeks at the castle in August 1323, the wooden outer defences were replaced by a stone wall with towers, which we can still see today (fig. 104).[22] It is interesting that even in a royal work the local tradition of square towers was respected.

In the south the enemy came by sea,[23] not land, and the attacks also had an influence on castle construction; much new work of the second half of the century (Bodiam, Dartmouth, Cooling, Hadleigh, Queen-borough, Southampton) was prompted by fears of attack from across the Channel. Sometimes this is specifically referred to, as in the licence for Bodiam.[24] The threats also led to the strengthening of town defences as the new town gates at Southampton and Canterbury testify. In the south curved shapes were always preferred for towers in contrast to the north, and, possibly not unrelated, fortifications on the south coast were furnished with those curious keyhole gunports that I have discussed elsewhere.[25] Although only large enough for use with small handguns they imply the use of firearms, and clearly round surfaces were more likely to deflect shot than flat ones with square angles.

Turning now to the Midlands there was no immediate threat of inva-

104 Pickering castle, N. Yorkshire. The rectangular tower of north-country form on the curtain wall, built from 1324 to 1326, showing latrine discharge points and the door to the wall walk

sion. Indeed there is a remarkable transformation between the Welsh border in the twelfth century, thickly studded with mottes (p. 53) and the state we find it in during the fourteenth century. The chief witness of disorder on the Scottish border, the profusion of pele-towers, a large number of which were constructed in the fourteenth century, is absent from the Welsh border if we except two or three examples like Hopton castle and Wattlesborough in Shropshire. New castle construction in this period was slight on the Welsh border (Broncroft, Myddle, Tong). Lordship was thriving, as R. R. Davies has shown,[26] but the mere fact that records survive to make such an economic study possible for the period from 1282 to 1400 tells us not a little about the area itself. There is no doubt about the hostility between Welsh and English that culminated just after 1400 in Glyndŵr's rebellion, which engulfed the whole of the Principality. The widespread destruction associated with it was confined to Wales. The Edwardian conquest of 1282 destroyed an organised Welsh state and seems to have made the construction of new castles on the border superfluous, and indeed led to the neglect of some of the existing ones.

The rest of the Midlands has no very exciting innovations to attract our attention. Norfolk and Suffolk have very little to offer; the shape of the moat at Wingfield, Suffolk, where the gatehouse and adjoining curtain survive, suggests that it held more in the nature of a courtyard house with a cross-range (perhaps with hall) dividing it into courts. There is little in the east Midlands to detain us, but the west Midlands has more of interest. Maxstoke castle in Warwickshire, remarkably symmetrical in shape with polygonal corner towers, is both well preserved and still inhabited; it will be discussed below (fig. 108). Excavations on the mound at Stafford castle have disentangled from later alterations the striking elongated tower with circular turrets at the corners recalling Nunney in shape and Warkworth in situation (p. 174). The fine domestic buildings at Kenilworth have already been mentioned (p. 157). The poor showing of the Midlands compared to north or south is redeemed by the splendid frontage to Warwick castle erected by the earls of Warwick in the second half of the fourteenth century: Guy's and Caesar's towers and the gatehouse (fig. 105).

By the fourteenth century, water-filled moats, usually rectangular, were becoming a normal accompaniment for a manor house, as much as a castle. They abound in great profusion in Essex and Suffolk and other low-lying parts of East Anglia, as well as on the impermeable clays of the west Midlands. The areas are noted for their timber-

105 Warwick castle. Machicolations forming a *chemin de ronde* of French style on Caesar's tower built in the later fourteenth century. Note also the lobate shape

framed buildings and the moat could no doubt serve as a fire hydrant or static water tank. Apart from protection they evidently had a status element, as well as important practical uses for sewerage (the water was normally flowing or at any event drainable), fish-breeding and watering stock. Excavation has shown that the buildings of the manor house, scattered in the twelfth and thirteenth centuries, were drawn together into enclosures of this kind in the later middle ages.

Controversy has recently arisen over whether the ease with which the moat could be drained from the outside by an enemy at Bodiam (fig. 106) meant that the castle was not designed for serious defence.[27] The outlet (and inlet) valve or sluice for a moat had, for obvious reasons, to be on its outside, so that sometimes elaborate measures were taken to protect it or them, as at Kenilworth or the Tower of London which was fed by tidal water. Even if the enemy managed to let the water out there was likely to be a couple of feet of soft ooze in the moat bottom, kept soft for some time by the drainage and latrines in the castle and, of course, the weather. Froissart described a siege in 1385 in the Low Countries: 'The Frenchmen could not well come to the walls because the dykes were full of mire, for had it been rainy weather the host would have had much ado'.[28] The French raiders at Bodiam would presumably have had little time to wait for the moat to dry out. I have few doubts that defence was a major consideration in the construction of that castle, defence against the 'king's enemies', to quote the licence.[29]

106 Bodiam castle, Sussex. View across the moat of the corner towers and gatehouse of the castle built in the late fourteenth century with an eye to protection from French raids

There are several other noteworthy changes in the appearance of castles in the fourteenth century. The general shape tended towards a rectangle with corner towers, although the scale, shape and size varied. Complete departure from this, as at Queenborough or Old Wardour, was unusual. In the latter case the ground plan was polygonal as were the corner towers at Maxstoke or the faceted exterior at Guy's tower, Warwick. The intention may have been to cause shot to ricochet off or it may have been merely for effect.

Appearance has already been mentioned as a central consideration (p. 159). For this reason the castle was not normally subdivided into wards; a single uniform design, as at Bolton or Wressle or Danby, had a far more dramatic impact then and still does today. An outer circuit detracted from the appearance of the inner circit, so the concentric castle vanished. Height always impresses, as at Warwick (fig. 105), Wardour or Sheriff Hutton (fig. 113). Ashlar or regular face-dressed masonry with tight joints gave a smooth and elegant finish, and so became far more usual in the late fourteenth century. The use of ashlar in French castles from the twelfth century gives them a much more elegant appearance than English castles. Much larger windows were opened in the curtain walls, often with tracery, as at Kenilworth or Wardour. Much bolder use of corbelled-out projections for flues, latrine shafts, turrets (bartisans) and so on was made possible by the employment of more dressed stone (fig. 104).

One of the most striking alterations in the appearance of castles in the later middle ages was the 'machicolation' that crowned the top of the walls. The wall walk was projected forward on a series of little arches springing from corbels just below wall walk level. The defender behind the parapet, looking down through the gap between the corbels, commanded a view of the base of the wall and could drop missiles on an enemy trying to scale or pierce the wall. They were a replacement in stone of the temporary wooden platform, the *hourds*, that had been previously set up in the same position when required. Machicolation altered the form of a tower and counteracted the recession caused by perspective, and although functional in origin its aesthetic effect was soon appreciated. When set below the top of the tower and encircling it (the *chemin de ronde* of the French castles or the *Très Riches Heures*) machicolation produced the effect of a crown. Although rare in England, it occurs at Caesar's tower at Warwick (fig. 105) and at Nunney (fig. 111).

For the student of the castle, the fourteenth century has a special fascination, not only because of the regional variation already discussed but also because of the remarkable changes in style between the early and late parts of the century. A good point to begin is with the castle at Dunstanburgh, Northumberland.[30] Set on a rocky headland defended by cliff on one side, the earliest castle, enclosing a substantial area and dominated by a massive twin-towered gatehouse, was erected by Thomas, earl of Lancaster, in the early years of the century (fig. 107). The aggressive gatehouse, redolent of Edwardian work, reveals the overriding importance of defence for the warlike earl. The towers on the gatehouse are round, although those on the curtain are square, conforming to the regional variation. Possibly fine domestic buildings were intended, but if so the execution of the earl in 1322 prevented their erection. The gatehouse had grand rooms on the first and second floors, recalling the gatehouses of Harlech or Beaumaris. The alterations of John of Gaunt involved blocking the gate passage and so turning the whole building into a keep, at the same time moving the entry to the north-west, where it was reached through a barbican formed parallel to the curtain wall. The new gate was a simple opening through the wall. The changes epitomise the difference in attitude between the early and the late fourteenth century: the self-dramatisation of living in a gatehouse (without the inconvenience of it being a thoroughfare) recalls the late fourteenth-century structure at Hylton, Tyne and Wear, so ably described for us by Beric Morley.[31]

Castles from the early part of the century are uncommon in England.

107 Dunstanburgh castle, Northumberland. The ruined gatehouse built c. 1310 by Thomas, earl of Lancaster

Goodrich on the Welsh border has been referred to more than once (pp. 115, 160), but whether the complete reconstruction of the castle should be referred to William de Valence or his son Aymer we cannot say, for the dating is architectural only: it could have taken place either before or after 1300. The style suggests post-1300, but if so the builder seems to have been strangely oblivious of the altered situation on the border produced by Edward I's conquest of Wales in 1282. The domestic buildings are tucked into a defensive envelope, partially concentric, with great corner towers, gatehouse and half-moon barbican (plan in fig. 77).

By the mid-fourteenth century at Maxstoke castle we are in a different atmosphere altogether (fig. 108). Built in the 1340s by Sir William Clinton, the castle consists of a 55 m regular square enclosure with octagonal towers at each corner, the vaulted gatehouse projecting into the moat on the east side and terminating in polygonal turrets.[32] There is a broad encircling moat. The domestic buildings were on three sides of the courtyard with the hall opposite the gatehouse. The hung shutters between the merlons, no doubt restored, give the castle a feeling of active use heightened by the fact that it is still inhabited. The ashlar, with fine joints of gatehouse and corner towers, make it an elegant structure. Appearance was clearly a major factor in the mind of the builder, so that we can perhaps regard this as a transitional stage between the purely defensive castle of the early part of the century and the 'cult-castle' of the later part.

108 Maxstoke castle, Warwicks. An aerial view of the mid-fourteenth-century castle showing its general symmetry, octagonal corner towers and gatehouse turrets, with the hall range (unroofed) opposite the gatehouse

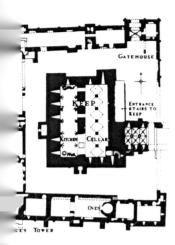

99 Middleham castle, N. Yorkshire. Plan showing the twelfth-
century keep (compare fig. 55)
with enclosing fourteenth-century
ranges built on the earlier curtain.
Scale c. 1:1,200

110 Middleham castle, N. Yorkshire. Discharge points from the
latrine tower on the N. side

The pattern continues in the latter part of the century at, for example, Farleigh Hungerford, Somerset, where Thomas de Hunger-ford was licensed to raise his manor to castle status in 1383.[33] A larger area was enclosed, perhaps around earlier buildings in the centre which exist today only as foundations, apart from a chapel in the outer ward.[34]

We have already met the twelfth-century keep at Middleham, York-shire (p. 77) where the resemblance of the large room, over a vault sup-ported on spinal columns and entered directly from outside, to a French hall has been commented on. In a most unusual and remarkable adaptation (fig. 109) the keep was kept in use in the later middle ages by erecting ancillary ranges around it on four sides, built at least in part against an earlier curtain wall.[35] At two points there were bridges ex-tending from the later ranges to the earlier central keep. The ranges are not subdivided into the independent cellular lodgings of fifteenth-century type, the latrines being housed in central towers on each side (fig. 110); this favours a dating to before 1400. Cellular lodging ranges are found in fourteenth-century castles (Windsor, Amberley, Oke-hampton) but stacking vertically in towers was preferred, as at Bodiam. Free-standing ranges of this form, in a courtyard house, do not seem to be known before their occurrence at the end of the century at Dartington, Devon. The rectangular towers at the corners, of Bolton type, again point to a pre-1400 date.

The starting-point for 'cult-castles' is 1347, when Ralph de Stafford entered into an agreement with a mason to erect a 'chastelle sur la moete', a castle on the motte at Stafford.[36] From this indenture, a plan made before destruction and the stump uncovered by excavation it is known that it stood on the motte and had a rectangular block plan, measuring about 35 by 15 m. There was an octagonal turret at each corner and another in the middle on the north side. There is something a little unreal about this miniature castle on the mound, but it recalls the keep with exaggerated corner turrets at Mulgrave, Yorkshire, thought to date to about 1300,[37] and even more strikingly the structure built 25 years later at Nunney, Somerset.

Because they were still in use, or at least usable, many of these fas-cinating late fourteenth-century castles were demolished or severely slighted in the Commonwealth period, but among those which escaped largely intact was Nunney castle in Somerset (fig. 111). On 28 Novem-ber 1373 John de la Mare 'chivaler', received licence to crenellate his dwelling-place at Nunney.[38] A completely new structure was erected with undoubted claims to be a castle. It was moated with entry by a

111 Nunney castle, Somerset, from the air. Built in the 1370s, it has a whimsical form like a keep with great round corner turrets or towers and the French-style *chemin de ronde*

bridge. It was of block design (no internal court), about 18 by 8 m internally, with a large round tower at each corner, the whole constructed of finely dressed stone. The principal level with hall was on the second floor, with service rooms below and a chamber above. The machicolation encircling the whole structure, forming a *chemin de ronde* of French style around the towers, a very rare feature in this country (Warwick is the only contemporary example), combined with the fine masonry, contributed to create an impressive building that recalls a manuscript illumination.[39] Although elegance was an overriding consideration, defence was by no means ignored, windows being largely suppressed in the lower part of the building. The raised great hall – and in a sense that is what the whole structure embodies – can leave little doubt that here, as in the other 'cult castles', cultural winds were blowing strongly from the other side of the English Channel.

One other castle from late in Edward III's reign (1327–77), built this time by the Crown, deserves notice, although unfortunately it has completely vanished and is known only from a later plan and drawing.[40] This is at Queenborough in the Isle of Sheppey, Kent, where the construction of the castle between 1361 and 1370 was accompanied by the foundation of a town, the last one so founded. It was a circular moated enclosure some 95 m in diameter with crenellated parapet and gatehouse enclosing at its centre the castle itself, 40 m in diameter with six round towers, two juxtaposed to form a gatehouse on the opposite side to the outer gatehouse. In Hollar's view, the towers appear to be machicolated. An innermost circular wall of diameter 20 m formed the inner wall of a circular range against the curtain. The geometric regularity of the plan is remarkable. The space between the inner and outer curtain was so great (25 m or 40 m to the outside of the moat) that it is not easy to conceive of the castle being 'concentric' in the Edwardian sense: defenders on the inner wall walk would have been hard put to it to assist those on the outer. Possibly the outer wall was intended to act as sort of *Fausse braie*, a shield to protect the inner curtain from enemy artillery fire. The enemy were French raiders in the Thames estuary, who probably would have had cannon even at this date. That is guesswork, however; what is clear is that by its rigid geometry Queenborough can be placed firmly among the 'cult-castles'. Appearance was dominant, although it was an entirely functional defensive structure assisting with the protection of the estuary on the south side in the same way that the castle at Hadleigh, largely reconstructed at the same time, did from Essex on the north side.

It is to Richard II's reign that some of the most interesting, not to say fanciful, castles belong. This was a period of considerable artistic achievement, in the architecture of Canterbury or Westminster cathedrals or in the roof of Westminster Hall, as well as in literature, with the sudden appearance of a native literature best known from the poetry of Chaucer or Langland; artistic achievement found expression also in other media, such as painting. The castles of the last two decades of the century fit into this background, both in the north and the south of the country. It will be sufficient to describe three, in addition to the one at Bolton already mentioned, which are well enough preserved to justify it, two *sui generis* and one of a fairly normal northern pattern.

Old Wardour castle, Wiltshire, is one of the most whimsical of the late fourteenth-century castles, erected presumably after a grant of a licence to crenellate to John, fifth Lord Lovell, in 1393;[41] it was the raising of the status of the manor to castle that was sought and granted with the licence. In this case, the structure resembles more a castellated hunting-lodge: a hexagon about 32 m across with a small open court in the centre with a well in the middle, and one side of the hexagon projected forward for the gatehouse with hall above. The ground floor of the ranges are vaulted in part, including the gate passage, and the principal rooms were on the first floor. The hall, with fine large traceried windows facing outward, measures only 14 by 8 m internally, and this, together with the limited supporting accommodation, suggests the building was designed to house hunting-parties rather than a full-scale household. The outer wall is substantially (75 cm) thicker than the inner that forms the ranges, which, together with the provision of arrow slits, indicates a serious defensive intention. The plan suggests a shell keep, or the thirteenth century castles of Castel del Monte or Boulogne, but there was no doubt something closer in date that had suggested this odd shape; Oudon (Loire Inferieure) or Largret-en-Elven (Morbihan) have polygonal keeps of about this date.[42]

The castle at Warkworth has already been mentioned (p. 106), but the end of the fourteenth century saw the construction there of a most remarkable 'keep' on top of the twelfth-century motte.[43] This was a quite independent residential unit recalling the tower on the motte at Stafford, or the residential unit created for the bishop within the shell at Farnham. It is probably to be attributed to the famous Harry Hotspur, but the dating just before or just after 1400 is uncertain. There is a donjon element in most of these late fourteenth-century castles, and in most of them one has the feeling of an expanded keep. The smaller the building the more fanciful the design could be. In the case of Warkworth there is a tower about 21 m square with bevelled corners and a rectangular turret with semi-octagonal end projecting from each side (fig. 112). It is three-storeyed, with a central light well. The hall, measuring 12 by 7 m was on the first floor with a chapel on its north side at the upper end, the eastern turret giving it a polygonal apse. No lodg-

112 Warkworth castle, Northumberland. The late fourteenth-century keep of highly individual form erected on top of the twelfth-century motte

ings were provided, so that the main household must have lived in the bailey below. The plan recalls the much earlier keep at Trim in Ireland but its real antecedents elude us. The lateral turrets may have had a buttressing purpose to counter any subsidence on the made-up ground of the motte.

Bolton castle, already mentioned (p. 160) is perhaps the earliest of the northern-style castles with a contract of 1378,[44] followed by Sheriff Hutton in Yorkshire, licence in 1381, now a ruin but with impressive towers (fig. 113), then Wressle in Humberside (licences in 1380 and 1390), with two of its towers still standing after Commonwealth demolition; but the most attractive and still occupied is Lumley castle in County Durham. Ralph, Lord Lumley, was licensed to construct it by the bishop of Durham in 1389 and the king in 1392.[45] It has undergone alteration in Tudor times and later at the hands of Vanbrugh, but the basic shape of the castle has not been altered (fig. 114). It has rectangular towers at the corners and the ground floor is vaulted throughout, the principal rooms are on the first floor and include the hall, 18 by 9 m on the west side opposite the gate. The gate has a segmental head and is ornamented above with a striking display of heraldic shields and crested helms. Such displays are characteristic of the period, perhaps best seen at Hylton castle in Tyne and Wear. The towers form part of

113 Sheriff Hutton castle, N. Yorkshire. The ruins of the four great corner towers of northern style, with three-storey ranges in between, of the late fourteenth century

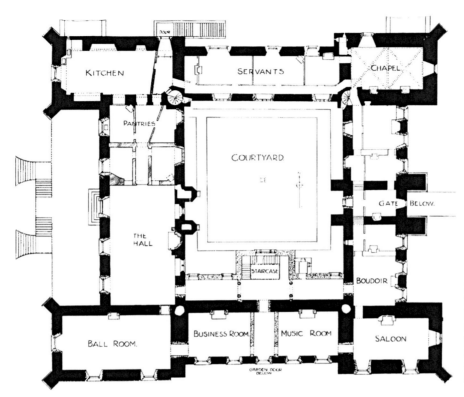

114 Lumley castle, County Durham. First-floor plan of the late fourteenth-century castle with rectangular corner towers. The principal rooms were in ranges above vaults on the first floor, and the hall was opposite the gatehouse. Scale *c.* 1:500

the accommodation with a fine vaulted chapel in the north-east one. A turret rises from each tower with projecting corbelled-out parapet at the top.

The stacked lodgings in the towers of Warwick and Bodiam have been described in *The Decline of the Castle* (p. 77). Guy's tower, Caesar's tower and the gatehouse at Warwick form a magnificent *ensemble* of the 'cult' style, with their machicolations and *chemin de ronde*, vividly demonstrating the French origins of these features (fig. 105). Although not closely dated, the whole of the front was erected by the earls of Warwick in the mid- to late fourteenth century. Bodiam, where Dalyngrigge was licensed in 1385 to crenellate his manor 'by the sea . . . and make a castle thereof in defence of the adjacent country against the king's enemies', is clearly more of a defensive structure than, say, Old Wardour; its more traditional accommodation was probably due to the fact that its defences had to take a more serious, old-fashioned form. Its moat and gunports have already been commented on (p. 106). Nevertheless, its symmetry, so gratifying when reflected in the water of the moat, leaves no doubt that it should be placed in the 'cult' style of Richard II's reign.

Looking back over the century, the change of style impresses us as much as the purpose associated with it. The grim aggressive defence of Edwardian form gave way to one where appearance was the overriding consideration. Symmetry and agreeable shapes were the order of the day: defence and accommodation had to play second fiddle. The normal accommodation of a manor house had to be packed into some unusual containers and in no two cases was the solution exactly alike. The primary objective was to insert the hall. In the fifteenth-century manor at South Wingfield, Derbyshire, the building account[46] leaves us in no doubt that the hall was the initial point of the whole operation; all the rest of the courtyard ranges followed. Occasionally the design had to be modified to accommodate the hall, as with Old Wardour, where symmetry was suspended to fit it in.

Apart from the hall, kitchen, chapel and latrines we do not positively know the functions of any of the rooms. To a great extent we seek to impose our own views of what a medieval household ought to be like when we seek to 'identify' the rooms. As explained above (p. 111) the absence of furniture made for great flexibility of function; a point not always familiar to a modern architect who thinks in terms of rigid functions. The intercommunication diagrams show that there was a greater complexity in the design than we might have suspected, but without reliable knowledge of the functions of the rooms the interpretation still remains to a great extent a closed book. It is like trying to read some undeciphered script. All we can say with full confidence is that a great deal more people required separate rooms in the second half of the fourteenth century than in the first half.

This may be an appropriate point to end this book. For the historian the fourteenth-century has its grim aspects of which the student of material culture of the period is often happily unaware. The Black Death has left no mark in the architecture, costume, pottery, and is, indeed, something to which Froissart characteristically omits reference in his chronicle; the subject is best left to the sombre lucubrations of the economic historians. The fear of contagion may have accelerated the desire for separate accommodation, but this must be speculative. Other events, like the Peasants' Revolt of 1381 (fully described by Froissart) cannot be ignored, since they almost certainly affected the architecture of the period: the strengthening of monastic closes and gatehouses, even the prolongation of the life of the castle in this country by a short period. It is very difficult to put one's finger on concrete evidence in the way one can on Scottish invasions or French raids. But some attention must be given to one major event.

The beginning of the Hundred Years War in the mid-fourteenth century meant that for Englishmen warfare was something that took place in France, not England. Furthermore, the war was popular and profitable, about which Froissart leaves us in no doubt. Thanks largely to the longbow, the English met with great success in the field in the early stages, and even in the sieges the longbow proved to be a valuable weapon. Although ideas about castles were brought back, it was the ornamental aspect, the cult attitude then flourishing in France, that most interested the builders, especially the association with raised social status. Sieges were more associated with France. The full consequences were visible in the fifteenth century, when castles were no longer constructed in this country but remained very much in use in France.[47] There is at first an easy transition and then there is a quite distinct bump at the turn of the century; the fourteenth-century cult castle was still functional, but with few exceptions the same cannot be said of the fifteenth-century show castles. The full-blown consequences of what has been discussed here have been described in *The Decline of the Castle*.

For three centuries the castle had been a grim but serviceable structure with unpleasant associations. In the late fourteenth century it seemed to reveal how nice it could look: at what better point than this for us to take our leave of it?

115 Luttrell Psalter (early fourteenth century). Margin illuminations showing a castle attacked by knights and defended by ladies who hurl roses at the 'enemy', a parody of *Le Roman de la Rose*

The sequence of halls in bishops' palaces in England and France

The intention of this appendix is to illustrate the contrast between England and France, the halls in the former sometimes undergoing a remarkable alteration in the twelfth or thirteenth centuries, generally from first to ground floor (usually aisled), while in the latter they remain constantly on the first floor throughout the middle ages. The open hall with twin arcades is apparently unknown not only in French bishops' palaces, but also in French aristocratic accommodation generally. Episcopal and archiepiscopal palaces were far more numerous in France than in England; the handful of surviving medieval examples cited here are those referred to in the literature. The *salle basse* was almost invariably vaulted on spinal columns.

Abbreviations
GF: ground floor
A: aisled
U: undercroft
1F: first floor

ENGLAND

Place	Notes	Reference
Acton Burnell, Shropshire	1F, ?with spinal columns in main hall, corner turrets, 1284 (licence)	J. West in A. Detsicas (ed.) *Collectanea Miscellanea* (Maidstone 1981), pp. 86–103.
Bishop Auckland, Durham	GF, A, 4 bays, late 12th century (Pudsey)	*EMH*, pp. 38–9.
Bishop's Waltham, Hants.	1. GF ?12th century converted to 2. 1F 14th. century	J. N. Hare in *AJ*, 145, (1988), pp. 222–54.
Buckden, Cambs	GF ?A	*RCHM, Hunts.* (1926), pp. 34–8.
Canterbury	GF A, 8 bays, early 13th century but with earlier hall?	F. Woodman, The *Arch. Hist. of Canterbury Cathedral* (1981), pp. 133–5.
Durham castle	1. 1F 3-storeyed. Late 12th century adjoining 2-storeyed chapel. 2. GF; U early 13th century replacing earlier hall?	*VCH, Durham*, III, pp. 64–9.
Exeter, Devon	GF; A ?3 bays, c. 1220	J. F. Chanter, *The Bishop's Palace at Exeter* (1932).
Farnham castle, Surrey	1. 1F? (inferred) converted to 2. GF; A, 4 bays	*VCH, Surrey*, II, p. 600.
Hereford	GF; A, 4 bays with 3-storeyed wing. Late 12th century	John Blair in *MA*, 31 (1987), pp. 59–71.
Lincoln	1. GF; U or 1F. E. hall late 12th century 2. GF; A, 4 bays. W. hall c. 1200	*Lincs. Museums Inf. Sheet, Archaeology*, 18.
Newark, Notts.	1. GF; U or 1F? converted to 2. GF, much longer. Partly U	*Trans. Thoroton Soc.* XXXIX (1935), pp. 53–92.
Norwich, Norfolk	1. 1F, early 12th century (Losinga) 2. GF; A 6 bays c. 1320 (Salmon)	A. B. Whittingham's plan of 1938.
Salisbury, Wilts. Old Sarum	GF; A 6 bays early 12th century	*RCHM, Salisbury,* I, p. 15.
City	GF; A 5 bays c. 1226 (Poore)	*Wilts Arch. Mag*, 57, pp. 405–6.
Sherborne, Dorset	1F, early 12th century	*RCHM, Dorset* (W.), I, pp. 64, 73.
Southwark, London	1F, c. 1340	*RCHM, London*, V, p. 67.
Taunton, Somerset	1. U or 1F? converted to 2. GF	*Proc. Som. Arch. and N. H. Soc.* 98 (1952), pp. 55–96.
Wells, Somerset	1. 1F early 13th century (Jocelyn) 2. GF; A 5 bays c. 1280	*EMH*, p. 24.
Winchester, Hants.	1. 1F early 12th century 2. E. Hall GF; A? single arcade, 4 bays	M. Biddle, *Wolvesey* (1986), HMSO.

FRANCE

Place	Notes	Reference
Aix en Provence, Bouches du Rhône	1F 13th century	*BM*, (1986), pp. 255ff.
Angers, Maine et Loire	1F early 12th century. *Grande salle* 20 years later than *salle basse*. Earliest bishop's hall in France	Enlart, I, pp. 61, 63
Auxerre, Yonne	1F 13th century	Viollet, VII, p. 18; Caumont, *Abécédaire* p. 137.
Avignon papal palace Vaucluse	1F 14th century	Viollet, VII, pp. 303–5.
Beauvais, Oise	1F, 12th century. Excavated basement	*BA* XX/XXI (1984–5), pp. 7–88.
Fréjus, Var	1F 14th century	*CAF* (1932), pp. 305–6.
Laon, Aisne	1F 13th century (fig. 17)	Viollet, VII, pp. 18–20.
Meaux, Seine-et-Marne	1F 12th century (fig. 117)	Enlart, I, p. 68; Caumont *Abécédaire*, pp. 138–9.
Narbonne, Aude	1F 14th century	Viollet, VII, pp. 19–25.
Paris	1F 12th century (fig. 18).	Viollet, VII, pp. 14–17.
Reims, Marne	1F 14th century	Viollet, VII, p. 18.
Sens, Yonne	1F 13th century. Hall itself vaulted (fig. 116)	Viollet, VII, pp. 74, 75; P. Frankl, *Gothic Architecture* (1962), p. 245, pl. 187a; Enlart, I, p. 17.

116 Sens, Yonne. Viollet-le-duc's section of the thirteenth-century hall of the bishop's palace showing vaults at three levels, including the first-floor hall itself

117 Meaux, Seine-et-Marne. Nineteenth-century view of the thirteenth-century bishop's palace, showing external stairs to the main hall

The spiritual castle

In a mid-twelfth-century sermon on the Assumption of the Virgin Ailred (1110– 66), Abbot of the Cistercian monastery of Rievaulx in Yorkshire, using as a text Luke x, 38 (*Intravit Jesus in quoddam castellum . . .*), made some analogies that are of interest to the student of the castle.

J. P. Migne, *Patrologiae, Cursus Completus . . .*, CXCV, pp. 303–5.

Therefore we will make ready this castle. In a castle there are three things that are strong, that is the ditch, the wall and the keep (*turris*). First the ditch, and next the wall above the ditch, and so to the keep which is stronger and finer than the rest. Wall and ditch give mutual defence; because unless the ditch precedes, men can reach and undermine the wall by some means; and unless there is a wall above the ditch they can reach the ditch and fill it up. The keep guards, all, because it is higher than all else . . . What is a ditch except deep ground . . . so that in our heart there is a ditch, that is deep and low soil. Therefore brothers this ditch is humility . . .

After the ditch we must make the wall. This spiritual wall is chastity . . . and as you have this ditch of humility and wall of chastity so must we build the keep of charity. The great keep (*magna turris*), my brothers, is charity. Just as the keep should be higher than all other structures in the castle, so charity is higher than all other virtues.

Abbreviations

AC	*Archaeologia Cantiana*
AJ	*Archaeological Journal*
AM	*Archéologie médiévale*
Ant. J.	*Antiquaries Journal*
Arch.	*Archaeologia*
Arch Camb.	*Archaeologia Cambrensis*
BA	*Bulletin archéologique*
BM	*Bulletin monumental*
BSAF	*Bulletin de la société nationale des antiquaires de France*
Cah. A.	*Cahiers archéologiques*
CA	*Current Archaeology*
CAF	*Congrès archéologique de France*
CBA	Council for British Archaeology
CC	*Cahiers de civilisation*
CG	*Château Gaillard*
CPR	*Calendar of Patent Rolls*
EETS	*Early English Text Society*
EHR	*English Historical Review*
EMH	M. Wood, *The English Medieval House*
Enlart	C. Enlart, *Manuel d'archéologie française*, 2nd edn (1932)
FS	*Frühmittelalterliche Studien*
HMSO	Her Majesty's Stationery Office
JBAA	*Journal of the British Archaeological Association*
JSAH	*Journal of the Society of Architectural Historians*
KW	*A History of the King's Works*, vols. I and II.
MA	*Medieval Archaeology*
MGH	*Monumenta Germaniae Historica*
Moy. A.	*Moyen Age*
PBA	*Proceedings of the British Academy*
RCHM	*Royal Commission on Historical Monuments*
RS	Rolls Series
VA	*Vernacular Architecture*
VCH	*Victoria County History*, Inventories
Viollet	E. Viollet-le-duc, *Dictionnaire raisonnée de l'architecture française*, vols. I–X
ZAM	*Zeitschrift für Archäologie des Mittelalters*

Notes

1 Introduction

1 Cf. the replacement of public buildings by palaces and ecclesiatical foundations in B. Ward-Perkins, *From Classical Antiquity to the Middle Ages: Urban Public Buildings in Northern and Central Italy AD 300–850* (Oxford, 1984).

2 K. Crossley-Holland, *The Anglo-Saxon World: An Anthology* (Oxford, 1984).

3 A. Verdier and F. Cattois, *Architecture civile et domestique* (Paris, 1855).

4 A. Owen, *The Ancient Laws and Institutes of Wales*, 2 vols. (London, 1841).

5 *ibid.*, p. 79.

6 S. Laing and J. Simpson (eds.) *Snorri Sturluson, Heimskringla* (London, 1964), pp. 1, 158.

7 G. Garmonsway and J. Simpson, *Beowulf and its Analogues* (London, 1968).

8 I. Gollancz, (ed.), *The Exeter Book*, Pt. 1, Early English Text Society (1895), pp. 295–6.

9 *ibid.*, p. 1.

10 *ibid.*, pp. 287–91.

11 K. H. Jackson, *A Celtic Miscellany* (London, 1951), p. 276.

12 H. Hamerow, 'Mucking: the Anglo-Saxon Settlement', *CA* 10 (1988), 128–31.

13 B. Hope-Taylor, *Yeavering, An Anglo-British Centre of Early Northumbria* (HMSO, 1977).

14 C. Plummer, *Venerabilis Baedae Historiam Ecclesiasticam Gentis Anglorum* . . . (Oxford, 1896) I, pp. 112, 115.

15 K. Baumgarten, *Das deutsche Bauernhaus, eine Einführung in seine Geschichte von 9. bis zum 19. Jahrhundert* (Berlin, 1980), pp. 37–41; W. Haarnagel, 'Die prähistorische Siedlungsformen in Küstengebiet der Nordsee', in *Beiträge zur Genese der Siedlungs-Agrarlandschaft in Europa* (Wiesbaden, 1968), pp. 67–84. Haarnagel thought that the houses without cattle stalls, which date to just before the migration to England, discovered in his excavations at Feddersen Wierde, near Bremerhaven could be identified as halls: *Die Grabung Feddersen Wierde*, II (Wiesbaden, 1979), p. 89.

16 Horn does not seem to distinguish between a Roman basilican use of arcades and a native bay system: W. Horn, 'On the Origin of the Medieval Bay System', *JSAH*, 17 (1900), 2–23.

17 P. Rahtz, *The Saxon and Medieval Palaces at Cheddar: Excavations 1960–62* (Oxford 1979).

18 J. H. Williams, M. Shaw and V. Denham, *Middle Saxon Palaces at Northampton* (Northampton, 1985).

19 W. H. Stevenson, *Asser's Life of King Alfred* (Oxford, 1904) p. 44. 'De aulis et cambris regalibus, lapideis et ligneis, suo iussu mirabiliter constructis.'

20 G Beresford, *Goltho, the Development of an Early Medieval Manor c. 850–1150* (London, 1987).

21 M. W. Thompson, 'Excavation of the Fortified Medieval Hall at Hutton Colswain at Huttons Ambo, nr Malton, Yorkshire', *AJ*, 114 (1957), fig. 3.

22 M. W. Thompson, 'A Single-Aisled Hall at Conisbrough Castle, Yorkshire', *MA*, 12 (1968), 153.

23 B. K. Davison, 'Excavations at Sulgrave, Northamptonshire, An Interim Report', *AJ*, 134 (1977), 105–14.

24 D. J. C. King and L. Alcock, 'Ringworks of England and Wales', *CG*, 3 (1966), 90–127.

25 R. Glasscock, 'Mottes in Ireland', *CG*, 7 (1975), 95–110.

26 G. N. Garmonsway (ed.), *The Anglo-Saxon Chronicle* (London, 1953), p. 123 n. 2.

27 A. J. Taylor in A. L. Poole (ed.), *Medieval England*, 2nd edn (Oxford, 1958) I, pp. 98–102.

28 D. Barthelemy, 'Kinship', in G. Duby (ed.), *A History of Private Life*, II, *Revelations of the Medieval World* (London, 1988), pp. 85–157.

2 Germany

1 Jankühn in H. Pätze (ed.), *Die Burgen im deutschen Sprachraum: ihre rechtliche und verfassungsgeschichtliche Bedeutung*. Vorträge and Forschungen, 19 (1976), I, 368ff.

2 M. Bloch, *Feudal Society* (London, 1961), pp. 179–81; L. Reynaud, *Etude sur l'histoire comparée de la civilisation en France et en Allemagne pendant le période précourtoise (950–1150)* (Paris, 1913).

3 *MGH, Capitularia Regum Francorum* (Hanover, 1883), I, p. 254.

4 A. Kleinelausz, *Charlemagne* (Paris, 1934), pp. 178–201.

5 The plans are conveniently reproduced in J. H. Williams, M. Shaw and V. Denham, *Middle Saxon Palaces at Northampton* (Northampton, 1985), pp. 34–5.

6 Reconstruction drawing in W. Hotz, *Kleine Kunstgeschichte der deutschen Burg* (Darmstadt, 1979), p. 77.

7 N. Duval, 'Le Palais de Diocletian à Spoleto à la lumière des récents découverts', *BSAF* (1961), 76–116.

8 J. M. P. Andrade, *Arte Asturiano* (Madrid, 1963), pp. 22–5, pl. 16–23.

9 W. Winkelmann, 'Der Königspfalz und Bischofspfalz des 11. und 12. Jahrhundert in Paderborn', *FS*, 4 (1976), 398–415.

10 Hotz, *Kleine Kunstgeschichte*, pp. 82–5.

11 *Ars Hispaniae*, 22 vols. (Madrid, 1947–77), V, pp. 114, 182.

12 K. L. Swoboda, *Römische und romanische Paläste*, 3rd edn (Vienna, 1968), chap. vii.

13 Pätze (ed.), *Die Burgen in deutschen Sprachraum*, I, 210ff.

14 A. T. Hatto, (ed.), *The Nibelungenlied* (Harmondsworth, 1965), pp. 242–74.

15 A. Antonow, *Planung und Bau von Burgen im süddeutschen Raum* (Frankfurt, 1983), pp. 24–5.

16 R. von Uslar, *Studien zu frühgeschictlichen Befestigungen zwischen Nordsee und Alpen* (Cologne, 1964).

17 *ibid.*, pp. 74–112.

18 *Lexikon des Mittelalters*, II, p. 1003.

19 Von Uslar, *Studien zu frühgeschichtlichen Befestigungen*, pp. 68ff.

20 E. Riesdahl, 'The Viking Fortress of Fyrkat in the Light of the Objects found', *CG*, 6 (1972), 195–202.

21 M. Müller-Wille, *Mittelalterliche Burghügel im nördlichen Rheinland* (Cologne, 1966).

22 *ibid.*, p. 12.

23 M. W. Thompson, 'A Group of Mounds on Seasalter Level, nr Whitstable, and the Medieval Imbanking in this Area', *AC*, 70 (1966), 44–67.

24 A. Herrnbrodt, *Der Husterknupp, eine niederrheinische Burgenanlage des frühen Mittelalters* (Cologne, 1958).

25 For examples, such as Xanten, see G. Binding, 'Spätkarolingischottonische Pfalzen und Burgen am Niederrhein', *CG*, 5 (1972), 23–35.

26 D. Lütz in M. Bey (ed.), *La Maison forte au moyen âge* (Paris, 1986).

27 Antonow, *Planung und Bau von Burgen*, pp. 37, 45.

28 *ibid.*, p. 21.

29 *ibid.*, p. 163.

30 H. Hinz, *Mote und Donjon: Zur Frühgeschichte der mittelalterlichen Adelsburg* (Cologne, 1981), 53ff.

31 G. Binding, *Burg Münzenberg, eine staufische Burganlage* (Bonn, 1963).

32 G. Binding, *Pfalz Gelnhausen, eine Bauuntersuchung* (Bonn, 1965).

33 Hotz, *Kleine Kunstgeschichte der deutschen Burg*, pp. 151–66, plan of Castel del Monte, p. 163.

3 France

1 L. Reynaud, *Les Origines de l'influence française en Allemagne. Etude sur l'histoire comparée de la civilisation en France et en Allemagne pendant la période précourtoise (950–1150). I. L'offensive politique et sociale de la France* (Paris, 1913), pp. 280–81.

2 P. Heliot, 'Sur les résidences princières

bâties en France du Xe au XIIe siècle',
Moy. A, 61 (1955), 27–62, 291–317; J.
Gardelles, 'Les Palais dans l'Europe occidental chrétienne du Xe au XIIe siècle',
CC, 19 (1976), 115–34; K. L. Swoboda,
Römische und romanische Paläste, 3rd
edn (Vienna, 1969).

3   Heliot, '*Sur les résidences princières
bâties en France*', 31.

4   I. Hacke-Sück, 'La Sainte Chapelle de
Paris et les chapelles palatines du moyen
âge en France', *Cah. A.* 13 (1982),
217–57.

5   Heliot, 'Sur les résidences princières
bâties en France'; Gardelles, 'Les palais',
and especially Swoboda, *Römische und
romanische Paläste*. pl. XV shows the
Badia in Orvieto.

6   J. S. Cotman, *Architectural Antiquities
of Norman Lands* (London, 1822), pl.
LXIX; J. Valéry-Radot, 'Le Donjon de
Lillebonne', in P. Gallais and Y. Rion
(eds.) *Mélanges offerts à René Crozet*
(Poitiers, 1966), II, pp. 1, 105–13; plan in
Comte de Caylus, *Recueil d'antiquités*
(Paris, 1764), VI, pp. 393–6, pl.
CXXVI–VII; *BM*, 4 (1838), 170, for visit
by Gully Knight; also *Gentleman's
Magazine*, 102 (1832), 322. '. . . large
Gothic hall . . . the style of early Norman
architecture.'

7   V. Mortet, *Etude historique et archéologique sur la cathédrale et palais
épiscopal de Paris du VIe au XIIe siècle*
(Paris, 1888); entries for *salle* and *palais*
in Viollet.

8   J. M. Cohen (ed.), *Rabelais: Gargantua
and Pantagruel* (Harmondsworth, 1955),
p. 64.

9   G. Fournier, *Le Château dans la France
médiévale* (Paris, 1978), pp. 38, 267.

10   M. de Bouard, 'Quelques données
françaises et normandes concernant le
problème de l'origine des mottes', *CG*, 2
(1967), pp. 19–26.

11   'Colloque de Caen, 1980; les fortifications de terre en Europe occidentale du
X^e au XIIe siècles', *AM*, 11 (1981), 5–123.

12   H. Hinz, *Motte und Donjon: Zur Frühgeschichte der mittelalterlichen Adelsburg* (Cologne, 1981), pp. 88ff.

13   V. Mortet, *Recueil de textes relatifs à
l'histoire de l'architecture et la condition
des architectes en France du Moyen âge
XIe–XIIe siècles* (Paris, 1911), p. 10.

14   A. J. Holden (ed.), *Le Roman de Rou de
Wace* (Paris, 1970), p. 126, lines
6, 509–29.

15   M. W. Thompson, 'Recent Excavations
in the Keep of Farnham Castle, Surrey',
MA, 4 (1960), 81–94.

16   M. de Bouard, 'De l'aula au donjon: les
fouilles de la motte de la Chapelle à
Doué la Fontaine (X^e–XIe siècle)', *AM*,
3/4 (1973–4), 1–110.

17   *Dictionnaire de biographie française*. II,
col. 1,264–66; M. Deyres, Les Châteaux
de Foulque Nerra', *BM*, 132 (1974),
4–28.

18   H. Woquet (ed.), *Suger, Vie de Louis VI
le Gros* (Paris, 1929), p. 140.

19   Gautier de Thérouanne, *Vie de Jean
Thérouanne, évêque de Thérouanne*,
quoted in Fournier, *Le Château*, p. 327.

20   B. K. Davison, 'Normandy Field Survey',
AJ, 126 (1968), 179–80.

21   A. Chatelaine, *Donjons romans des pays
d'Ouest: Etude comparative sur les donjons romans quadrangulaires de la
France de l'Ouest* (Paris, 1973).

22   P. Heliot, 'La Genèse de plan quadrangulaire des châteaux en France et en
Angleterre', *BSAF* (1965), 238–57.

23   Viollet, III, pp. 86–102; M. Powicke, *The
Loss of Normandy 1189–1209*, 2nd edn
(Manchester, 1961), 116, 178ff, 253ff.

24   Heliot, 'La Genèse de plan
quadrangulaire'.

25   Viollet, III, pp. 107–17.

26   M. N. de Wailly, *Jean, sire de Joinville:
Histoire de St Louis* (Paris, 1878), pp. 54,
56, English translation, M. R. B. Shaw
(ed.), *Joinville and Villehardouin,
Chronicles of the Crusades* (Harmondsworth, 1963); for Henry II at
Saumur see W. Stubbs (ed.), *Benedict of
Peterborough, Chronicle*, RS, 1867, II,
pp. 61, 69; Stubbs (ed.), *Roger of
Hoveden, Chronicle*, RS, 1869, pp. 362,
364.

27   W. Braunfels, *Monasteries of Western
Europe, the Architecture of the Orders*
(London, 1977), pp. 96–102.

28   The wooden aisle posts at Hereford and
Leicester are now thought to be late
twelfth century: *MA*, 31 (1987), 59–79.
For St John's Hospital, Angers: J.
Bonssard, *Le Comté d Anjou sous Henri
Plantagenet et son fils* (Paris, 1938),
p. 99.

29 Lucheux, *CAF* (1936), 227ff.
30 In the English area at Bordeaux it looks like a single aisle on the eighteenth-century plan of the destroyed Palais de l'Ombrière: J. Gardelles, *Les Châteaux du moyen âge dans la France du Sud-Ouest: la Gascogne anglaise de 1216 à 1327* (Geneva, 1972), p. 106.
31 G. I. Meirion-Jones, 'The Vernacular Architecture of France: an Assessment', *VA*, 16, (1985), 1–18.
32 Viollet, VIII, pp. 81–5.

4 Wooden castles

1 T. Wright (ed.), *The Historical Works of Giraldus Cambrensis* (London, 1905), p. 288.
2 *ibid.*, p. 311.
3 M. Chibnall, (ed.), *The Ecclesiastical History of Orderic Vitalis* (Oxford, 1969), p. 219.
4 T. E. Lawrence, *Crusader Castles*, ed. by D. Pringle (Oxford, 1988).
5 See the introduction to R. Foreville (ed.), *Guillaume de Poitiers, Histoire de Guillaume le Conquérant* (Paris, 1952); F. Stenton (ed.), *The Bayeux Tapestry, A Comprehensive Review*, 2nd edn (London, 1965); D. M. Wilson, *The Bayeux Tapestry* (London, 1965). The most realistic version is the French continuous paper strip, *Tapisserie de la Reine Mathilde* (Bayeux, n.d.).
6 D. J. C. King and L. Alcock, 'Ringworks of England and Wales', *CG*, 3 (1966), 90–127.
7 M. W. Thompson, 'Trial Excavation in the West Bailey of a Ring Motte and Bailey at Long Buckby, Northants', *Journal of the Northants. Natural History Society and Field Club, 33* (1956), 55–66.
8 M. W. Thompson, 'Excavation of the Fortified Medieval Hall of Hutton Colswain at Huttons Ambo, nr Malton, Yorkshire', *AJ*, 114 (1959), 69–91.
9 *VCH, Yorkshire, North Riding*, II, pp. 202 and 242.
10 L. Alcock, 'Castle Tower, Penmaen, a Norman Ringwork in Glamorgan', *Ant. J*, 46 (1966), 178–210; B. K. Davison, 'Excavations at Sulgrave, Northamptonshire, An Interim Report', *AJ*, 134 (1977), 105–14.

11 Foreville (ed.), *Guillaume de Poitiers*, p. 236.
12 *MA*, 8 (1964).
13 C. J. Spurgeon, 'Mottes and Ringworks in Wales', in J. R. Kenyon and R. Avent (eds.), *Castles in Wales and the Marches, Essays in Honour of D. J. Cathcart King* (Cardiff, 1987), pp. 23–51.
14 M. W. Thompson, 'Motte Substructures', *MA*, 5 (1961), 305–6.
15 B. Hope-Taylor, 'The Norman Motte at Abinger, Surrey, and its Wooden Castle', in R. L. S. Bruce-Mitford (ed.), *Recent Archaeological Excavations in Britain* (London, 1956), pp. 223–50.
16 *MA*, 5 (1960), 318; *MA*, 6/7 (1961), 322; *MA*, 8 (1964), 255.
17 *VCH*, Surrey, II, pp. 599–605; M. W. Thompson, 'Recent Excavations in the Keep of Farnham Castle, Surrey', *MA*, 4 (1960), 81–94.
18 P. Barker and R. Higham, *Hen Domen, Montgomery: a Timber Castle on the English–Welsh Border* (London, 1982); P. Barker, 'Hen Domen' *CA*, 11 (1988), 137–42.
19 P. Mayes and L. A. S. Butler, *Sandal Castle Excavations, 1964–73* (Wakefield, 1983).
20 R. A. Brown, 'A List of Castles, 1154–1216', *EHR*, 74 (1959), 249–80.
21 For example, *Pipe Roll Society*, XIX (1895), p. 117 and XXI (1896), p. 50.
22 M. W. Thompson, *Pickering Castle, Yorkshire* (HMSO, 1956).
23 M. W. Thompson, *Farnham Castle Keep, Surrey* (HMSO, 1961).
24 O. E. Craster, *Skenfrith Castle, Gwent* (HMSO, 1970).

5 Stone towers

1 D. R. Renn, *Norman Castles in Britain*, 2nd edn (London, 1973).
2 R. Willis, *Architectural History of the Conventual Buildings of Christchurch, Canterbury* (London, 1869).
3 J. G. Coad and A. D. F. Streeten, 'Excavation at Castle Acre Castle, Norfolk. Country House and Castle of the Norman Earls of Surrey', *AJ*, 139 (1982), 138–302.
4 J. C. Perks, *Chepstow Castle, Monmouthsire* (HMSO, 1955).

5 W. St J. Hope, 'The Castle of Ludlow', *Arch*, 61 (1909), 257–328.

6 *KW*, I, pp. 29–32; R. A. Brown, 'Architectural History and Development to *c*. 1547 and Architectural Description', in J. Charlton (ed.), *The Tower of London: its Buildings and Institutions* (HMSO, 1978), pp. 28–54.

7 P. J. Drury, 'Aspects of the Origins and Development of Colchester Castle', *AJ*, 139 (1982), 302–419.

8 *RCHM, City of Oxford*, p. 158, pl. 211.

9 G. T. Clark, *Medieval Military Architecture* (1884), II, pp. 291–3.

10 R. A. Brown, *Castle Rising, Norfolk* (HMSO, 1978).

11 M. W. Thompson, *Kenilworth Castle, Warwickshire* (HMSO, 1976).

12 C. Peers, *Middleham Castle, Yorkshire* (HMSO, 1943).

13 S. E. Rigold, *Portchester Castle, Hampshire* (HMSO, 1974).

14 R. A. Brown, *Rochester Castle, Kent* (HMSO, 1969), p. 10.

15 R. A. Brown, 'Royal Castle-Building in England, 1154–1216', *EHR*, 70 (1955), 353–98.

16 *ibid.*, 359.

17 O. E. Craster, 'Skenfrith Castle: when was it built?', *Arch. Camb.* (1967), 133–58.

18 R. A. Brown, *Dover Castle, Kent* (HMSO, 1961).

19 W. H. Knowles, 'The Castle, Newcastle upon Tyne', *Archaeologia Aeliana*, 2 (1926), 2–50.

20 R. A. Brown, *Orford Castle, Suffolk*, (HMSO, 1964).

21 M. W. Thompson, *Conisbrough Castle, Yorkshire* (HMSO, 1959); S. Johnson, *Conisbrough Castle, Yorkshire* (HMSO, 1984).

22 The scale of Henry I's castle-building in Normandy is made known to us from Robert de Torigni, an almost contemporary writer: L. Delisle (ed.), *Chronique de Robert de Torigni* (Rouen, 1872), pp. 164–5, 196–7.

6 **Dwelling and defence divided**

1 M. W. Thompson, *The Decline of the Castle* (Cambridge University Press, 1988), chapter 2.

2 P. Barker and R. Higham, *Hen Domen, Montgomery: a Timber Castle on the English–Welsh Border* (London, 1982).

3 S. E. Rigold, *Portchester Castle, Hampshire* (HMSO, 1963).

4 S. E. Rigold, *Eynsford Castle, Kent* (HMSO, 1964).

5 *RCHM, Dorset*, II, pt.1, pp. 57–78 and coloured plan at back. The dating obviously is very tentative.

6 *KW*, II, pp. 629–40.

7 F. J. E. Raby and P. K. Baillie Reynolds, *Framlingham Castle, Suffolk* (HMSO, 1959); D. Renn, 'Defending Framlingham Castle', *Proc. Suff. Inst. Arch.* 33, (1975), 59–67.

8 J. G. Coad, 'Recent Excavations within Framlingham Castle', *Proc. Suff. Inst. Arch*, 32, pt 2 (1971), 152–63.

9 N. Pevsner, *Buildings of England: Sussex*, p. 93.

10 A. J. Taylor, *Monmouth Castle and Great Castle House* (HMSO, 1976); D. J. C. King and J. C. Perks, 'Manorbier Castle, Pembrokeshire', *Arch. Camb.*, 119 (1970), 83–124.

11 Attributed to Paris in Walsingham's work, since it took place in Abbot John's time, 1235–60: H. C. Riley (ed.), *Gesta Abbatum Monasterii Sancti Albani*, RS, 1877, I, p. 314.

12 M. W. Thompson, 'Three Stages in the Construction of the Hall at Kenilworth Castle', in M. R. Apted *et al.* (eds.), *Ancient Monuments and their Interpretation* (Chichester, 1977), pp. 211–19.

13 P. Mayes and L. A. S. Butler, *Sandal Castle Excavations, 1964–73* (Wakefield 1983).

14 W. H. St J. Hope, 'The Castle of Ludlow', *Arch.*, 61 (1909), 257–328.

15 *KW*, II, pp. 910–18.

16 C. A. R. Radford, 'Oakham Castle', *Arch. J.*, 112 (1955), 181–4.

17 *KW*, II, pp. 766–8.

18 T. H. Turner and J. H. Parker, *Some Account of Domestic Architecture in England* (Oxford, 1851), I, chaps. 3–4; *KW*, I, chap. 4.

19 *KW*, II, pp. 856, 858; *VCH, Hants*, V, pp. 9–12; M. Portal, *The Great Hall of Winchester Castle* (Winchester, 1897).

20 M. W. Thompson, *Kenilworth Castle, Warwickshire* (HMSO, 1976).

21 M. W. Thompson, 'The Origins of Bol-

ingbroke Castle, Lincs.', *MA*, 10 (1966), 152–6.

22 W. H. St J. Hope, 'The Castle of Ludlow'.

23 M. W. Thompson, 'Bolingbroke Castle'.

24 M. W. Thompson, *Kenilworth Castle*.

25 O. E. Craster, *Cilgerran Castle, Dyfed* (HMSO, 1957).

26 S. Johnson, *Conisbrough Castle, S. Yorkshire* (HMSO, 1984); M. W. Thompson, 'A Single-Aisled Hall at Conisbrough Castle, Yorkshire', *MA*, 13 (1968), 152.

27 *KW*, II, pp. 829–37; Anon., *Scarborough Castle, Yorkshire* (HMSO, 1955), p. 7.

28 M. W. Thompson, 'The Origins of Bolingbroke Castle, Lincs.'.

29 M. W. Thompson, 'The Green Knight's Castle', in C. Harper-Bill *et al.* (eds.), *Studies in Medieval History Presented to R. A. Brown* (London, 1989), pp. 317–25.

30 M. W. Thompson, 'Bolingbroke Castle'; P. Heliot, 'Boulogne-sur-mer', *CAF* (1936), 349–77.

31 C. H. Hunter Blair and H. L. Honeyman, *Warkworth Castle, Northumberland* (HMSO, 1954).

32 *VCH, Surrey*, II, pp. 599–605.

33 *VCH, Northants*, III, pp. 70–2.

34 J. C. Perks, *Chepstow Castle, Monmouthshire* (HMSO, 1957).

35 O. E. Craster, *Skenfrith Castle, Gwent* (HMSO, 1970).

36 C. A. R. Radford, *Grosmont Castle, Gwent* (HMSO, 1980).

37 C. A. R. Radford, *White Castle, Gwent* (HMSO, 1962); A. J. Taylor, 'White Castle in the Thirteenth Century', *MA*, 5 (1961), 169–75.

38 R. Avent, *Castles of the Princes of Gwynedd* (Cardiff, 1983).

7 **Defence paramount**

1 J. Goronwy Edwards, 'Edward I's Castle-Building in Wales', *PBA*, 32 (1967), 15.

2 Listed in M. R. Apted *et al.* (eds.), *Ancient Monuments and their Interpretation* (Chichester, 1977) pp. 349–57.

3 M. E. Wood, 'Thirteenth-Century Domestic Architecture in England', *AJ*, 105, supplement (1950), 62–70; T. H.

Turner and J. H. Parker, *Some Account of Domestic Architecture in England* (1851), I, pp. 158–61.

4 W. H. St J. Hope, 'The Castle of Ludlow', *Arch.* 61 (1909), 257–328.

5 C. N. Johns, *Caerphilly Castle, Mid-Glamorgan* (HMSO, 1978). There is a simpler, more illustrated guide by D. F. Renn, *Caerphilly Castle* (CADW 1989).

6 C. A. R. Radford, *Llawhaden Castle, Pembrokeshire* (HMSO, 1969).

7 For both bishop's palaces, see the official guides by C. A. R. Radford.

8 D. J. King and J. C. Perks, 'Carew Castle, Pembrokeshire', *AJ*, 119 (1962), 270–307.

9 G. and T. Jones (eds.), *The Mabinogion* (London, 1949), pp. 137–8.

10 T. H. Turner and J. H. Parker, *Domestic Architecture*, I, pp. 172–3.

11 C. A. R. Radford, *Goodrich Castle, Herefordshire* (HMSO, 1958). Excavations at Sandal castle, Yorkshire, have revealed a remarkable semi-circular barbican of the same kind as Goodrich, protecting the bridgehead at the foot of the motte ramp leading up to the thirteenth-century keep: P. Mayes and L. A. S. Butler, *Sandal Castle Excavations, 1964–73* (Wakefield, 1983), p. 48.

12 R. E. M. Wheeler, *Maiden Castle, Dorset* (London, 1943).

13 M. R. B. Shaw (ed.), *Joinville and Villehardouin, Chronicles of the Crusades* (New York, 1985), pp. 70ff.

14 M. W. Thompson, 'Kenilworth since 1962', *MA*, 13 (1969), 218–20.

15 M. W. Thompson, *Kenilworth Castle, Warwickshire* (HMSO, 1976).

16 C. N. Johns, *Caerphilly Castle*.

17 *KW*, II, pp. 695–703.

18 A. J. Taylor, 'Castle-Building in Thirteenth-Century Wales and Savoy', *PBA* 62 (1978), 265–92.

19 A. J. Taylor's section of the *King's Works in Wales* has been published separately (HMSO, 1974), and he has written guidebooks to the principal castles: Rhuddlan, Conwy, Caernarfon, Harlech and Beaumaris. Conwy and Caernarfon castles are also described in the *RCHM* volumes for Caernarvonshire. I have drawn on all these.

20 A. J. Taylor, 'Master Bertram, Ingeniator Regis', in C. Harper-Bill *et al.*

(eds.), *Studies in Medieval History presented to R. Allen Brown* (Woodbridge, 1989), pp. 289–316.

21 Apted *et al.* (eds.), *Ancient Monuments*; A. J. Taylor, 'Castle-Building', *King's Works in Wales*, 'Master Bertram', see note 20 above.

22 See Taylor, *KW* and note 19 above.

23 *ibid.*

24 *ibid*, pp. 1,027–29.

25 *ibid*, p. 293. The substantial but fragmentary remains at Hope and Ruthin are omitted.

26 The reconstructed motte and bailey at Hawarden, Clwyd, is omitted, although the keep was built at this date. Holt castle, although subsequently completely destroyed, is known from an Elizabethan plan of 1562: Lawrence Butler, 'Holt Castle: John de Warenne and Chastellion', in J. R. Kenyon (ed.), *Castles in Wales and the Marches, Essays in Honour of D. J. Cathcart King* (Cardiff, 1987), pp. 105–25.

27 M. W. Thompson, *The Decline of the Castle* (Cambridge University Press, 1988), p. 180.

28 Butler, 'Holt Castle'.

29 L. A. S. Butler, *Denbigh Castle, Clwyd* (HMSO, 1976).

30 M. W. Thompson, *The Journeys of Sir Richard Colt Hoare* (Gloucester, 1983), pp. 179–81.

31 T. and G. Jones (eds.) *The Mabinogion*, p. 83.

8   The castle as midwife: monasteries

1 C. V. Langlois, *La Société française au XIIIᵉ siècle d'après dix romans d'aventure* (Paris, 1904), p. xxii.

2 L. Gautier, quoted in E. Lavisse and A. Rimbaud, *Histoire générale du IVᵉ siècle à nos jours* (Paris, 1893), II, p. 35.

3 G. G. Coulton, *Five Centuries of Religion* (Cambridge University Press, 1923), I, chaps. 3–10.

4 P. Zeller, *Die täglichen Lebensgewohnheiten im altfranzösichen Karls-Epos* (Marburg, 1885).

5 A. J. Taylor, *Harlech Castle, Gwynedd* (HMSO, 1977).

6 I. Hacke-Sück, 'La Sainte-Chapelle de Paris et les chapelles palatins du moyen âge en France', *Cah. arch*, 13 (1962), 217–57.

7 R. A. Brown, *Castle Rising, Norfolk* (HMSO, 1978).

8 D. Knowles and R. N. Hadcock, *Medieval Religious Houses in England and Wales* (London, 1971), p. 385.

9 A. J. Taylor, 'Evidence for the Pre-Conquest Origin for the Chapels in Hastings and Pevensey Castles', *CG*, 3 (1970), 144–51.

10 W. H. St J. Hope, 'The Castle of Ludlow', *Arch.* (1908), 271–5.

11 D. Renn, ' "Chastel de Dynan": the First Phases of Ludlow', in J. R. Kenyon and R. Avent, *Castles in Wales and the Marches* (Cardiff, 1987) p. 64.

12 Guillaume de Poitiers, *Histoire de Guillaume le Conquérant*, ed. by R. Foreville (Paris, 1952), p. 125.

13 D. Knowles, *The Monastic Order in England* (Cambridge University Press, 1952), p. 125.

14 *ibid.*, pp. 128–40.

15 The largest collection of foundation and confirmation charters is to be found in William Dugdale, *Monasticon Anglicanum* (1830 edition).

16 M. W. Thompson, 'Associated Monasteries and Castles in the Middle Ages', *AJ*, 142 (1986), 305–21.

17 P. Heliot, 'Sur les résidences princières bâties en France du Xᵉ au XIIᵉ siècle', *Moy. A.*, 61 (1955), 27–61, 291–317.

18 T. B. Ross (ed.), *The Murder of Charles the Good, Count of Flanders, by Galbert of Bruges* (New York, 1960).

19 R. Graham, 'Four Alien Priories in Monmouthshire', *JBAA*, 30 (1929), 102–21.

20 Excavations by R. Shoesmith.

21 Knowles and Hadcock, *Medieval Religious Houses*, p. 73.

22 *ibid.* pp. 60 and 421.

23 *VCH, Essex*, II, p. 93.

24 *VCH, Sussex*, II, p. 64; *VCH, Norfolk*, II, p. 356.

25 *VCH, Norfolk*, II, p. 363

26 J. C. Dickinson, *The Origins of the Austin Canons and their Introduction into England* (London, 1950).

27 *VCH, Hunts*, I, p. 393.

28 M. W. Thompson, *Kenilworth Castle, Warwickshire* (HMSO, 1976); *VCH, Warwicks*, II, p. 86; Dugdale, *Monasticon Anglicanum*, VI (1), 220–2.

29 Dugdale, *Monasticon Anglicanum*, pp. 220–1.
30 Knowles and Hadcock, *Medieval Religious Houses*, p. 117.
31 *VCH, Yorks*, III, p. 149; C. R. Peers, *Rievaulx Abbey, Yorkshire* (HMSO, 1948).
32 *VCH, Staffs*, III, p. 230.
33 *VCH, Shropshire*, II, p. 47.
34 P. E. Curnow, 'The Tower House at Hopton Castle and its Affinities', in C. Harper-Bill *et al.* (eds.) *Studies in Medieval History* presented to R. Allen Brown (Woodbridge, 1989) pp. 97–8.
35 *VCH, Warwicks*, II, p. 91.
36 Knowles and Hadcock, *Medieval Religious Houses*, p. 444.
37 *VCH, Cumberland*, II, p. 204.

9 **The castle as midwife: towns**

1 I. Soulsby, *The Towns of Medieval Wales* (Chichester, 1983), p. 34.
2 W. St J. Hope, 'The Ancient Topography of the Town of Ludlow, in the County of Salop', *Arch.* 61 (1909), 383–8.
3 M. W. Beresford, *New Towns of the Middle Ages* (London, 1967), p. 183.
4 C. Drage, 'Urban Castles', in *Urban Archaeology in Britain*, CBA Research Reports 61 (1987), pp. 117–32.
5 E. S. Armitage, *Early Norman Castles of the British Isles* (London, 1912).
6 M. W. Barley, 'Town Defences in England and Wales', in M. W. Barley (ed.), *The Plans and Topography of Medieval Towns in England and Wales*, CBA Research Report, 14 (1976), p. 59.
7 K. R. Potter (ed.), *Gesta Stephani* (London, 1955), p. 38.
8 William Dugdale, *Monasticon Anglicanum* (London, 1830), VI (1), 222–3.
9 M. W. Beresford and H. P. R. Finberg, *English Medieval Boroughs, a Handlist* (Totowa, NJ, 1973), p. 174. The authors merely quote Dugdale.
10 P. E. Curnow and M. W. Thompson, 'Excavations at Richards Castle, Herefordshire, 1962–64', *JBAA* 22 (1969), 105–22.
11 Beresford, *New Towns*, pp. 451–1.
12 Potter, *Gesta Stephani*, pp. 9–10.
13 T. Wright (ed.), *The Historical Works of Giraldus Cambrensis* (London, 1905), p. 311.
14 Soulsby, *Towns of Medieval Wales*; Barley, 'Town defences'.
15 E. A. Lewis, *The Medieval Boroughs of Snowdonia* (London, 1912), p. 37.
16 Beresford, *New Towns*, pp. 506–8.
17 *KW*, II, pp. 793–804.
18 T. Arnold (ed.), *Symonis Monachi Opera Omnia*, RS, London, 1885, 211; R. F. Walker, *The Origins of Newcastle upon Tyne* (Newcastle, 1976); *Newcastle upon Tyne Charters* (Newcastle, 1980).
19 *KW*, II, pp. 746–8.
20 Arnold, *Symonis Monachi*, p. 211.
21 Beresford, *New Towns*, pp. 435–6; *RCHM, Essex*, II, pp. 200–2; P. A. Rahtz, *Pleshey Castle, First Interim Report, 1960* (Ipswich, 1961).
22 Soulsby, *Towns of Medieval Wales*.
23 Beresford, *New Towns*, p. 559.
24 Soulsby, *Towns of Medieval Wales*, pp. 152–54.
25 Beresford, *New Towns*, pp. 250–3. For a fuller historical account of Tenby, see Walker's chapter in R. A. Griffiths, *Boroughs of Medieval Wales* (Cardiff, 1978), pp. 289–320.
26 Soulsby, *Towns of Medieval Wales*, pp. 214–17.
27 *KW*, I, p. 341.
28 *KW*, I, pp. 342, 348–50.
29 *KW*, I, pp. 337–40.
30 *KW*, I, pp. 369–70. For an historical account, see chapter by Williams-Jones in Griffiths, *Boroughs of Medieval Wales*, pp. 73–103.

10 **Indian summer: the fourteenth century**

1 *KW*, II, pp. 864–88.
2 M. W. Thompson, *Kenilworth Castle, Warwickshire* (HMSO, 1976).
3 M. W. Thompson, *The Decline of the Castle* (Cambridge University Press, 1988), pp. 46, 50–1.
4 *KW*, II, pp. 876; I, pl. 11a.
5 M. W. Thompson, 'Three Stages in the Construction of the Hall at Kenilworth Castle,' in M. R. Apted *et al.* (eds.) *Ancient Monuments and their Interpretation* (Chichester, 1977), pp. 211–18.
6 W. E. Henley (ed.), *The Chronicle of*

Froissart Translated by Lord Berners, 6 vols. (London, 1901–3), V, pp. 281–2.

7 J. Longnon (ed.), *Les Très Riches Heures du Duc de Berry* (London, 1969).

8 P. A. Faulkner, 'Castle Planning in the Fourteenth Century', *AJ*, 120 (1963), 215–35.

9 *ibid.*, 222.

10 M. W. Thompson, *Decline of the Castle*, chap. 4.

11 Faulkner, 'Castle Planning'.

12 Henley (ed.), *Chronicle of Froissart*.

13 *ibid.*, e.g. I, pp. 182, 210, 244; II, p. 370; III, p. 26; IV, p. 400.

14 *ibid.*, e.g. I, pp. 99, 296; II, pp. 245, 278.

15 *ibid.*, e.g. III, p. 132; IV, p. 293.

16 *ibid.*, e.g. III, pp. 332, 347, 441.

17 *ibid.*, e.g. III, pp. 461, 497; IV, pp. 305, 347.

18 *ibid.*, e.g. VI, p. 156.

19 *ibid.*, V, pp. 139, 386.

20 C. L. H. Coulson, 'A Handlist of English Royal Licences to Crenellate, 1200–1576,' Ms.

21 *KW*, II, pp. 793–804.

22 M. W. Thompson, *Pickering Castle, Yorkshire* (HMSO, 1958), p. 9.

23 Henley (ed.), *Chronicle of Froissart*, III, p. 497; IV, pp. 305ff, 347.

24 *CPR*, 21 October 1385.

25 M. W. Thompson, *Decline of the Castle*, pp. 36–8.

26 R. R. Davies, *Lordship and Society in the March of Wales, 1282–1400* (Oxford, 1978).

27 Discussion in D. J. Turner, 'Bodiam, Sussex: True Castle or an Old Soldier's Dream House?' in W. M. Ormrod (ed.), *England in the Fourteenth Century* (Woodbridge, 1986), pp. 267–77.

28 Henley (ed.), *Chronicle of Froissart*, p. 41; C. Morton, *Bodiam Castle, Sussex* (National Trust, 1986).

29 *CPR*, 21 October 1385.

30 C. L. Hunter Blair and H. L. Honeyman, *Dunstanburgh Castle, Northumberland* (HMSO, 1955).

31 B. M. Morley, *Hylton Castle, County Durham* (HMSO, 1979).

32 *VCH, Warwicks*, IV, pp. 133–7.

33 *CPR*, 26 November 1383.

34 *Farleigh Hungerford Castle, Somerset* (HMSO, 1962).

35 B. M. Morley, 'Aspects of Fourteenth Century Castle Design', in A. Detsicas (ed.), *Collectanea Historica* (Maidstone, 1981), pp. 104–13.

36 L. F. Salzman, *Building in England down to 1540* (Oxford, 1952), pp. 438–9; *VCH, Staffs*, V, pp. 85–6.

37 *VCH, Yorks, N. Riding*, I, pp. 391–2.

38 *CPR*, 28 November 1373.

39 S. E. Rigold, *Nunney Castle, Somerset* (HMSO, 1956).

40 *KW*, pp. 793–804, pl. 47b.

41 R. B. Pugh and A. D. Saunders, *Old Wardour Castle, Wiltshire* (HMSO, 1968); also Morley, 'Castle Design'.

42 R. Ritter, *Donjons, châteaux et places fortes* (Paris, 1953), p. 119.

43 C. H. Hunter Blair and H. L. Honeyman, *Warkworth Castle, Northumberland* (HMSO, 1958).

44 Salzman, *Building in England*, pp. 454–6.

45 W. St J. Hope, 'Lumley Castle, Durham', *Country Life*, (18 June 1910), pp. 896–905.

46 M. W. Thompson, 'The Construction of the Manor at South Wingfield, Derbyshire', in G. de G. Sieveking *et al.*, (ed.) *Economic and Social Archaeology* (London, 1976), pp. 417–38.

47 M. W. Thompson, *Decline of the Castle*, chaps. 2 and 3.

Select bibliography

Antonow, A., *Planung und Bau von Burgen im suddeutschen Raum*, Frankfurt on Main, 1983

Armitage, E. S., *Early Norman Castles of the British Isles*, London, 1912

Barker, P. and Higham, R., *Hen Domen, Montgomery: a Timber Castle on the English–Welsh Border*, London, 1982

Barley, M. W., *The Plans and Topography of Medieval Towns in England*, CBA Research Report, 14, London, 1967

Baumgarten, K., *Das deutsche Bauernhaus, eine Einführung in seine Geschichte von 9. bis zum 19. Jahrhundert*, Berlin, 1980

Benton, J. F. (ed.), *Self and Society in Medieval France: the Memoirs of Abbot Guibert of Nogent*, New York, 1970

Beresford, G., *Goltho, the Development of an Early Medieval Manor, c. 850–1150*, London, 1987

Beresford, M., *New Towns of the Middle Ages*, London, 1967

Binding, G., *Burg Münzenberg, ein staufishce Burganlage*, Bonn, 1963
Pfalz Gelnhausen, ein Bauuntersuchung, Bonn, 1965

Bloch, M., *Feudal Society*, London, 1961

Bouard, M. de, 'De l'aula au donjon: les fouilles de la motte de la Chapelle à Doué la Fontaine (X^e–XIe siècle)', *AM* 3/4 (1973–4)
Le Château de Caen, Caen, 1979

Braunfels, W., *Monasteries of Western Europe: the Architecture of the Orders*, Princeton, 1980

Brown, R. A., 'Royal Castle-Building in England', *EHR*, 70 (1955), 353–98
English Medieval Castles, 3rd edn, London, 1976
Castles from the Air, Cambridge, 1989
Calendar of Patent Rolls, Public Record Office

Caumont, M. de, *Abécédaire ou Rudiment d'Archéologie*, Paris, 1853

Chatelaine, A., *Donjons romans des pays d'Ouest. Étude comparative sur les donjons romans quadrangulaires de la France de l'Ouest*, Paris, 1973

Chibnall, M. (ed.), *The Ecclesiastical History of Orderic Vitalis*, Books III and IV, Oxford, 1969

Chronique de Robert de Torigni, edited by L. Delisle, Rouen, 1872

Coad, J. G. and Stretten, A. D. F., 'Excavations at Castle Acre, Norfolk, 1972–77: Country House and Castle of the Norman Earls of Surrey', *AJ*, 139 (1982), 138–301

Colloque de Caen: Les fortifications de terre en Europe occidentale du Xe au XIIe siècles', *AM*, II (1981), 5–123

Colvin, H. M., Taylor, A. J. and Brown, R. A., *A History of the King's Works*, I and II, HMSO, 1963

Contamine, P., *La Vie quotidienne pendant la guerre de cent ans, France et Angleterre (XIVe siècle)*, Paris, 1976

Cotman, J. S., *Architectural Antiquities of Normandy*, London, 1822

Coulson, C. L. H., 'Handlist of English Royal Licences to Crenellate, 1200–1578', Ms, 1982

Coulton, G. G., *Five Centuries of Religion*, I, Cambridge, 1923

Crossley-Holland, K., *The Anglo-Saxon World, An Anthology*, Oxford, 1984

Deyres, M. D., 'Les Châteaux de Foulque Nerra', *BM*, 132 (1974), 7–28

Drage, C., 'Urban Castles', in *Urban Archaeology in Britain*, CBA Research Report 61 (1987), 117–32

Dugdale, W., *Monasticon Anglicanum*, edited by Carey, Ellis, and Bandihel, 6 vols. in 8, London 1817–30

Edwards, G., 'Edward I's Castle Building in Wales', *PBA*, 32 (1947), 16

Ellis, T. P., *Welsh Tribal Law and Custom in the Middle Ages*, Oxford, 1926

Emery, A., *Dartington Hall*, Oxford, 1970

Enlart, C., *Manuel d'archéologie française depuis les temps mérovingiennes jusqu'à la Renaissance*, pt 2, 2nd edn, Paris, 1932

Faulkner, P. A., 'Castle Planning in the Fourteenth Century', *AJ*, 120 (1963), 215–35

Fournier, G., *Le Château dans la France médiévale. Essai de sociologie monumental*, Paris, 1978

Fredegar, *The Fourth Book of the Chronicle of Fredegar*, edited by J. M. Wallace-Hadrill, London, 1960

Gardelles, J., *Les Châteaux du moyen âge dans la France du Sud-Ouest: la Gascogne anglaise du 1216 à 1327*, Geneva, 1972

'Les Palais dans l'Europe occidentale chrétienne du Xe au XIIe siècle', *CCM*, 19 (1976), 115–34

Garmonsway, G. N. (ed.), *The Anglo-Saxon Chronicle*, London, 1953

Garmonsway, G. N. and Simpson, J. (eds.), *Beowulf and its Analogues*, London, 1968

Gesta Stephani, edited by K. R. Potter, London, 1955

Giraldus Cambrensis, Historical Works of, edited by T. Wright, London, 1905

Glasscock, R., 'Mottes in Ireland', *CG*, 7 (1975), 95–110

Hatto, A. T. (ed. and trans.), *The Nibelungenlied*, Harmondsworth, 1965

Heliot, P. 'Sur les residences princières bâties en France du Xe au XIIe siècle', *Moy. A.* 61 (1955) 27–62, 291–317

'La Genèse des châteaux de plan quadrangulaire en France et Angleterre', *Bull. Soc. Nat. Ant. de France* (1965), 238–57

'Les Châteaux-forts en France du Xe au XIIe siècle', *Journal des Savants* (1965), 483–514

'L'Evolution des donjons dans le Nord-Ouest de la France et en Angleterre au XIIe siècle', *Bull. arch. com. trav. historiques et scientifiques*, NS, 5(1969) 141–94.

Henley, W. E. (ed.), *The Chronicle of Froissart Translated out of French by Sir John Bourchier, Lord Berners, 1523–5*, 6 vols. London, 1901–3

Heyne, M., *Das deutsche Wohnungswesen von altesten geschichtlichen Zeiten bis zum 16 Jahrhundert*, Leipzig, 1899

Hinz, H., *Motte und Donjon: zur Frühgeschichte der mittelalerischen Adelsburg*, ZAM Monograph (1981)

Hope-Taylor, B. K., 'The Excavation of a Motte at Abinger, Surrey', *AJ*, 107 (1950), 15–43

Yeavering, An Anglo-British Centre of Early Northumbria, Dept. of Environment Report 7, HMSO, 1977

Horn, W., 'On the Origins of the Medieval Bay System', *JSAH*, 17 (1958), 2–23

Hotz, W., *Kleine Kunstgeschichte der deutschen Burg*, Darmstadt, 1979

Pfalzen und Burgen der Stauferzeit, Darmstadt, 1981

Kenyon, J. R., *Medieval Fortifications*, Leicester, 1990

Kenyon, J. R. and Avent, R. (eds.), *Castles in Wales and the Marches. Essays in Honour of D. J. Cathcart King*, Cardiff, 1987

King, D. J. C., *Castellarium Anglicanum*, 2 vols., New York, 1983

The Castle in England and Wales, London, 1987

King, D. J. C. and Alcock, L., 'Ringworks of England and Wales', *CG*, 3 (1966), 90–127

Kleinelausz, A., *Charlemagne*, Paris, 1934

Landais, H., 'Le Château de Saumur', *CAF* (1964), 523–58

Lawrence, T. E., *Crusader Castles*, edited by D. Pringle, Oxford, 1988

Leask, H. G., 'Irish Castles, 1180–1310', *AJ*, 93 (1936), 144–99

Lewis, E. A., *The Medieval Boroughs of Snowdonia*, London, 1912

Lobel, M. D. (ed.), *Historic Towns*, I, London, 1969

Longnon, J. (ed.), *Les Très Riches Heures du Duc de Berry*, London, 1969

Malmesbury, William, *Historia Novella*, edited by K. R. Potter, London, 1955

Map, W., *De Nugis Curialum*, edited by M. R. James, Oxford, 1914

Mayes, P. and Butler, L. A. S., *Sandal Castle Excavations, 1964–73*, Wakefield, 1983

Meirion-Jones, G., 'The Vernacular Architecture of France: An Assessment', *VA*, 16 (1985), 1–18

Meyer, W., *Deutsche Burgen*, 2nd edn, Frankfurt on Main 1969

Mortet, V., *Recueil de textes relatifs à l'histoire de l'architecture et la*

*condition des architectes en France du
moyen âge, XIe–XIIe siècles*, Paris, 1911

Müller-Wille, M., *Mittelalterliche Burghügel
("Motten") im nördlichen Rheinland*,
Cologne, 1966

Owen, A., *The Ancient Laws and Institutes
of Wales*, 2 vols., London, 1841

Planitz, H., *Die deutsche Stadt im
Mittelalter*, Cologne, 1965

Powicke, M., *The Loss of Normandy,
1189–1204*, 2nd edn, Manchester, 1961

Rahtz, P., *The Saxon and Medieval Palaces
at Cheddar: Excavations in 1960–62*,
British Archaeological Report 65,
Oxford, 1979

Renn, D. F., 'The Anglo-Norman Keep,
1066–1138', *JBAA*, 3rd ser., 23 (1960),
1–23

   Norman Castles in Britain, 2nd edn,
London, 1973

Rigold, S. E., *Nunney Castle, Somerset*,
HMSO, 1955

   Eynsford Castle, Kent, HMSO, 1964

Ritter, R., *Châteaux, donjons et places
fortes*, Paris, 1955

Ross, J. B. (ed.), *The Murder of Charles the
Good, by Galbert of Bruges*, New York,
1960

Salzman, L. F., *Building in England to 1540*,
Oxford, 1952

Sandall, K., 'Aisled Halls in England and
Wales', *VA*, 6 (1975), 19–26

Saunders, A. D. *et al.*, 'Five Castle
Excavations: Reports on the Institute's
Research Project into the Origins of the
English Castle in England', *AJ*, 134
(1977), 1–156

Schultz, A., *Der höfische Leben zur Zeit der
Minnesinger*, 2nd edn, 2 vols., Leipzig,
1889

Soulsby, I., *The Towns of Medieval Wales*,
Chichester, 1983

Swoboda, K. M., *Romische und Romanische
Paläste*, 3rd edn, Vienna, 1969

Taylor, A. J., *The King's Works in Wales,
1277–1330*, HMSO, 1974

   'Castle-Building in Thirteenth Century
Wales and Savoy', *PBA*, 63 (1978),
265–92

   'Master Bertram, Ingeniator Regis', in
C. Harper-Bill *et al.* (eds.), *Studies in
Medieval History presented to R. Allen*

Brown, Woodbridge, 1989, pp. 289–316

Thompson, A. H., *Military Architecture in
England during the Middle Ages*,
Oxford, 1912

Thompson, M. W., 'Recent Excavations in
the Keep of Farnham Castle, Surrey',
MA, 4 (1960), 81–94

   'Motte Substructures', *MA*, 4 (1960),
305–6

   Kenilworth Castle, Warwickshire,
HMSO, 1976

   'Associated Monasteries and Castles in
the Middle Ages: a Tentative List', *AJ*,
143 (1986), 305–21

   The Decline of the Castle, Cambridge,
1988

   'The Green Knight's Castle', in C.
Harper-Bill et al., *Studies in Medieval
History presented to R. Allen Brown*,
Woodbridge, 1989, 317–26

Turner, T. H. and Parker, J. H., *Domestic
Architecture of the Middle Ages*, 4 vols.,
Oxford 1851

Uslar, R. von, *Studien zu frühgeschictlichen
Befestigungen zwischen Nordsee und
Alpen*, Cologne, 1964

Viollet-le-duc, E., *Dictionnaire raisonné de
l'architecture française du XIe au XVIe
siècle*, 10 vols., Paris, 1875 (see
especially entries for *château, donjon,
palais, salle*)

Wailly, M. N. de (ed.), *Jean sire de Joinville:
Histoire de Saint Louis*, Paris, 1874

Ward-Perkins, B., *From Classical Antiquity
to the Middle Ages. Urban Public
Building in Northern and Central Italy,
AD 300–850*, Oxford, 1984

William of Poitiers, *Histoire de Guillaume le
Conquérant*, Paris, 1952

Wilson, D. M. (ed.), *The Bayeux Tapestry*,
London, 1985

Wood, M., *The English Medieval House*,
London, 1965

Woquet, H. (ed.), *Suger: Vie de Louis VI, le
Gros*, Paris, 1929

Wright, T., *A History of Domestic Manners
and Sentiments in England during the
Middle Ages*, London, 1862

Yver, J., 'Les Châteaux forts en Normandie',
*Bulletin de la Société des Antiquaires de
Normandie*, 53 (1955–6), 33–115

Grateful acknowledgement is made to the persons and bodies mentioned in brackets for permission to make use of their original illustrative material.

Page numbers in italics refers to illustrations. Castle and Palace are abbreviated to C. and P. respectively.

Lightning Source UK Ltd.
Milton Keynes UK
UKOW021206080812

197211UK00003B/42/P

9 780521 088534